Moral Development in a Global World

D1430154

Questions addressing people's moral lives, similarities and differences in the moral concepts of cultural groups, and how these concepts emerge in the course of development are of perennial interest. In a globalizing world, addressing what is universal and what is culturally distinctive about moral development is pressing. More than ever, well-substantiated knowledge of diverse peoples' moral compasses is needed. This book presents the cultural-developmental theory of moral psychology, findings from numerous countries, and four instruments for conducting cultural-developmental research. The central thesis is that humans are born with a shared moral heritage and that, as we develop from childhood into adulthood, we branch off in diverse directions shaped by culture – resulting in novelty and contention. An international group of eminent and cutting-edge scholars from anthropology, psychology, and linguistics addresses this timely topic and explores how gender, social class, and "culture wars" between liberals and conservatives play into moral development across cultures.

LENE ARNETT JENSEN is Associate Professor of Psychology at Clark University. She is the originator of the "cultural-developmental" theoretical approach to research on human psychology. This approach encompasses what is universal and what is culturally distinctive about human development. Unlike one-size-fits-all psychological theories of the twentieth century, the cultural-developmental approach provides a flexible and dynamic way to think about psychological development in today's global world. Dr. Jensen's research addresses moral development and cultural identity formation in the contexts of "culture war" tensions, migration, and globalization, and she has conducted research with her colleagues in Denmark, India, Thailand, Turkey, and the United States. Her recent books include *Bridging Cultural and Developmental Psychology: New Syntheses for Theory, Research, and Policy* (2012) and the *Oxford Handbook of Human Development and Culture* (2015).

Moral Development in a Global World

Research from a Cultural-Developmental Perspective

Edited by

Lene Arnett Jensen

CAMBRIDGE
UNIVERSITY PRESS

CAMBRIDGE
UNIVERSITY PRESS

University Printing House, Cambridge CB2 8BS, United Kingdom

Cambridge University Press is part of the University of Cambridge.

It furthers the University's mission by disseminating knowledge in the pursuit of education, learning and research at the highest international levels of excellence.

www.cambridge.org
Information on this title: www.cambridge.org/9781316635674

First published 2015
First paperback edition 2016

A catalogue record for this publication is available from the British Library

Library of Congress Cataloguing in Publication data
Moral development in a global world : research from a cultural-developmental perspective / edited by Lene Arnett Jensen.
    pages   cm
Includes bibliographical references and index.
ISBN 978-1-107-03714-4 (hardback)
1. Ethics – Cross-cultural studies.   2. Moral development – Cross-cultural studies.
3. Conduct of life – Cross-cultural studies.   I. Jensen, Lene Arnett.
GN468.7.M67   2015
170 – dc23   2015005502

ISBN   978-1-107-03714-4   Hardback
ISBN   978-1-316-63567-4   Paperback

Contents

Contributors

RACHANA BHANGAOKAR is an assistant professor at the Department of Human Development and Family Studies, the Maharaja Sayajirao University of Baroda, India. Her research interests include cultural psychology, moral development, youth civic engagement, and positive youth development. She is the recipient of a number of awards, including a Fulbright Junior Research Fellowship at the University of Chicago. She was the co-investigator for a project funded by Indian Council of Social Science Research, New Delhi, on the development of morality in Indian families. Currently, she is involved in two research projects on the interface of youth civic engagement with Gandhian philosophy and human rights funded by the Indian Council of Philosophical Research and University Grants Commission of New Delhi.

ALLISON DIBIANCA FASOLI is a visiting assistant professor at Middlebury College in Vermont, United States. She received her PhD from the Department of Comparative Human Development at the University of Chicago and BAs in Psychology and Philosophy from Middlebury College. Her research seeks to understand the nature of moral psychology by examining the role of culture in moral development. Her current work examines the social processes through which children reconstruct the moral concepts of their cultures.

ROGER S. GINER-SOROLLA is a professor of social psychology at the University of Kent, United Kingdom. He received his PhD from New York University in 1996. His research interests, funded by British and European agencies, cover the role of specific social emotions in such fields as morality, self-control, and intergroup relations. He is currently an associate editor of the *Journal of Experimental Social Psychology.* His publications on such emotions as anger, disgust, guilt, and shame can be found in *Journal of Personality and Social Psychology, Psychological Science,* and *Psychological Bulletin.* He is the author of *Judging Passions: Moral Emotions in Persons and Groups* (2012). He is also a frequent contributor to the activities of the Center for Open Science, focusing on the role of publishing in encouraging replicable research and replication.

VALESCHKA MARTINS GUERRA is a lecturer in research methods and social psychology at the Universidade Federal do Espírito Santo, Brazil. As a PhD candidate in social psychology at the University of Kent, UK, she developed the CADS, an instrument to measure the three Ethics of Community, Autonomy, and Divinity. She has collected data with CADS in six different national cultures. Her research is published in international periodicals, such as the *Journal of Cross-Cultural Psychology, Journal of Applied Social Psychology, Group Processes & Intergroup Relations, Personality and Individual Differences,* and *Archives of Sexual Behavior.* Her primary research interests are in human values, religiosity, honor, well-being, and positive psychology. Additional interests are in human sexuality and cultural adaptation.

JACOB R. HICKMAN is an assistant professor in the Department of Anthropology at Brigham Young University, Utah, United States, where he specializes in psychological anthropology and cultural psychology. He did his graduate work at the University of Chicago in the Department of Comparative Human Development. He has conducted ethnographic fieldwork in Hmong communities in Southeast Asia and in the United States (Alaska, Wisconsin, and Minnesota) since 2004. His research interests include understanding how moral thinking, ritual practice, family life, religious movements, and subjectivities have been adapting to different social and political circumstances in the Hmong diaspora. In this research Hickman takes a person-centered ethnographic approach that integrates perspectives from psychology and anthropology in order to understand both cultural and psychological influences on morality and religious life.

LENE ARNETT JENSEN is an associate professor of psychology at Clark University in Massachusetts, United States. She aims through scholarship and professional collaboration to move the discipline of psychology toward understanding human development in terms of both what is universal and what is cultural. She calls this a cultural-developmental approach. Her research addresses moral development and cultural identity formation in the contexts of "culture war" tensions, migration, and globalization. She and her colleagues have conducted research in different countries, including Denmark, India, Thailand, Turkey, and the United States. Her books and monographs include *New Horizons in Developmental Theory and Research* (2005, with Reed Larson), *Immigrant Civic Engagement: New Translations* (2008, with Constance Flanagan), *Bridging Cultural and Developmental Psychology: New Syntheses for Theory, Research, and Policy* (2012), and the *Oxford Handbook of Human Development and Culture* (2015). She served as Editor-in-Chief of *New Directions for Child and Adolescent Development* from 2004 to 2014 and as conference chair for the 2012 biennial Conference of the

Society for Research on Adolescence. A native of Denmark, Dr. Jensen has resided in a number of countries, including Belgium, India, and France. She lives in Massachusetts, United States, with her husband and twin children.

SHAGUFA KAPADIA is a professor in the Department of Human Development and Family Studies and the Director of the Women's Studies Research Center at the Faculty of Family and Community Sciences, the Maharaja Sayajirao University of Baroda, India. Her theoretical perspective encompasses cultural and developmental issues among children, adolescents, and emerging adults. She has conducted research on morality, immigrant acculturation, and gender issues. In 2009 she was Visiting Psychology Faculty at James Madison University, Virginia, United States. She is on the review and editorial boards of a number of journals, including *Psychological Studies* and *Culture and Psychology.* She is also a founding board member of the Society for the Study of Emerging Adulthood and the India coordinator of the International Society for the Study of Behavioural Development. She has received a number of prestigious awards and fellowships, including the Shastri Indo-Canadian Faculty Research Award (2006–7 and 2009–10) and the Fulbright Senior Research Fellowship (2003–4).

JOAN G. MILLER is a professor and the director of Undergraduate Studies in the Department of Psychology at the New School for Social Research in New York, United States. She is a fellow of the Association for Psychological Science and served as past newsletter editor for the International Society for the Study of Behavioural Development. She obtained her doctorate in human development from the University of Chicago and has held past faculty positions at Yale University and the University of Michigan. Her research interests center on culture and basic psychological theory, with a focus on interpersonal motivation, moral development, family and friend relationships, and theory of mind.

LARRY J. NELSON is a professor in the School of Family Life at Brigham Young University, Utah, United States. He examines factors that contribute to flourishing or floundering during the third decade of life. He has published more than 70 peer-reviewed journal articles and chapters in edited books on topics including conceptions of adulthood, social withdrawal, and the role of parents and culture in the transition to adulthood. His professional citizenship contributions include service on the Governing Counsel of the Society for the Study of Emerging Adulthood and the editorial board of *Emerging Adulthood* as well as being the editor of a series of books on emerging adulthood. He is a devoted teacher-scholar who has received numerous awards for excellence in teaching, including being rated as one of "The Best 300 Professors" in the United States by the Princeton Review.

LAURA M. PADILLA-WALKER is an associate professor in the School of Family Life at Brigham Young University, Utah, United States. Her research focuses on how parents and other socialization agents, such as media and siblings, help to foster prosocial and moral development during adolescence and emerging adulthood. She has published more than 50 peer-reviewed articles and book chapters and has co-edited a volume entitled *Prosocial Development: A Multidimensional Approach* (2014). She is currently an associate editor of the journal *Emerging Adulthood*.

NIYATI PANDYA is a PhD student in the Department of Psychology at Clark University, Massachusetts, United States. She holds an MS in Human Development and Family Studies from the Maharaja Sayajirao University of Baroda, India. Her research interests focus on examining the role of culture and development in moral reasoning, particularly in the Indian context. She is also interested in how intracultural differences of social class and religion shape moral reasoning. Her research takes the cultural-developmental approach to study moral reasoning across the life span, with recent work including longitudinal and cross-sectional analysis. She has received travel awards from the Society for Research on Adolescence, and one of her posters was selected as the model poster for submissions to the 2014 conference.

RICHARD A. SHWEDER is a cultural anthropologist and the Harold Higgins Swift Distinguished Service Professor in the Department of Comparative Human Development at the University of Chicago, United States. He is author of *Thinking Through Cultures: Expeditions in Cultural Psychology* and *Why Do Men Barbecue? Recipes for Cultural Psychology* and editor of many books in the areas of cultural psychology, psychological anthropology, and comparative human development. His recent research examines the scopes and limits of pluralism and the multicultural challenge in Western liberal democracies. He has co-edited two books on this topic (with Martha Minow and Hazel Markus) entitled *Engaging Cultural Differences: The Multicultural Challenge in Liberal Democracies* and *Just Schools: Pursuing Equality in Societies of Difference*.

GISELA TROMMSDORFF is head of the Division of Developmental and Cross-Cultural Psychology at the University of Konstanz and Research Professor at the German Institute for Economic Research in Berlin. She is a member of several scientific and advisory committees, including the German Institute for Japanese Studies in Tokyo and the Research Center for Psychological Science in Taiwan. She also serves on several editorial boards, including for the *Asian Journal of Social Psychology* and the *Journal of Cross-Cultural Psychology*. She has published more than 20 books (co-edited), 145 book chapters, and 100 journal articles. Her research interests center on intergenerational relations, transmission of values, and socioemotional development in cultural contexts. She is the president of the German-Japanese Society for Social Sciences and a recipient of the Federal Cross of Merit, 1st Class, Federal Republic of Germany.

ANNUKKA VAINIO works as Principal Research Scientist at Natural Resources Institute Finland where she conducts research on sustainable consumption. She is also Docent in Social Psychology at the University of Helsinki. Her publications focus on morality, justice, and environmental responsibility. Her newest research examines moral reasoning in the context of climate change.

Foreword

Richard A. Shweder

I have been fortunate over the years to have several brilliant predoctoral and postdoctoral students who have creatively developed and applied the "Big Three" framework and made it both visible and theoretically and empirically accessible to researchers in the fields of cognitive, developmental, and social psychology. Lene Jensen, the editor of this volume, was the first moral psychologist to see the relevance of the Big Three of morality (Autonomy, Community, Divinity) for "culture war" issues in the United States – as a way of characterizing the tensions between liberal and conservative views of the world and as a way of describing the ontogenetic development or life course trajectories of moral thinking in liberal and conservative communities around the globe. *Moral Development in a Global World: Research from a Cultural-Developmental Perspective* adds substance to that insight through a series of comparative studies of moral development, including critical reflections on the Big Three framework by scholars from around the world.

The chapters in this volume explore the empirical and theoretical dimensions of the Big Three. These chapters are especially significant for two reasons. The first is their developmental focus on cultural variations in the life course trajectories of the Big Three and their interconnections. In some moral communities (for example, among Evangelical Christians in New England), the developmental story is about how Autonomy reasoning in children becomes the basis for the development of Divinity reasoning (via a process of social communication from parents to children), whereas in other communities (for example, among low- and high-socioeconomic-status Indians from Baroda) younger children display higher levels of Divinity thinking than do older children. In general, the researchers also discover that gender differences in these trajectories are relatively minor or nonexistent. Ditto for the relative salience of Autonomy, Community, and Divinity thinking in the moral judgments of males and females in any particular cultural group, which is noteworthy given the history of debates in moral psychology about gender differences in moral reasoning. In light of these and other studies, the claim that males and females speak with different moral voices seems overblown. That is just one take-home message. There are many others.

For example, one commends the collection for its distinctive attention to the Ethic of Divinity. The Ethics of Autonomy and Community (and cognate notions of individualism and collectivism, or independent and interdependent selves) are much discussed in the moral psychology literature, and that is true of this collection as well. The Ethic of Divinity, however, is a subdomain of moral thinking that has not been treated with equal regard in psychology in general or in developmental psychology in particular. We live in a world in which global-ization (with its ecumenical, border-erasing, universalizing impulse) and ethnic and religious nationalism (with their localizing, border-patrolling, parochial impulses to revivify thick cultural identities) seem to go hand in hand. Nor has the rise of modernity in the "West" and its global expansion brought an end to the spiritual side of human nature or to the transcendental goods favored by religious traditions. It is a great virtue that the present chapters examine the Ethic of Divinity or in some cases even place the Ethic of Divinity on the center of the morality stage.

A thumbnail sketch or bare-bones summary of the Big Three framework might read as follows: in the social communicative contexts in which one's moral judgments must be accounted for, justified, and explained, the moral truths or goods embraced around the world are many, not one. The moral character of an action or practice is typically established by connecting that action through a chain of factual, means-ends, and causal reasoning to some argument-ending "terminal good": that point in the provision of a verbal justi-fication at which the goodness of the action seems obvious and nothing more needs to be said or can be said by way of justification. On a worldwide scale, the argument-ending terminal goods that play a part in the deliberative moral justifications privileged in various cultural communities are rich and diverse and include such valued ends as personal freedom, family privacy, equity, just deserts, harm avoidance, loyalty, benevolence, courage, piety, duty, respect, gratitude, sympathy, modesty, chastity, purity, and sanctity.

The Big Three is a classification of these goods into a smaller set. At its core, the Big Three (Autonomy, Community, Divinity) is a theory about the different aspects of the self (as a preference structure, as an office holder in a particular community, or as connected to a sacred realm) that are made salient and institutionalized in different traditions of value and belief and that are made manifest in everyday life in the customary practices of any cultural community. The scheme is an induction of the different clusters of moral goods or virtues associated with each of those aspects of the self and a theory of the inherent multiplicity of the moral domain.

Replication and generalization are both virtues in science. One of the great virtues of the chapters in this volume is the respect shown for disciplined inquiry, replication of findings, and the scope and limits of generalizations in the psychological sciences. As a result of these studies, which were conducted across diverse population samples using somewhat diverse methods, a compelling case can be made for the robustness of the Big Three framework. Working in different cultural regions and national sites, the authors discover the presence of all three ethics and are able to put the Big Three and the cultural-developmental approach to work to illuminate the particular processes of moral development at play in each cultural context. The universal and the particular go hand in hand, and that which is ecumenical or global (the Big Three) makes it possible to understand that which is parochial or local in moral attitudes toward particular sorts of actions.

One of my central claims of the Big Three approach is that the illiberality of an action or cultural practice is not necessarily a measure of its immorality. This is both an eye-opening insight and a very big claim. Much academic research in North America and Western Europe on the psychology of morality has limited itself to the study of the liberal values associated with the Ethic of Autonomy and has even tended to define the very meaning of the domain of morality in liberal terms, leaving little space for either the Ethic of Community (and reducing it to mere "convention" or the conditioning of habits) or the Ethic of Divinity (and reducing it to religion, which has not been a topic of interest for most academic psychologists despite its universality and importance as a motivator of human behavior).

Liberalism itself is based on the principle of equal regard for all persons viewed as individuals and not as social categories or members attached to particular "in-groups." Varieties of liberal thought about the meaning of equal regard for persons implicate such moral aspirations as expressive liberty, merit-based justice, equal opportunity, harm avoidance, and the benevolent safeguarding of the vulnerable so as to assist them in becoming self-governing individuals regardless of social-status-defining characteristics such as gender, religion, ethnicity, social class, or group membership. In my view, liberalism's ideological home is the Ethic of Autonomy with its emphasis on rights to noninterference and the liberty to make self-determined "free choices" (short of harming others or denying them equal opportunity or their just deserts). In contrast, according to the Big Three, the reach of the domain of morality is much broader than the core moral concepts of liberalism; the moral domain also encompasses the normative concepts mentioned earlier, such as loyalty, duty, the hierarchical interdependency of social statuses, purity, sanctity, and pollution.

But what makes a judgment a moral judgment at all? What makes it a judgment of a moral kind? This is hardly a settled issue in the moral philosophy literature, but one possible definition of the moral domain might go like this: a moral judgment is the expressed or (more typically) implied judgment that person P *ought to* do X under such and such circumstances, where the doing of X under those circumstances is thought to be the right thing to do because it is presumed to be productive of some objective good. In other words, members of every cultural community behave as if they assume they are parties to an agreement to uphold a certain ideal way of life, to praise or permit certain kinds of actions and practices and to condemn and prohibit others. Characteristically, judgments that are moral judgments presuppose the existence of an objective normative reality (a realm of moral truths – the touchstones of an objective moral charter) that serves as an ostensible nonsubjective standard for judging what is right and wrong.

In some moral communities the posited moral charter is quite concrete and specific, in the sense that it sets forth clear and determinate instructions, principles, or commands for the actual behavior of the members of a group (do's and don'ts such as "thou shall not bow down before carved images" or "thou shall never use physical punishment to discipline a child" or "thou shall always permit widows to remarry if they want to, but never require them to do so"). The Big Three can be viewed as a moral charter as well, albeit one that is far more abstract in its posit of a heterogeneous set of moral "goods" such as justice, loyalty, and sanctity, which are classified and summarized as "autonomy," "community," and "divinity."

It is especially noteworthy that there is considerable cross-cultural and intra-cultural variation in the degree to which all the social norms of a society are moralized and viewed as manifestations of an objective moral charter. Indeed, that criterion itself may be one mark of the difference between liberal and conservative cultural communities. One is delighted that several of the chapters in this volume elaborate on specific ways this is the case. It is also noteworthy that what is viewed as an objective moral issue in some traditions of value (for example, the particular restrictions on diet or clothing among some Jews, Hindus, or Muslims) may be viewed as a subjective issue (a mere opinion, convention, preference, or distinctive taste of a group or a person) in some other traditions of value. Drawing this fact to our attention, and doing so with evidence on a global scale, is one of the features of this book that makes it so innovative and path-breaking for researchers of moral development.

Regardless of the scope of the moral charter – whether it encompasses all social norms or only a few, whether it is concrete or abstract in its prescriptions – perceived objectivity is one feature of those judgments that count as moral judgments. In other words, judgments that are moral judgments purport to represent normative requirements (obligations, duties, rights, prohibitions) that are, and always have been, binding on all persons or groups to whom they apply, and they are obligatory regardless of a person's or people's subjective or conventional acceptances or personal likes and dislikes. In other words, this feature of perceived or purported objectivity is an ontological claim, not only an epistemological one.

Of course, any developmentai study of moral thinking will want to document the epistemologies or mental processes at play as moral motives, reactions, and judgments get formed, including (perhaps even especially) the way metaphysical beliefs are acquired in childhood and adolescence. On the basis of my own fieldwork experiences in a Hindu temple town on the east coast of India, I have in mind the acquisition in childhood of such metaphysical beliefs as these: moral careers extend over many lifetimes, you are reborn into the world bearing spiritual debts, and nature itself is just and governed by moral laws that guarantee that in the long run "you reap what you sow." Consequently, according to temple town residents, one's position in society is not an example of "there but for fortune goes you or goes I" but is rather a matter of personal responsibility, carrying with it implications for one's future behavior and demanding morally relevant self-control in order to unburden oneself of spiritual debts and improve one's prospects in this and future lives. The study of moral judgments must address both the ontological and epistemological sides of the moral psychology of any cultural community. Happily, the research projects reported in this book often focus on the acquisition of these kinds of morally relevant beliefs of members of different cultural communities and draw them to our attention.

Undoubtedly, the coding schemes used for identifying moral concepts in everyday conversations and in interview responses and for classifying them as autonomy-based, community-based, or divinity-based will forever be objects of criticism and progressive development. Good theory and good evidence are likely to interact with each other as new measures get devised. Given the distinctive recognition in this volume of the inclusion of the Ethic of Divinity within the moral domain and the obvious importance of the study of religion in the contemporary world, permit me to use this occasion to briefly comment on what I view as productive approaches to the study of that subdomain of the Big Three.

In addition to the Big Three of morality, I suspect there may also be a "Big Three" of religion. In the history of thought about the religions of the world, it seems to me theorists tend to come in three kinds. There are those who define religion by focusing on the concepts of the soul, the sacred, and superior or supernatural beings. The soulful, the sacred, and the supernatural are the three Ss of religion. Reflecting on the Ethic of Divinity, it is not hard to see how that particular realm of the moral is an application of all three Ss (soul, sacred, supernatural) to a fourth S – the "self." Human selves are capable of experiencing and recognizing themselves as soulful and supernatural in the sense of being capable of being the "unmoved mover," able to initiate action in ways that distinguish the "I" from other moved movers such as robots and other facts and artifacts of the material or "natural" world. (The equation of *Atman*, the animated personal self, with *Brahman*, the world soul or the divine, is a Hindu doctrinal version of this recognition.)

Human persons are also capable of feeling a direct connection to some elevated or dignifying realm of truth and value (a sacred realm, in the sense of being unquestionably good) that is inherently a potential source of human integrity. "Cleanliness is next to Godliness" is but one rather theistic way to express the virtues or goods associated with the Ethic of Divinity, but one can even be an atheist and still experience the moral domain guided by self-regulatory goods such as cleanliness, purity, pollution, sin, salvation, and sanctity.

The Enlightenment recoil against the institutions of organized religion, the ultimate distrust of all metaphysical notions expressed by many positive scientists may have inoculated many contemporary secular social scientists against words like *soul, sacred,* and *supernatural.* This may be one reason contemporary moral psychologists do not typically include the Ethic of Divinity in their studies of morality. But the concepts underlying those words are deeply embedded in the human experience of value and choice, and they play a part in the socialization of children and in the significance and meanings conveyed in daily activities such as the preparation of food, eating, bathing, going to bed, and even how one dresses in the morning and prepares to meet the world. Fortunately, the Ethic of Divinity is capable of rendition in less tendentious terms. Mathematical and logical truths, for example, arguably have a "supernatural" status in the sense that they are nonmaterial and nonmental yet nonetheless really real. The analogy between moral reality and mathematical reality has not gone unnoticed in the history of moral philosophy. Happily, the Big Three of the morality empirical research tradition as expressed in this very readable book on moral development in a global world seems well positioned to bridge the fields of developmental psychology and psychology of religion and to elaborate more and more sophisticated methods and concepts for comparative study.

Finally, although there are analytic distinctions to draw among the Big Three domains of morality, there is no reason to view Autonomy thinking, Community thinking, and Divinity thinking as mutually exclusive with respect to the particular social practices of a cultural community. Consider, for example, some Amish communities in the United States where late-adolescent youth are given the opportunity to go off into the world of the "English" and see what life is like in other communities. Most of the youth return to the farm after they see modern life, choose to become baptized, and commit themselves to the strictures and moral charter of and for the Amish cultural and religious community. This ritual seems to combine Ethics of Autonomy, Community, and Divinity in a rather powerful identity-defining way. Every essay in this book is testimony both to the heterogeneity and inherent tensions in the moral domain and to the potential of each of the ethics to reinforce the others in creative and often culture-specific ways.

I am delighted to have been invited to write the Foreword to this brilliant and very coherent collection of chapters on the Big Three of morality.

Congratulations to the contributors. One looks forward to future research that builds on this volume. "Onward and upward" is the sentiment I experienced reading the book. *Moral Development in a Global World: Research from a Cultural-Developmental Perspective* is an inspiration to move onward to the interdisciplinary developmental study of comparative ethics, with developmental psychologists and cultural anthropologists working together to investigate the moral psychology of particular customary practices in the diverse cultural regions of the world. The book's truly great achievement is to move us upward to the rightful inclusion of the Ethic of Community and the Ethic of Divinity in the moral domain.

Acknowledgments

No woman is an island. Here I would like to acknowledge key groups that over the years have influenced my thinking on psychological development, morality, and culture. To the Committee on Comparative Human Development at the University of Chicago, where as a graduate student I studied the complexities of culture. To the Department of Sociology at the University of California, Berkeley, where as a postdoctoral fellow I learned about subtleties of individuality and spirituality in the United States. To the Life Cycle Institute at Catholic University of America, where hiring a psychologist whose unorthodox scientific research addressing moral psychology and "culture wars" seemed worthwhile. To the Department of Psychology at Clark University, where a history of welcoming original ideas about human development continues. To the Bridging Culture and Development Group sponsored by the Society for Research on Child Development, whose members gave me the assurance and friendships to switch out one-size-fits-all social science models of the twentieth century with a "cultural-developmental" approach where local and global knowledge come together.

I also appreciate the support of the administrative, production, and marketing teams at Cambridge University Press. I thank my editors, Adina Berk, Hetty Marx, and Rebecca Taylor, who embraced the idea of a book on moral development with an international and interdisciplinary team of authors.

1 Theorizing and researching moral development in a global world

Lene Arnett Jensen

In recent decades, an argument for multiplicity has gained traction in the study of human psychology. Instead of a focus on one kind of self, one kind of intelligence, and one kind of creativity, for example, researchers have described multiple selves (Kağitçibaşi, 1996; Markus & Kitayama, 1991), intelligences (Gardner, 1993; Sternberg, 1985), and creativities (Csikszentmihalyi, 1988; Lubart, 1999). Moral psychology, too, has seen calls for the inclusion of more than one kind of moral reasoning (Colby & Damon, 1992; Damon & Colby, in press; Dien, 1982; Gilligan, 1982; Miller, 1989; Shweder, 1990) in lieu of conceptualizations of morality as a unitary structure (Kohlberg, 1984) or domain (Turiel, 1983). More often than not, the arguments for multiplicity have been inspired by consideration of culturally diverse individuals and groups.

What has so far received less attention is the development, from childhood into adulthood, of some of these multiplicitous psychological phenomena. This is because it takes time to build knowledge about new constructs, such as "interdependent self" (Triandis, 1995), "naturalistic intelligence" (Gardner, 2004), "spiritually-oriented creativity" (Lubart & Sternberg, 1998), and "Ethic of Community" (Jensen, 1995; Shweder, 1990). It also takes novel theoretical thinking to capture the development of a multiplicitous phenomenon (Greenfield, Keller, Fuligni, *et al.*, 2003). Additionally, when it comes to policy, it may seem more straightforward to work toward one goal than to figure out how to balance or select among two or more.

Nonetheless, a new focus in moral psychology is how the development of diverse kinds of reasoning occurs across the life course and the extent to which developmental trajectories vary across cultures. This is the focus of the theory known as the "cultural-developmental approach" (Jensen, 2008, 2011, 2012). This approach introduces the theoretical concept of a *template*. The template for moral development charts trajectories across the life course for three kinds of moral reasoning, the Ethics of Autonomy, Community, and Divinity. The cultural-developmental approach is not a one-size-fits-all model, however. The developmental trajectories are proposed as a template in the sense that they accommodate the different hierarchies of the ethics held by culturally diverse

1

peoples. For example, there is a more pronounced emphasis on the Ethic of Community in Taiwan than in the United States and a stronger emphasis on the Ethic of Autonomy in the United States than in Taiwan (Miller, Fung, Lin, *et al.*, 2012; see also Li, 2011, 2012). These different hierarchies interact with development. Thus the Ethics of Community and Autonomy are likely to emerge at different points in childhood in Taiwan and in the United States, to develop along somewhat different slopes, and to reach different endpoints in adulthood. The cultural-developmental approach, then, aims to capture how moral development and culture comodulate. From this perspective, ontogenetic development is not determinative, but neither is there a limitless cultural range.

The purpose of this book is to present the cultural-developmental approach to moral psychology, new research findings with highly diverse age and cultural groups that test and expand the theory, and four different research instruments for collecting and coding cultural-developmental research on morality. The international group of contributing authors represents anthropology, human development, linguistics, and social psychology. The authors bring a range of questions and methods to focus on the cultural-developmental nature of human morality. The hope is that the book provides a fresh conceptual approach to moral psychology along with concrete research tools for future scholarship. Perhaps, too, it may inspire ideas for how to address the development of multiplicity for other human psychological characteristics.

Here, I will begin with an overview of the cultural-developmental approach. I will then highlight a set of insights and issues that emerged across the chapters. This will include both how findings support cultural-developmental predictions and how they give rise to intriguing and fruitful new research ideas. The highlights, of course, represent a selection. Each chapter elucidates a number of additional findings on its own. In light of their specific findings, the authors of each chapter also discuss where they see a need for future scholarship.

The cultural-developmental approach

The cultural-developmental approach builds on a review of a large set of valuable findings from different research traditions. The findings come from traditions as varied as structural-developmental and domain theory (e.g., Kohlberg, 1984; Piaget, 1932/1965; Turiel, 1983), cultural psychology and anthropology perspectives on morality (e.g., Shweder, Mahapatra, & Miller, 1990; Trommsdorff & Chen, 2012; Whiting & Edwards, 1988), and research on the origins and development of prosocial emotions and norms (e.g., Padilla-Walker & Carlo, 2014; Thompson, 2012; Vaish & Tomasello, 2014; Warneken & Tomasello, 2006). These findings have been synthesized – and sometimes reinterpreted – to propose the cultural-developmental approach. Thus it is not a case of throwing out the baby with the bathwater, to use a fairly common idiom. Rather, it is a call to recognize that babies are instantly immersed in different cultural environments, and as they grow into adulthood they become increasingly culturally diverse. All babies may be moral (Bloom, 2013), but they are not particularly diverse in their morality. Adults from different cultures, however, are diverse. In short, the cultural-developmental approach proposes that there is universality and also increasing multiplicity with development.

As mentioned, the cultural-developmental approach introduces a template that charts developmental trajectories across the life course for the three Ethics of Autonomy, Community, and Divinity – a tripartite differentiation originally proposed by Shweder and his colleagues (Jensen, 1995; Shweder, 1990; Shweder, Much, Mahapatra, *et al.*, 1997). Briefly, the Ethic of Autonomy involves a focus on the self as an individual. Moral reasons within this ethic include the interests, well-being, and rights of individuals (self or other) and fairness between individuals. The Ethic of Community focuses on persons as members of social groups, with attendant reasons such as duty to others, and concern with the customs, interests, and welfare of groups. The Ethic of Divinity focuses on people as spiritual or religious entities, and reasons encompass divine and natural law, sacred lessons, and spiritual purity. Research has shown the presence of these three ethics among varied age and cultural groups (Arnett, Ramos, & Jensen, 2001; Guerra & Giner-Sorolla, 2010; Haidt, Koller, & Dias, 1993; Jensen, 1997a, 1997b, 1998, 2008; Padilla-Walker & Jensen, 2014; Rozin, Lowery, Imada, *et al.*, 1999; Vasquez, Keltner, Ebenbach, *et al.*, 2001). As we will see later, too, the present chapters substantiate their presence and differentiation in highly diverse samples.

The cultural-developmental approach describes moral development in terms of consistencies and changes in the *degree* of use of the three ethics across the life course. For example, does overall use of the Ethic of Community go down, remain stable, go up, or fluctuate with age? It also speaks to the specific *types* of moral reasons used within an ethic. Do children use different Ethic of Community reasons as compared to adolescents or adults?

In the standard manual for coding oral and written moral reasoning (*Coding Manual: Ethics of Autonomy, Community, and Divinity*, Jensen, 2004; see Appendix A in this volume), each reason is coded into one of the three ethics, allowing for an assessment of the *degree* to which a person uses each of the Ethics of Autonomy, Community, and Divinity. Each reason is also coded into one of numerous subcategories. The manual provides thirteen to sixteen subcategories for each ethic, such as "Self's Psychological Well-Being" and "Rights" for Autonomy, "Duty (to others)" and "Social Order or Harmony Goals" for Community, and "Scriptural Authority" and "Conscience (when God-given)" for Divinity. Apart from ensuring careful and comprehensive coding of all of a person's moral reasoning, the use of subcategories allows for an assessment of the specific *type* of moral concept used within an ethic. Distinguishing not only among the three ethics but also among types means that highly diverse concepts can be given consideration. For example, the Chinese concept of shame (Fung, 1999) and the Indian concept of role-based obligations (Miller, 1994) would both be coded into the Ethic of Community. However, they would be coded into the different subcategories "Virtues (community-oriented)" and "Duty (to others)," respectively. Likewise, a child's invocation of parental authority (Piaget, 1932/1965) and an adult's concern with social coordination (Zimba, 1994) would be coded as Ethic of Community reasons but with the former exemplifying the subcategory "Important Socially Defined Person's Author-ity" and the latter "Social Order or Harmony Goals."

The three questionnaires that have been developed based on the standard cod-ing manual also allow for assessment of both degree and type of usage of the three ethics. The Community, Autonomy, and Divinity Scale (CADS) assesses moral reasoning in regard to unspecified actions judged to be either right or wrong (Guerra & Giner-Sorolla; see Appendix B in this volume). The Ethical Values Assessment (EVA) measures the extent of endorsement of value state-ments that reflect the three ethics (Jensen & Padilla-Walker; see Appendix C in this volume). Both of these questionnaires come in standard and short ver-sions. The Three Ethics Reasoning Assessment (TERA) assesses reasoning in regard to a selection of specific moral issues, namely, abortion, divorce, sui-cide, and suicide in the case of terminal illness (Jensen; see Appendix D in this volume). Reasoning for other specific issues, however, could be assessed using the same format.

The development of Ethics of Autonomy, Community, and Divinity

In regard to the development of the three ethics, Figure 1.1 shows the template of trajectories for each ethic from childhood into adulthood. As illustrated, the argument is that Ethic of Autonomy reasoning emerges early in childhood and that the degree to which persons use this ethic stays relatively stable across adolescence and into adulthood. The specific types of Autonomy reasons that persons use are likely, however, to change with age. A substantial body of research has shown that from early on, children in different cultures focus on harm to the self and the interests of the self (Colby, Kohlberg, Gibbs, *et al.*, 1983; Snarey, 1985; Walker, 1989), as well as the needs and interests of other individuals (Bloom, 2013; Carlo, 2006; Gilligan, 1982; Miller, 1994; Turiel, 2002; Warneken & Tomasello, 2006). As persons in different cultures grow into adolescence and adulthood, some consideration of the welfare of the self and other individuals remains (Eisenberg, Carlo, Murphy, *et al.*, 1995; Gilligan, 1982; Vasquez, Keltner, Ebenbach, *et al.*, 2001; Walker, Pitts, Hennig, *et al.*, 1995; Zimba, 1994). However, in a consistent manner adolescents and adults

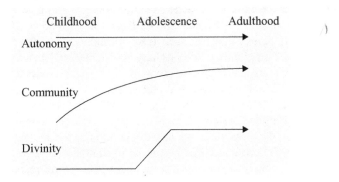

Figure 1.1   The cultural-developmental template of moral reasoning
(Reprinted from *Developmental Review* 28[3], Jensen, L. A., 'Through two
lenses: A cultural-developmental approach to moral psychology,' © 2008,
with permission from Elsevier.)

also begin to speak of reasons such as individual rights and equity – even
if these do not prevail across cultures (Killen, 2002; Miller & Luthar, 1989;
Piaget, 1932/1965; Snarey, 1985; Walker, 1989; Zimba, 1994).

The proposal, then, is that Autonomy reasoning stays relatively stable across
the life course but with some changes in types of Autonomy reasoning. However, it is noteworthy that in cultures in which there is a very strong push for
collectivity or submission to divinity, there may be somewhat of a decline in
Autonomy reasoning with age. In such cultures, considerations of the needs,
desires, and interests of individuals – especially the self – would be seen as
either irrelevant or even morally objectionable, and hence by adulthood such
considerations might diminish.

The Ethic of Community, according to the cultural-developmental approach,
rises throughout childhood and into adolescence and adulthood both in degree
of usage and in the diversity of types of reasons. Findings have consistently indicated that younger children in diverse cultures invoke Community reasons such
as family interests and customs (Kohlberg, 1984; Miller, Bersoff, & Harwood,
1990; Olson & Spelke, 2008; Shweder, Mahapatra, & Miller, 1990; Thompson,
2012). Cross-cultural research with the domain approach also shows this, even
as domain researchers have regarded the reasoning as "conventional" rather
than moral (Turiel, 1983, 2002). Moral reasoning related to the family is likely
to find continued expression past childhood and probably even more so in the
course of adolescence and adulthood as a person's awareness of and experiences
with diverse types of family considerations increase, such as duty to family in
addition to family interests and customs (Miller, Bersoff, & Harwood, 1990).
By late childhood and adolescence, Community reasons that pertain to social

groups other than the family are added (Carlo, 2006; Whiting & Edwards, 1988), including concern for friends (Rubin, Bukowski, & Parker, 2006) and peers and authority figures in places such as school and work (Schlegel, 2011). Cross-sectional and longitudinal findings have shown that, by late adolescence or adulthood, even more Community reasons are added, such as a focus on societal organization (Eisenberg, Carlo, Murphy, *et al.*, 1995; Eisenberg, Guthrie, Cumberland, *et al.*, 2002; Nisan, 1987; Walker, 1989; Zimba, 1994).

Turning to the Ethic of Divinity, for which much less research on moral reasoning is available, the proposal is that its use will often be low among children but will rise in adolescence and become similar to adult use. Diverse religions have ceremonies in early or midadolescence that confer moral responsibility on adolescents and link that responsibility to knowledge of religious teachings (Mahoney, Pargament, Murray-Swank, *et al.*, 2003). Adolescence appears to be a notable time for the development of religiosity or spirituality, even in societies in which affiliation with religious institutions is low (Trommsdorff, 2012). Research has also indicated that adults, including adults from relatively secular communities (McAdams, Albaugh, Farber, *et al.*, 2008; Walker, Pitts, Hennig, *et al.*, 1995), often explain their moral behaviors in terms of Divinity concepts (Colby & Damon, 1992; Shweder, Mahapatra, & Miller, 1990).

This potential infusion of Divinity reasoning in adolescence, however, may especially characterize religious cultures that emphasize scriptural authority or cultures in which people conceive of supernatural entities (e.g., God) as largely distinct from humans (e.g., omniscient and omnipotent). In these communities, the culturally articulated concepts pertaining to supernatural entities are of such an abstract nature that they may be readily translated into moral reasoning only by adolescents, whose cognitive skills allow for more abstraction than do those of younger children (Adelson, 1971; Keating, 1990; Kohlberg, 1976; Piaget, 1972; see also review in Trommsdorff, 2012).

In cultures where scriptural accounts of supernatural or transcendent entities are less salient or where people regard such entities as less distinct from humans, however, it is possible that Divinity concepts are more accessible to and hence more used by children in moral reasoning (Saraswathi, 2005). In some Hindu Indian communities, for example, religious devotion finds expression in tangible and recurrent activities (e.g., bathing, dressing, and feeding the gods); there are many places within and outside the home for worship (e.g., household and roadside shrines, temples); and there are a variety of persons seen to have godlike status or special connections with the gods (e.g., gurus, *sadhus* [renouncers], temple priests) (Jensen, 1998; Shweder, Mahapatra, & Miller, 1990). In such cultures, children may reason about moral issues in terms of Ethic of Divinity concepts from fairly early on because these concepts are tied repeatedly to specific everyday activities and objects. Then, in the course of adolescence and adulthood, additional Divinity concepts may become part of a person's moral reasoning. In Chapter 2 of the present volume, Pandya and Bhangaokar address the question of whether the Ethic of Divinity emerges early in Indian children. They use quantitative analyses to examine the degree to which the children reason in terms of Divinity and in-depth qualitative analyses to elaborate on the specific types that they bring up. In Chapter 4, Kapadia and Bhangaokar focus on adolescents and adults from the same Indian community, including their use of the Ethic of Divinity.

The comodulation of development and culture

The developmental trajectories in Figure 1.1, as noted, are intended to be a template that accommodates the different hierarchies of ethics held by culturally diverse peoples. The argument is that in order to make reasonably specific predictions about the development of each of the three ethics, we need to know not only about ontogeny but also about culture. In other words, the slopes and endpoints of the developmental trajectories are dependent on how the ethics are hierarchized within a culture.

For example, I have conducted research with Americans from religiously liberal and conservative cultures for more than two decades. On the basis of interview, questionnaire, and ethnographic research, as described in Chapter 8, I have found that religiously liberal adults emphasize the Ethics of Autonomy and Community, but not Divinity. Religiously conservative adults, in comparison, reason substantially in terms of the Ethics of Divinity and Community, but they deemphasize the Ethic of Autonomy. On the basis of these findings, I have proposed different developmental trajectories of moral reasoning within the two religious cultures (Jensen, 2008, 2011). I have illustrated these in Figures 1.2A and 1.2B. Within religiously liberal groups, as shown in Figure 1.2A, the expectation is that children, adolescents, and adults frequently will use the Ethic of Autonomy. Community reasons will be rarer among children but will then become quite common among adolescents and adults. Divinity will be used infrequently at all ages, and if it emerges, this will only occur in the course of adolescence. Figure 1.2B shows predictions for religiously conservative groups. The expectation is that these children, adolescents, and adults will use Autonomy infrequently. There may be some decrease over the life course because of the strong emphasis among religious conservatives on renouncing self-interest. With respect to Community, the expectation is that its prevalence will rise steadily from childhood to reach a high level in adulthood. The Ethic of Divinity will be low among children but will then rise markedly in adolescence and remain high throughout adulthood.

Chapter 8 of this volume includes a description of research with children, adolescents, and adults from religiously liberal and conservative American cultures that aimed to test and extend the predictions proposed in Figures 1.2A

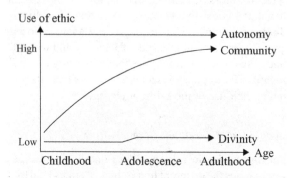

Figure 1.2A Hypothesized expression of template among religious liberals (Reprinted from *Developmental Review* 28[3], Jensen, L. A., 'Through two lenses: A cultural-developmental approach to moral psychology,' © 2008, with permission from Elsevier.)

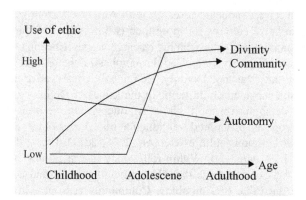

Figure 1.2B Hypothesized expression of template among religious conservatives (Reprinted from *Developmental Review* 28[3], Jensen, L. A., 'Through two lenses: A cultural-developmental approach to moral psychology,' © 2008, with permission from Elsevier.)

and 1.2B. In Chapter 3, Vainio also addresses these predictions in regard to religiously liberal and conservative adolescents from Finland. Furthermore, Chapter 7 by Hickman and DiBianca Fasoli includes a linguistic analysis of conversations between young children and parents from a religiously conservative American congregation. It aims to compare the moral reasoning of the two age groups and also to delve into the ways that parents and children respond to one another. As it turns out, the parents regularly sought to reroute their children's reasoning from a focus on Autonomy to Divinity considerations.

This chapter, then, speaks to not only the comodulation of moral development and culture but also a process whereby that comodulation takes place.

Other predictions follow from the cultural-developmental approach. One is the expectation of a particularly early and strong emergence of the Ethic of Community within collectivistic cultures. Taiwanese toddlers, for example, have been shown already to give repeated expression to community-oriented concepts such as shame (Fung, 1999; Miller, Fung, Lin, *et al.*, 2012). Furthermore, one might expect that Community considerations would come to exceed Autonomy and Divinity concepts in the course of adolescence and adulthood in such cultures. Studies with Indian adults, for example, have documented an elaborate emphasis on Community concepts such as duty, beneficence, social custom, and familial relations (Miller, Bersoff, & Harwood, 1990; Shweder, Mahapatra, & Miller, 1990). In Chapter 4, Kapadia and Bhangaokar pick up on these lines of research by comparing adults to adolescents on Ethic of Community reasoning and also by delving into the extent to which the two age groups resolve moral dilemmas through a process of autonomous decision making or interpersonal and role-based negotiation.

In cultures that afford young people in their twenties a prolonged period of identity exploration, also termed emerging adulthood (Arnett, 2004), the cultural-developmental prediction is for an upsurge in the Ethic of Autonomy. The hallmarks of emerging adulthood – independent decision making, financial self-sufficiency, and accepting responsibility for oneself – all center on Ethic of Autonomy considerations. Some research with American emerging adults supports the prediction (Arnett, Ramos, & Jensen, 2001). In this volume, Chapters 5 and 6 further test this proposal. In Chapter 5, Padilla-Walker and Nelson examine the moral reasoning of American emerging adults from a religiously conservative community of Latter-Day Saints (LDS, or Mormons). As they note, this sample constitutes an interesting test because of the potential pull toward Autonomy for American emerging adults and the simultaneous pull toward Divinity in LDS culture. Guerra and Giner-Sorolla, in Chapter 6, look at the use of the three ethics among younger and older emerging adults from five countries. Specifically, they compare emerging adults from Brazil, Israel, Japan, New Zealand, and the United Kingdom.

In sum, the cultural-developmental approach provides a developmental template that can be merged with knowledge of one or more cultures to generate new and well-defined hypotheses. Although it should be clear from the preceding research examples, I would like to note that the cultural-developmental approach defines *culture* as symbolic, behavioral, and institutional inheritances that are shared and coconstructed by members of a community (Goodnow, 2010; Heine, 2012; Shweder, Goodnow, Hatano, *et al.*, 2006). Culture is not synonymous with country or ethnicity, for example, but rather describes communities whose members share key beliefs, values, behaviors, routines, and institutions.

As scholars addressing cultural issues have long observed, cultural communities include heterogeneity among groups and individuals (Gramsci, 1971; Salzman, 1981). Variation also exists among cultural communities, including their degree of heterogeneity, intergroup contest, and change over time (Strauss, 1992; Weisner, Bradley, & Kilbride, 1997; Whiting & Edwards, 1988). Finally, access to power varies both within and among cultures.

New insights and ideas across chapters

As described earlier, every chapter examines its own set of hypotheses or questions. Across chapters, however, a set of collective insights emerges. I will highlight three. They include findings that support the cultural-developmental approach as well as intriguing new observations.

Widespread presence and differentiation of the three ethics

First, as mentioned briefly, the chapters in this volume substantiate the presence and differentiation of the three Ethics of Autonomy, Community, and Divinity in highly diverse samples. With respect to age, the samples ranged from 6 to 85 years. Also, across chapters, samples came from a total of nine countries and four continents. These samples also varied widely on religion, socioeconomic status, and rural versus urban residence. Across chapters, interrater reliabilities for interview responses coded with the standard coding manual for the three ethics ranged from 0.78 to 0.97. The researchers using the CADS and EVA questionnaires obtained reliabilities in the range of 0.64 to 0.91. These reliabilities speak to the robustness of the tripartite differentiation.

Recognition of the robustness of the three ethics does not preclude a finer-grained focus. In fact, attention to types of reasons that are characteristic of particular groups (or individuals) can be very fruitful. As described previously, all three questionnaires for assessing use of the three ethics also allow for assessment of subcategories. Furthermore, the standard coding manual for the Ethics of Autonomy, Community, and Divinity allows researchers to add subcategories to encompass new and distinctive reasons. Similarly, the EVA and TERA questionnaires include open-ended questions that provide participants with the option of adding ethical values and reasons not included on the closed-ended sections. In this volume, every chapter includes discussion of existing or new types of reasons in addition to the overarching focus on the three ethics. For example, in Chapter 8 I discuss the emphasis on the Ethic of Divinity subcategory "Scriptural Authority" that is characteristic of Protestant American samples of religious conservatives. This specific type of reason is a keystone of the ethical edifice of Divinity constructed by members of this cultural community. Pandya and Bhangaokar propose a distinctive Divinity subcategory of "Paap" for their sample of Indian children. As they explain, this Hindu concept encompasses not only a concrete notion of divine punishment but also a much broader metaphysics pertaining to *karma* and purity of one's soul. In sum, this volume supports the differentiation among Autonomy, Community, and Divinity. The extent to which research focuses on the three main ethics, existing subcategories, or new subcategories hinges on the questions asked by the researchers.

The cultural-developmental trajectories: support and surprise

A number of chapters in this volume also support the trajectories laid out in the cultural-developmental template. As predicted, the Ethic of Autonomy is lower among adults than among children or adolescents in cultures that emphasize familism and communalism (Kapadia & Bhangaokar, Chapter 4, this volume) or submission to divinity (Hickman & DiBianca Fasoli, Chapter 7, this volume; Jensen, Chapter 8, this volume).

Autonomy reasoning also decreased with age among religiously liberal Americans rather than remaining steady as predicted (Jensen, Chapter 8, this volume). This is rather striking since most major developmental theories of moral development, from Piaget to Kohlberg to Turiel, have positioned Autonomy reasoning at the endpoint of moral development. After all these years, room remains for more examination of the actual extent of adult use of the Ethic of Autonomy – even in cultures where Autonomy ranks high.

Speaking of which, three chapters add further evidence that the Ethic of Autonomy may be particularly high among people in their late teens and twenties who live in cultures where there is a period of emerging adulthood. The emphasis and precedence of this ethic were observed by Guerra and Giner-Sorolla for four of the five cultures they examined: emerging adults in Brazil, Israel, New Zealand, and the United Kingdom reasoned more in terms of Autonomy than in terms of the other two ethics. The interesting, if not entirely surprising, exception was Japan, where Autonomy was equal with Community.

Hickman and DiBianca Fasoli also found that Hmong emerging adult immigrants to the United States emphasized the Ethic of Autonomy, whereas their parents did not. As the authors poignantly explain:

They are dealing with the competing demands of Hmong moral models handed to them by their parents and relatives versus those that are more prevalent in American society (such as their non-Hmong peers) and more typical of American emerging adults in particular (see Jensen, 1995). This is an important dynamic for understanding the moral worlds of these migrant youth, and it suggests a more complicated picture of the development of moral identity (see Hardy, Walker, Olsen, *et al.*, 2013). (Chapter 7, this volume)

Finally, even among LDS emerging adults, Padilla-Walker and Nelson found evidence for considerable attention to the Ethic of Autonomy, even as the Ethic of Divinity was generally rated as significantly more important. These two authors engaged in an extensive exploration of how the two ethics were related in the thoughts and behaviors of their sample. I return to this question later in a discussion of relations among ethics.

The Ethic of Community, as predicted by the cultural-developmental approach, was found to be higher among adults than among children and adolescents. This was the case among Indian participants (Kapadia & Bhangaokar, this volume) and among both religiously liberal and conservative participants in the United States (Jensen, Chapter 8, this volume). There is clearly a need, however, for more research. The present findings are cross-sectional. They are also limited to three cultural groups, even if those are notably diverse.

With respect to the Ethic of Divinity, the thesis that an infusion of Divinity reasoning takes place in adolescence in religious cultures that emphasize scriptural authority and abstract conceptions of the supernatural was supported in Jensen's findings with American evangelical children, adolescents, and adults. Hickman and DiBianca Fasoli, too, observed low use of the Ethic of Divinity among American evangelical children but high use among their parents, and they surmise that adolescence must be when the shift occurs.

In a different religious tradition, Pandya and Bhangaokar examine the cultural-developmental proposal (described earlier) that the use of Divinity in moral reasoning may emerge at a fairly young age in cultures such as those in India where religion suffuses everyday life. They found that Divinity reasoning in Indian children is common, and just as common as Autonomy reasoning. This certainly supports the thesis. Unexpectedly, however, they also found that third graders used Divinity significantly more than sixth graders did. Furthermore, Kapadia and Bhangaokar, who studied adolescents and adults from the very same city and context in India, found low use of the Ethic of Divinity as compared to use of the Ethics of Autonomy and Community. These findings would seem to call for replication, preferably with comparable stimulus materials across age groups of children, adolescents, and adults.

As Pandya and Bhangaokar write, there is a "lacuna in contemporary moral psychology" in research on Divinity considerations (see also Trommsdorff, 2012). It is a lacuna that at a minimum goes back to Piaget, who argued that any references to religion and the supernatural mask the structure of genuine moral reasoning. Consequently, he left all such references by his samples of children and adolescents in Geneva uncoded (Edwards, 1981). I would argue that attention to Divinity considerations in people's moral lives has been on the rise (e.g., de Waal, 2013; Markus & Conner, 2013) and that the present chapters contribute to this emerging scientific focus. The inclusion of the Ethic of Divinity in the cultural-developmental approach provides a theoretical starting point for additional research.

The broadening and deepening of moral development

As I have argued elsewhere, the study of development in diverse cultures consistently leads to the discovery of new concepts (Jensen, 2012). It broadens our understanding of human psychology. Obviously, starting with a focus on three kinds of ethics rather than one already represents broadening, as discussed at the outset. In these chapters, the bridging of cultural and developmental perspectives spawned a broadening in regard to additional moral phenomena. Vainio, for example, shows that a much broader array of issues than what has traditionally been included within the moral domain (e.g., Turiel, 1983) is discussed by her diverse Finnish participants as being moral. Kapadia and Bhangaokar, as briefly noted, detail how moral decision making may be either relatively autonomous or may entail considerable interpersonal negotiation and calibration. In other words, they differentiate two processes for reaching moral judgments. Jensen distinguishes two new "spheres" of morality, the public and the private, in which the former describes moral reasoning that is applied to people in general and the latter comprises moral reasons that one applies to one's own moral behaviors. One key finding is that this distinction is critical to understanding the nuanced nature of the division between religiously liberal and conservative groups in the United States – sometimes referred to as the "culture wars." This volume, then, broadens our research foci not only on moral reasoning but also on moral issues, moral decision making, and moral spheres.

While the study of moral development in diverse cultures expands our range of psychological concepts, it also deepens them. One step toward deepening our understanding of these ethics comes from probing their intersection. Some past research has addressed this. For example, Arnett, Ramos, and Jensen (2001) showed positive correlations between Autonomy and Community among American emerging adults and discussed participants' emic (or indigenous) views of their developmental relation and intersection. Guerra and Giner-Sorolla (2010) also found correlations among the three ethics and discussed how those were dependent on culture. Jensen (1995) described how all three ethics were invoked by middle and older American adults. Vasquez, Keltner, Ebenbach, et al. (2001) highlighted how the history of the Philippines lends itself to invocation of all three ethics, and that is also what they found.

This volume includes chapters that push the focus on intersections further. Padilla-Walker and Nelson differentiate three patterns of "negotiation" between the Ethics of Autonomy and Divinity among their LDS participants: congruence, dominance, and conflict. They examined the patterns of negotiation in a number of ways, including the relative degree to which their participants valued each of the two ethics and the strength and direction of the correlation between the ethics. They also conducted regression analyses to determine how each of the three patterns of negotiation was associated with a range of behavioral outcomes that are salient to emerging LDS adults, including pro-social behavior, cohabitation, religious faith, and sexual exploration. Hickman and DiBianca Fasoli, too, address intersections. Rather than the quantitative approach of Padilla-Walker and Nelson, they take a qualitative one in which they delve deeply into the reasoning of the participants at both the group and individual levels. They look for ways that two or three ethics are used together, are in conflict with one another, or are interwoven to an extent to which differentiation seems to run counter to participants' emic worldviews. This latter emic issue is one that researchers coding for the three ethics are particularly likely to ponder because they typically work with culturally diverse groups. One of the strengths of Hickman and DiBianca Fasoli's chapter is that the authors take this cultural consideration very seriously.

Conclusion

The purpose of this book, as stated at the outset, is to provide a theoretical approach and concrete research ideas and tools to examine moral development as a multiplicitous phenomenon. The present authors have advanced this purpose. Their methods and findings can also serve as inspirations for future work. For example, there is clearly a need for longitudinal and sequential research on the cultural-developmental trajectories to better understand the roles of ontogenetic development and culture. Such longitudinal research is now under way with the Indian children of Chapter 2, who are now in early adolescence. There is also a need for new kinds of research on cultural-developmental processes. The present examples of research with child-parent dyads and on the differentiation between public and private spheres of morality are two avenues. Currently, research is comparing adolescent-parent dyads from rural and urban Thailand on their reasoning about public and private moral issues (McKenzie, 2014). There are many other possibilities, however, including research tailored to other contexts such as peers, service and civic organizations, and media.

Richard Shweder, who authored the foreword to this volume, and Joan Miller and Gisela Trommsdorff, who each provided commentaries, offer still other ideas for future work. Each author's insights are based on decades of experience in the field.

I, like many of my colleagues (Jensen, 2015), am continuously struck by just how fast "fields" – the academic and the cultural ones – are changing. I think the universal aspirations of many theories of the last century are giving way to something more flexible that recognizes both universality and multiplicity. Furthermore, culturally insular communities are rapidly changing in the wave of globalization (e.g., Hermans, 2015; Hermans & Kempen, 1998; Silbereisen & Chen, 2010; Trommsdorff, 2000). Isolated cultures are a phenomenon of yore. Culture, too, is becoming something more flexible that involves both stability and hybridity. Thus I titled the present volume "Moral Development in a Global World" in an attempt to direct attention to the dynamic and divergent ways that morality develops across cultures in a time of globalization.

REFERENCES

Adelson, J. (1971). The political imagination of the young adolescent. *Daedalus*, 100, 1013–1050.

Arnett, J. J. (2004). *Emerging adulthood: The winding road from the late teens through the twenties*. New York, NY: Oxford University Press.

Arnett, J. J., Ramos, K. D., & Jensen, L. A. (2001). Ideological views in emerging adulthood: Balancing autonomy and community. *Journal of Adult Development*, 8, 69–79.

Bloom, P. (2013). *Just babies: The origins of good and evil*. New York, NY: Crown Publishers.

Carlo, G. (2006). Care-based and altruistically-based morality. In M. Killen & J. Smetana (Eds.), *Handbook of moral development* (pp. 551–580). Mahwah, NJ: Erlbaum.

Colby, A., & Damon, W. (1992). *Some do care: Contemporary lives of moral commitment*. New York, NY: Free Press.

Colby, A., Kohlberg, L., Gibbs, J., & Lieberman, M. (1983). A longitudinal study of moral judgment. *Monographs of the Society for Research in Child Development*, 48.

Csikszentmihalyi, M. (1988). Society, culture, and person: A systems view of creativity. In R. J. Sternberg (Ed.), *The nature of creativity: Contemporary psychological perspectives* (pp. 325–339). New York, NY: Cambridge University Press.

Damon, W., & Colby, A. (in press). *The power of ideals*. New York, NY: Oxford University Press.

de Waal, F. (2013). *The Bonobo and the atheist: In search of humanism among the primates*. New York, NY: Norton.

Dien, D. S. (1982). A Chinese perspective on Kohlberg's theory of moral development. *Developmental Review*, 2, 331–341.

Edwards, C. P. (1981). The comparative study of the development of moral judgment and reasoning. In R. H. Munroe, R. L. Munroe, & B. B. Whiting (Eds.), *Handbook of cross-cultural human development* (pp. 501–528). New York, NY: Garland STPM Press.

Eisenberg, N., Carlo, G., Murphy, B., & Van Court, P. (1995). Prosocial development in late adolescence. *Child Development*, 66, 1179–1197.

Eisenberg, N., Guthrie, I. K., Cumberland, A., Murphy, B. C., Shepard, S. A., Zhou, Q., Carlo, G. (2002). Prosocial development in early adulthood: A longitudinal study. *Journal of Personality and Social Psychology*, 82, 993–1006.

Fung, H. (1999). Becoming a moral child: The socialization of shame among young Chinese children. *Ethos*, 27, 180–209.

Gardner, H. (1993). *Multiple intelligences: New horizons*. New York, NY: Basic Books. (2004). *Frames of mind: The theory of multiple intelligences*. New York, NY: Basic Books.

Gilligan, C. F. (1982). *In a different voice: Psychological theory and women's development*. Cambridge, MA: Harvard University Press.

Goodnow, J. J. (2010). Culture. In M. H. Bornstein (Ed.), *Handbook of cultural developmental science*. New York, NY: Psychology Press.

Gramsci, A. (1971). *Selections from the prison notebook*. London, United Kingdom: Lawrence and Wishart.

Greenfield, P. M., Keller, H., Fuligni, A., & Maynard, A. (2003). Cultural pathways through universal development. *Annual Review of Psychology*, 54, 461–490.

Guerra, V. M., & Giner-Sorolla, R. (2010). Community, Autonomy, and Divinity Scale (CADS): Development of a theory-based moral codes scale. *Journal of Cross-Cultural Psychology*, 41, 35–50.

Haidt, J., Koller, S. H., & Dias, M. G. (1993). Affect, culture, and morality, or, Is it wrong to eat your dog? *Journal of Personality and Social Psychology*, 65, 613–628.

Hardy, S. A., Walker, L. J., Olsen, J. A., Woodbury, R. D., & Hickman, J. R. (2013). Moral identity as moral ideal self: Links to adolescent outcomes. *Developmental Psychology*, 50(1), 45–57.

Heine, S. J. (2012). *Cultural psychology*. New York, NY: Norton.

Hermans, H. J. M. (2015). Human development in today's globalizing world: Implications for self and identity. In L. A. Jensen (Ed.), *The Oxford handbook of human development and culture: An interdisciplinary perspective*. New York, NY: Oxford University Press.

Hermans, H. J. M., & Kempen, H. J. G. (1998). Moving cultures: The perilous problem of cultural dichotomies in a globalizing society. *American Psychologist*, 53, 1111–1120.

Jensen, L. A. (1995). Habits of the heart revisited: Autonomy, Community and Divinity in adults' moral language. *Qualitative Sociology*, 18, 71–86.

  (1997a). Culture wars: American moral divisions across the adult lifespan. *Journal of Adult Development*, 4, 107–121.

  (1997b). Different worldviews, different morals: America's culture war divide. *Human Development*, 40, 325–344.

  (1998). Moral divisions within countries between orthodoxy and progressivism: India and the United States. *Journal for the Scientific Study of Religion*, 37, 90–107.

  (2004). *Coding manual: Ethics of Autonomy, Community, and Divinity (Revised)*. Retrieved from www.lenearnettjensen.com.

  (2008). Through two lenses: A cultural-developmental approach to moral reasoning. *Developmental Review*, 28, 289–315.

  (2011). *Bridging cultural and developmental psychology: New syntheses in theory, research, and policy*. New York, NY: Oxford University Press.

  (2012). Bridging universal and cultural perspectives: A vision for developmental psychology in a global world. *Child Development Perspectives*, 6, 98–104.

  (2015). *The Oxford handbook of human development and culture: An interdisciplinary perspective*. New York, NY: Oxford University Press.

Kağitçibaşi, C. (1996). The autonomous-relational self: A new synthesis. *European Psychologist*, 1, 180–186.

Keating, D. (1990). Adolescent thinking. In S. S. Feldman & G. Elliott (Eds.), *At the threshold: The developing adolescent* (pp. 54–89). Cambridge, MA: Harvard University Press.

Killen, M. (2002). Early deliberations: A developmental psychologist investigates how children think about fairness and exclusion. *Teaching Tolerance*, 22, 44–49.

Kohlberg, L. (1976). Moral stages and moralization: The cognitive-developmental approach. In T. Lickona (Ed.), *Moral development and behavior*. New York, NY: Holt, Rinehart and Winston.

(1984). *The psychology of moral development*. San Francisco, CA: Harper & Row.

Li, J. (2011). Cultural frames of children's learning beliefs. In L. A. Jensen (Ed.), *Bridging cultural and developmental psychology: New syntheses in theory, research, and policy* (pp. 26–48). New York, NY: Oxford University Press.

(2012). *Cultural foundations of learning: East and West*. New York, NY: Cambridge University Press.

Lubart, T. I. (1999). Creativity across cultures. In R. J. Sternberg (Ed.), *Handbook of creativity*. New York, NY: Cambridge University Press.

Lubart, T. I., & Sternberg, R. J. (1998). Creativity across time and place: Life span and cross-cultural perspectives. *High Ability Studies*, 9(1), 59–74.

Mahoney, A., Pargament, K. I., Murray-Swank, A., & Murray-Swank, N. (2003). Religion and the sanctification of family relationships. *Review of Religious Research*, 44, 220–236.

Markus, H. R., & Conner, A. (2013). *Clash! 8 Cultural conflicts that make us who we are*. New York, NY: Hudson Street Press.

Markus, H. R., & Kitayama, S. (1991). Culture and the self: Implications for cognition, emotion and motivation. *Psychological Review*, 98, 224–253.

McAdams, D. P., Albaugh, M., Farber, E., Daniels, J., Logan, R. L., & Olson, B. (2008). Family metaphors and moral intuitions: How conservatives and liberals narrate their lives. *Journal of Personality and Social Psychology*, 95, 978–990.

McKenzie, J. (2014). *Morality, modernity, and globalization: A cross-generational study in rural and urban Thailand* (Unpublished doctoral dissertation). Clark University, Worcester, MA.

Miller, J. G. (1989). A cultural perspective on the morality of beneficence and interpersonal responsibility. In S. Ting-Tomey & F. Korzenny (Eds.), *International and intercultural communication annual* (Vol. 15, pp. 11–27). Newbury Park, CA: Sage.

(1994). Cultural diversity in the morality of caring: Individually oriented versus duty-based interpersonal moral codes. *Cross-Cultural Research*, 28, 3–39.

Miller, J. G., Bersoff, D. M., & Harwood, R. L. (1990). Perceptions of social responsibility in India and in the United States: Moral imperatives or personal decisions? *Journal of Personality and Social Personality*, 58, 33–47.

Miller, J. G., & Luthar, S. (1989). Issues of interpersonal responsibility and accountability: A comparison of Indians' and Americans' moral judgments. *Social Cognition*, 7, 237–261.

Miller, P. J., Fung, H., Lin, S., Chen, E. C.-H., & Boldt, B. R. (2012). How socialization happens on the ground: Narrative practices as alternate socializing pathways in Taiwanese and European-American families. *Monographs of the Society for Research in Child Development*, 77, 1–140.

Nisan, M. (1987). Moral norms and social conventions: A cross-cultural study. *Developmental Psychology*, 23, 719–725.

Olson, K. R., & Spelke, E. S. (2008). Foundations of cooperation in young children. *Cognition*, 108, 222–231.

Padilla-Walker, L. M., & Carlo, G. (2014). *Prosocial development: A multidimensional approach*. New York, NY: Oxford University Press.

Padilla-Walker, L. M., & Jensen, L. A. (2014). The Ethical Values Assessment (EVA): A validation study of the long- and short-form (Unpublished manuscript). Brigham Young University, Provo, UT.

Piaget, J. (1965). *The moral judgment of the child*. New York, NY: Free Press. (Original work published 1932)

(1972). Intellectual evolution from adolescence to adulthood. *Human Development*, 15, 1–12.

Rozin, P., Lowery, L., Imada, S., & Haidt, J. (1999). The CAD triad hypothesis: A mapping between three moral emotions (contempt, anger, disgust) and three moral codes (Community, Autonomy, Divinity). *Journal of Personality and Social Psychology*, 76, 574–586.

Rubin, K., Bukowski, W., & Parker, J. (2006). Peer interactions, relationships and groups. In W. Damon & R. M. Lerner (Eds.), *Handbook of child development*. New York, NY: Wiley.

Salzman, P. C. (1981). Culture as enhabilmentis. In L. Holy & M. Stuchlik (Eds.), *The structure of folk models* (pp. 233–256). London, United Kingdom: Academic Press.

Saraswathi, T. S. (2005). Hindu worldview in the development of selfways: The "Atman" as the real self. In L. A. Jensen & R. Larson (Eds.), *New Horizons in Developmental Theory and Research. New Directions for Child and Adolescent Development*, 109, 43–50.

Schlegel, A. (2011). Adolescent ties to adult communities: The intersection of culture and development. In L. A. Jensen (Ed.), *Bridging cultural and developmental approaches to psychology: New syntheses in theory, research, and policy* (pp. 138–157). New York, NY: Oxford University Press.

Shweder, R. A. (1990). In defense of moral realism. *Child Development*, 61, 2060–2067.

Shweder, R. A., Goodnow, J., Hatano, G., LeVine, R., Markus, H., & Miller, P. (2006). The cultural psychology of development: One mind, many mentalities. In W. Damon & R. M. Lerner (Eds.), *Handbook of child development* (pp. 716–792). New York, NY: Wiley.

Shweder, R. A., Mahapatra, M., & Miller, J. G. (1990). Culture and moral development. In J. W. Stigler, R. A. Shweder, & G. Herdt (Eds.), *Cultural psychology* (pp. 130–204). Cambridge, United Kingdom: Cambridge University Press.

Shweder, R. A., Much, N. C., Mahapatra, M., & Park, L. (1997). The "Big Three" of morality (Autonomy, Community, Divinity), and the "big three" explanations of suffering (pp. 119–170). In A. Brandt & P. Rozin (Eds.), *Morality and health*. New York, NY: Routledge.

Silbereisen, R. K., & Chen, X. (2010). *Social change and human development: Concepts and results*. London, United Kingdom: Sage.

Snarey, J. R. (1985). Cross-cultural universality of socio-moral development: A critical review of Kohlbergian research. *Psychological Bulletin*, 97, 202–232.

Sternberg, R. J. (1985). *Beyond IQ: A triarchic theory of human intelligence*. New York, NY: Cambridge University Press.

Strauss, C. (1992). Models and motives. In R. G. D'Andrade & C. Strauss (Eds.), *Human motives and cultural models* (pp. 1–20). Cambridge, United Kingdom: Cambridge University Press.

Thompson, R. A. (2012). Whither the preconventional child? Toward a life-span moral development theory. *Child Development Perspectives*, 6, 423–429.

Triandis, H. C. (1995). *Individualism and collectivism*. Boulder, CO: Westview Press.

Trommsdorff, G. (2000). Effects of social change on individual development: The role of social and personal factors and the timing of events. In. L. Crockett & R. K. Silbereisen (Eds.), *Negotiating adolescence in times of social change* (pp. 58–68). Cambridge, United Kingdom: Cambridge University Press.

(2012). Cultural perspectives on values and religion in adolescent development: A conceptual overview and synthesis. In G. Trommsdorff & X. Chen (Eds.), *Values, religion, and culture in adolescent development* (pp. 3–45). Cambridge, United Kingdom: Cambridge University Press.

Trommsdorff, G., & Chen, X. (2012). *Values, religion, and culture in adolescent development*. Cambridge, United Kingdom: Cambridge University Press.

Turiel, E. (1983). *The development of social knowledge: Morality and convention*. Cambridge, United Kingdom: Cambridge University Press.

(2002). *The culture of morality*. Cambridge, United Kingdom: Cambridge University Press.

Vaish, A., & Tomasello, M. (2014). The early ontogeny of human cooperation and morality. In M. Killen & J. G. Smetana (Eds.), *Handbook of moral development* (pp. 279–298). New York, NY: Psychology Press.

Vasquez, K., Keltner, D., Ebenbach, D. H., & Banaszynski, T. L. (2001). Cultural variation and similarity in moral rhetorics: Voices from the Philippines and the United States. *Journal of Cross-Cultural Research*, 32, 93–120.

Walker, L. J. (1989). A longitudinal study of moral reasoning. *Child Development*, 51, 131–139.

Walker, L. J., Pitts, R. C., Hennig, K. H., & Matsuba, M. K. (1995). Reasoning about morality and real-life moral problems. In M. Killen & D. Hart (Eds.), *Morality in everyday life: Developmental perspectives* (pp. 371–407). New York, NY: Cambridge University Press.

Warneken, F., & Tomasello, M. (2006). Altruistic helping in human infants and young chimpanzees. *Science*, 311, 1301–1303.

Weisner, T. S., Bradley, C., & Kilbride, P. (1997). *African families and the crisis of social change*. Westport, CT: Greenwood Press/Bergin & Garvey.

Whiting, B. B., & Edwards, C. P. (1988). *Children of different worlds: The formation of social behavior*. Cambridge, MA: Harvard University Press.

Zimba, R. F. (1994). The understanding of morality, convention, and personal preference in an African setting: Findings from Zambia. *Journal of Cross-Cultural Psychology*, 25, 369–393.

2 Divinity in children's moral development: an Indian perspective

Niyati Pandya and Rachana Bhangaokar

> If someone is doing wrong, like if he is in the habit of stealing other's money or harming them on purpose, then we should pray to God for him, we should collect blessings for him – if he is not bothered about himself, at least we are. We should pray to God so that God gives him blessings and helps him become a good person. By doing this for him, we will also get blessings and a good life in return.
>
> 11-year-old Indian girl

Morality is a fundamental aspect of human development, one that encompasses a multitude of values related to the interactions between the self, others, and the spiritual world. This intersection of the autonomous, interpersonal, and spiritual spheres in morality is a characteristic of the Indian moral worldview. The preceding quotation from a participant in our study illustrates this well. Much attention has been given to the role of autonomy and community in moral reasoning, whereas divinity remains insufficiently explored. In the present chapter, we show evidence for the need to include divinity in the study of moral reasoning. We focus on Indian children's use of divinity concepts in moral discourse and the influences of age and social class. We begin with an overview of traditional psychological theories and their propositions regarding divinity and moral reasoning. Following that, we review research that employs noncognitive and cultural perspectives in the study of morality. Next, we discuss the role of divinity in the Indian moral worldview and aspects of moral socialization that help children imbibe cultural meanings associated with moral reasoning, with special emphasis on divinity concepts. Last, adopting the cultural-developmental approach, we provide quantitative and qualitative evidence for the early emergence of divinity in children's moral reasoning in the Indian context.

This research was supported by a grant from the Indian Council of Social Science Research, New Delhi. Rachana Bhangaokar was the co-investigator for the project, with the principal investigator, Professor Shagufa Kapadia, the Maharaja Sayajirao University of Baroda, India. Niyati Pandya is grateful to both for their support and guidance.

Religion and divinity in moral psychology

Early theories and research in the field of moral psychology have largely been dominated by the cognitive development approach that emphasizes universal frameworks of moral reasoning and development (Kohlberg, 1981; Piaget, 1932/1965). These theories are developed from the vantage point of dominant Western traditions that emphasize autonomous and justice-based moral reasoning. In doing so, they have often neglected and undermined alternate moral conceptions that are integral to worldviews held by groups in other parts of the world, including those that have religious and spiritual underpinnings. A review of contributions made by early developmental theorists reflects a separation of the religious and moral spheres.

In his theory of cognitive development, Piaget (1932/1965) emphasized universal standards of rational and mature thinking. He distinguished between the logical, scientific, rational world of modern people and the religious, superstitious, and irrational world of "primitive" people. Thus, progressive moral thinking was strictly characterized by objective ideals of logic and justice, whereas beliefs in immanent justice (the idea that suffering is punishment for one's sins), animistic thinking (belief that inanimate objects have feelings and desires), and the role of social order (duties, obligations, and social roles) that are central to moral philosophies of several non-Western cultures were believed to be immature or less-developed modes of thinking and reasoning (Shweder, Much, Mahapatra, et al., 1997). Thus, Piagetian theory offers a rather narrow definition of morality, one that does not extend beyond principles of justice and fairness to encompass moral worldviews that involve religious or spiritual ideas.

Kohlberg's theory of moral development was an extension of Piaget's ideas, and he similarly began with the assumption that autonomy is reflective of a higher level of moral development compared to religious attitudes or principles (Kohlberg, 1981). Kohlberg and Power (1981) asserted that morality is independent of religion and that moral education should be based on universal principles of justice and fairness. The well-known six stages of moral development proposed by Kohlberg posit justice as the highest principle. The cultural appropriateness of Kohlberg's theory has long been debated, especially his claim for universality and the neglect of religious as well as community concepts in moral discourse. Kohlberg later proposed a seventh stage where he speculated the possibility of a cosmic orientation and a religious perspective. Presumably, this stage included concepts pertaining to the natural law as well as ideas such as universal love, service, and sacrifice. However, moral reasoning and religious reasoning were still seen as distinguishable, almost parallel areas in human development.

On similar lines, Turiel (2002) proposed that moral rules are ones that can be justified through reasoning based on universal ideas of justice and fairness.

According to Turiel, there may be nonmoral and moral rules of religion. The nonmoral rules are those that are the conventional type. These apply only to members of the religion and depend on religious authority. In contrast, moral rules have a different kind of connection with religion in that people outside the religion are also obliged to adhere to these rules, and moral acts are evaluated independent of God's word, as in the case of issues related to harm or justice. Thus, religion and morality share a complex relationship that includes what ought to be part of religious teachings. Hence, domain theorists distinguished between the relative or conventional aspects of religion and the absolute or universal aspects of the moral domain, which may also feature in what religions prescribe.

These early theories have given significant impetus for subsequent research, with many scholars arguing for a broader definition of morality – one that includes multiple moral concepts used by diverse cultures and groups (Edwards, 1987; Haidt, Koller, & Dias, 1993; Miller & Bersoff, 1995; Vasudev & Hummel, 1987; Zimba, 1994). This chapter also aims to highlight the role of culture and divinity concepts in children's emerging conceptualization of morality.

Cultural examinations of divinity in moral development

Research involving application of the universalistic approaches of Piaget, Kohlberg, and Turiel across cultures suggests the need for a more pluralistic and culture-inclusive framework of understanding morality. Research shows that Kohlberg's manual tends to overlook concepts of divinity, spirituality, and religion even though these concepts are foundational to morality in various cultural groups (Miller & Luthar, 1989; Shweder, Mahapatra, & Miller, 1990; Vasquez, Keltner, Ebenbach, *et al.*, 2001; Vasudev, 1994; Vasudev & Hummel, 1987). Further, Shweder and Much (1991) as well as Vasudev (1994) have shown that Kohlberg's theory portrays a limited view of postconventional thought and offers little scope to capture alternate forms of postconventional thinking.

Vasudev takes the example of *ahimsa* (nonviolence or harmlessness) to illustrate this point. *Ahimsa* is regarded as the ultimate religion and the highest moral virtue in the Mahabharata (Sanskrit epic of ancient India). This concept of nonviolence prescribes an obligation not to inflict harm by "mind, word or deed" (Chatterjee, 1995; Vasudev, 1994) to any form of life. It stems from and perpetuates a sense of deep connection and moral obligation toward all living beings, including fellow humans, animals, and plants. It is a foundational aspect of three important ancient religions of India – Hinduism, Jainism, and Buddhism. It permeates life and philosophy in India, including everyday moral preferences such as eating a vegetarian diet and avoiding animal products (e.g., animal fat, meat, and eggs) that are believed to pollute the soul. Further,

Gandhi (1951) developed the concept of *satyagraha* as a practical extension of *ahimsa*. *Satya* implies truth, and *agraha* implies firmness. Thus, *satyagraha* is the force that stems from truth and love, or nonviolence. He understood *ahimsa* as the love for all living beings, including one's enemy, and thus led the nation to engage in peaceful resistance against and noncooperation with the British rule in India. Moral reasoning pertaining to *ahimsa* cannot be coded using Kohlberg's manual even though it is regarded as one of the highest moral virtues in India and has immense religious as well as moral significance in Indian society.

Similarly, Huebner and Garrod (1991) examined moral views of Tibetan Buddhist monks through in-depth interviews. They argued that the monks' meta-ethical beliefs are remarkably different from Kohlberg's views. For instance, the authors draw attention to the moral significance of *dukkha*, or suffering in the karmic world (while cautioning the reader about *dukkha* being more than what the closest English word for it – *suffering* – suggests). In Buddhism, suffering is conceptualized as one means of undoing negative *karma* (deeds), the second being the involvement in positive karma. Additionally, this understanding of suffering endorses the prevention of and sensitivity to the suffering of others, including fellow nonhuman beings. For example, Huebner and Garrod explained how monks in their study were perceptive of the pain, vulnerability, and suffering endured by animals or insects because of being less developed compared to humans. By virtue of upholding these moral values and concepts, Buddhists are likely to come across moral dilemmas that are unfamiliar to Western thought. Thus, Huebner and Garrod claimed that the conceptualization of morality within the framework of assumptions established by Western philosophers is often inadequate in accounting for moral reasoning in Buddhist cultures and in other non-Western cultures. They advocated for the need to explore alternate ideologies and to understand moral worldviews in the context of the philosophy and language of a culture. Interestingly, research suggests that although divinity or supernatural concepts, such as *karma* and sacred self, run counter to the mainstream scientific discourse in the United States, they continue to exist in the moral conscience of certain groups in the country, even though they may be considered as part of one's personal realm (Jensen, 1998; Shweder, 2003). Contrary to this trend, religious and spiritual themes are openly acknowledged as central aspects of morality in several other cultures and are essential to moral socialization.

Additionally, we would like to note that ideas about God and divinity have been found to have several positive influences on development. For example, research in Canada suggests that priming for God concepts generates a sense of security and increases prosocial behaviors such as cooperation and generosity (Shariff & Norenzayan, 2007). Kumari and Pirta (2009) provide evidence that God serves as a secure base for Hindus in India. Findings from the study lend support to the proposition that religious phenomena such as the belief in God and supernatural power have important positive influences. Faith in traditional religious moral values continues to serve as a source of immense hope, courage to face difficulties in life, and thus promotes positive mental health outcomes throughout the course of development. In case of adverse situations, God serves as affirmative energy that instills in people hope and the determination to pursue a moral path, even if that entails undergoing temporary hardship. Thus, examining religious and spiritual beliefs from within the cultural frame of reference and value systems helps illuminate and acknowledge their role in moral reasoning. In the next section, we explain aspects of the Hindu Indian moral worldview to contextualize moral reasoning among participants in the present study.

The Hindu moral worldview

In the Indian philosophical tradition, *Vedas* (ancient religious texts) represent the ultimate religious authority, especially with respect to *dharma* (righteous duty) and *Brahmān* (universal order) (Sharma, 2000). Additionally, the *Vedas* inform us about specific qualities and values that should be upheld in life. For instance, *ahankar* (pride) should be eliminated, and qualities such as *manusa* (humanity), *daanam* (charity), *damyata* (self-control), *dayadhvam* (compassion), and *sama* (tranquility) are important. These qualities make one *vinamra* (humble/modest), lead to an ethical way of life, and, in turn, bring one closer to attaining the ultimate goal of *moksha* (Chatterjee, 1995). Research shows that in spite of the many influences brought about by invasions, migrations, reform movements (e.g., Buddhism and Sikhism), and modernization, the principal values of the Indian moral worldview remain integral to people's conscience and have an implicit influence on moral thought and behavior (Menon, 2003; Miller & Luthar, 1989; Saraswathi, Mistry, & Dutta, 2011).

The observance of *dharma* through good *karma* (actions) and pursuit of *moksha*, or liberation of the soul from the cycle of birth-death-rebirth, comprise the central goals of human life in Hinduism. *Karma* is believed to be a moral order, in which events take place for ethical reasons, and, in the long run, sins are punished and righteous conduct is rewarded (Bhangaokar & Kapadia, 2009; Huebner & Garrod, 1991; Paranjpe, 1996; Shweder, Mahapatra, & Miller, 1990). Thus, *karma* functions as a law of causality where consequences of good and bad deeds may be experienced in the present or future births.

According to the law of *karma*, souls progress from lower to higher forms till they achieve the human form. In their human birth, they accumulate credit and discredit through their good and bad deeds. Good deeds result in birth in the human form and bad deeds lead to birth in the form of an animal. The influence of the deeds is not limited to the form one's soul takes at rebirth; deeds also influence the quality of life and experiences in future births (Paranjpe, 1996). Thus, the goal of the karmic cycle is to achieve a better form of rebirth through *samsāra* (transmigration of souls) or to ultimately gain *moksha* (liberation from the delusion of individual existence) and attain the realization of one's true self, or *ātman*. We think it is important to note that the *Brahmān* in the Hindu worldview responds to human activity. It is not a fatalistic view. Thus, people suffer or enjoy benefits depending on their *karma* in their present as well as previous lives and depending on their good and bad deeds in everyday life (Clooney, 1989).

This Indian moral worldview is also highly contextual (Ramanujan, 1990). There are no absolute claims or rules that one must abide by; instead, one's deeds are judged as "good" or "bad" on the basis of social roles, duties, and circumstances. Additionally, these abstract philosophical ideas form the foundation of concrete practices and values that inform us of ways of leading a moral life. The ultimate goal of spiritual enlightenment and *moksha* can be attained by fulfilling one's duties and following moral discipline throughout life. For example, Krishnan and Manoj (2008) closely examined traditional Hindu writings to understand the concept of *daanam* in the purview of the Indian psychology of values. The word *daanam* literally means "giving" and loosely translates to charity. However, the authors assert that *daanam* is more than merely prosocial behavior or altruism, as is commonly conceptualized by social psychologists and the Western world. In the Hindu system of values, it has a deeper moral and religious significance, too. For example, as Krishnan and Manoj explain, *daanam* involves *nivrutti*, or withdrawal/detachment, and *tyaaga*, or relinquishment by the donor.

Paranjpe (2013) explained the concept of *dharma* – the cornerstone for understanding morality among Hindu Indians – by highlighting that *dharma* does not mean religion. It is also not tied to a single explanatory belief system, and it does not pose any threat to a science. Rather, the concept of *dharma* is pluralistic and concerns the "upholding" of a moral order in the world. This understanding has societal, interpersonal, and spiritual/individualistic implications.

Menon (2013) stated that the understanding of *dharma* is not duty based but, rather, goal based. One of the goals is cosmic in nature, and the other, individualistic. Moral development is a life-long process that depends on self-discipline and self-refinement, necessary ingredients for the upholding of *dharma* and the cultivation of nonattachment. The ultimate goal of spiritual enlightenment, or *moksha*, can be attained by fulfilling one's duties and performing actions (*karma*) with nonattachment (*niskama*). These views reiterate the fact that *dharma* should not be bound to narrow understandings of duty or righteousness. Rather, they provide a broad template to navigate individual moral concerns in a highly contextual, social, and spiritual framework.

From a very young age, children observe and participate in everyday familial and social practices that reiterate this Hindu Indian worldview. Thus, these moral values and philosophical ideas are transmitted over generations through socialization (Miller & Bersoff, 1995; Shweder & Much, 1991). Children have multiple sources of cultural learning. These include everyday habits enforced by adults such as touching the feet of elders to convey respect, removing footwear outside temples and homes to maintain their sanctity, and considering guests as a form of God and serving them with love, respect, and reverence. Additionally, participation in everyday rituals such as bathing, dressing, feeding, worshipping God, and feeding the needy to maintain the spirit of sharing with others is also encouraged. Last, listening to mythological stories from adults or grandparents (e.g., the Mahabharata, *Ramayana, Panchatantra*) plays a major role in inculcating the understanding of moral principles through the example of model characters and the way they lived their lives.

The present study is part of a larger cultural-developmental study on the development of morality in children, adolescents, and adults in the Indian context. Here we focused on children and their moral reasoning in terms of divinity concepts. Through quantitative and qualitative analyses, we address the extent of similarities and differences between younger and older children, and children of different socioeconomic statuses (SES). We also provide a detailed, culturally grounded elaboration and explication of the religious concepts used by these Indian children, with the aim of broadening the current literature on morality.

Present study

A cultural-developmental framework: the three ethics

Shweder and colleagues propose a pluralistic definition of morality and differentiate three Ethics of Autonomy, Community, and Divinity (Shweder, Much, Mahapatra, *et al.*, 1997). The Ethic of Autonomy defines the self as an autonomous being with rights, needs, and the freedom to make choices and protect individual interests. This ethic includes virtues such as self-expression, self-esteem, and independence. The Ethic of Community views the self as a member of social groups, with duties and obligations toward the group's well-being. Thus, self-moderation, respect, and loyalty toward the group are important virtues within this ethic. Last, the Ethic of Divinity focuses on the self as a spiritual being and involves reasoning that pertains to divine law, ancient scriptures, and purity of the soul. It encompasses virtues such as faithfulness, humility, and devotion.

Research across cultures such as Brazil, India, the Philippines, Finland, and the United States has shown the presence of the three ethics in moral reasoning

(Haidt, Koller, & Dias, 1993; Jensen, 2008; Vainio, 2003; Vasquez, Keltner, Ebenbach, *et al.*, 2001). Research also provides evidence for the utility of the Three Ethics framework in examining differences in moral reasoning in groups within cultures, for instance, groups of different socioeconomic and religious backgrounds (Haidt, Koller, & Dias, 1993; Jensen, 1998).

Jensen (2008) has proposed the cultural-developmental approach that charts the development of the three ethics across the life span. The developmental trajectories in the template have the potential to accommodate worldviews held by people of diverse cultural groups. Jensen has observed that there is very little research on the Ethic of Divinity. With this caveat in mind, she suggests that in cultures where divinity is prominent and conceptualized in abstract ways, the degree of use of divinity concepts is low among children and rises during adolescence to become similar to adult use of the ethic. The reason for this developmental trajectory is that abstract concepts, although available to children, may be incorporated into moral reasoning only upon development of the cognitive abilities for abstraction during adolescence (Kohlberg, 1981; Piaget, 1932/1965).

With respect to India, Jensen specifically suggests that the use of divinity in moral reasoning may emerge at a fairly young age. She explains that in India religious beliefs are accessible to children as aspects integral to daily routines and lives of individuals, as we also explained above. Thus, children grow up in a familial and community ethos where religious devotion and conceptions permeate everyday practice, thought, and interactions.

Thus, by examining the role of culture in moral development and the significance of divinity, the present chapter aims to address a lacuna in contemporary moral psychology. In the present chapter we extend research on the developmental and cultural aspects of morality in India. We examine children's use of divinity in moral reasoning and provide support for the hypothesis that in India, where divinity and morality are closely related and where everyday life and activities reflect religious beliefs, divinity concepts and ethical values of the Indian moral worldview feature early in children's moral reasoning. Specifically, we draw upon research with third- and sixth-grade children from the city of Vadodara, India. We approached children belonging to higher and lower socioeconomic class (SES) families for the study so as to ensure representation of both social classes from Indian society. Our aim is to focus on both culture and development in line with the cultural-developmental approach and to contribute to new theory and research on moral reasoning. Extending the cultural-developmental approach (Jensen, 2008, 2011), we expected Divinity reasoning to be present early and to rise with age. Thus, we expected older children to use more Divinity in their reasoning compared with their younger counterparts. Further, we did not expect to find a difference in the use of divinity in moral reasoning between lower and higher social class groups because the Hindu moral worldview represents a way of life available to all and, more importantly, because not much research is available to guide our hypothesis.

The participants and interview

A total of 144 children from Vadodara in the state of Gujarat, India, participated in in-depth interviews about five hypothetical scenarios. Participants were third graders ($M_{age} = 8.22$ years, $SD = 0.61$) and sixth graders ($M_{age} = 11.54$ years, $SD = 0.50$). Within each age group, an equal number of participants belonged to upper-middle and low socioeconomic families ($n = 36$). Additionally, an even gender distribution was maintained within each age and socioeconomic group. Participants from the higher social class were approached through a private school catering to children belonging to upper-middle-class families, whereas participants from the lower social class were identified through a local nongovernmental organization that provides educational assistance to children in urban slum communities of Vadodara. Additionally, in each urban slum community an enthusiastic group of youth volunteered to assist in snowballing additional participants. These youth, or peer leaders, helped build rapport with children and families in the slum communities. This approach was essential as it helped build a sense of trust in a community where research is rare, thereby aiding the process of recruitment.

The five hypothetical scenarios were about moral issues that children might experience in their everyday lives, such as lying, stealing, helping others, and participating in religious practices. They included moral issues that parents are likely to discuss with their children to inculcate moral values. Additionally, the scenarios involved diverse moral concepts and issues highlighted in theories and research in moral psychology, such as justice, fairness, interdependence, duty, spirituality, and divinity (Jensen, 2011; Kohlberg, 1981; Piaget, 1932/1965; Shweder, Mahapatra, & Miller, 1990; Snarey & Keljo, 1991; Vasudev & Hummel, 1987). These scenarios were presented to participants in a random order during the interviews. (The Interview Schedule at the end of this chapter provides verbatim descriptions of the five scenarios.)

Briefly, the first scenario pertained to a boy who is on his way to an important soccer game where he is to represent his school. On the way, he finds an injured kitten. The dilemma is whether to help the kitten or proceed to the match. The second scenario is about a girl whose mother gives her money to buy sweets. On her way home she loses the packet of sweets. She has to decide whether to take money from a wallet lying close by so she can purchase a new packet of sweets. The third scenario is based in the context of an Indian festival when a boy unintentionally breaks an idol of God while playing soccer. He has to choose between telling the adults in his neighborhood that he broke the idol or remaining quiet. In the fourth scenario, the participant has to resolve the dilemma by deciding whether to help a needy friend by lying to her teacher. Last, the fifth scenario is about a girl who tastes *prashad* before it is offered to God (*Prashad* is food offered to God before being eaten by worshippers, also believed to be a form of God's blessings.) The dilemma is whether to tell her mother the truth or allow her mother unknowingly to commit the sin of offering tasted *prashad* to God.

Participants responded to the following questions in each scenario: "What should the girl/boy do?" "Why?" "What would you have done if you faced such a dilemma?" "Why?" "What if you did otherwise?" and "Why would that be morally right or morally wrong?" These probes served to elicit moral evaluations (i.e., what course of action to take) and reasoning (i.e., why that course of action). Additional follow-up questions were asked as needed to ensure that participants carefully thought through each dilemma and discussed all their reasons. For example, if participants talked about punishment avoidance, they were asked to explain who would punish them, in what way, and why.

The five scenarios used language that all children could easily comprehend. They were constructed in a story-like format in consideration of the age of the participants and to make the interview process interesting for the children. Participants had the choice of using English or Gujarati, or both, during the interviews. All interviews were tape-recorded and transcribed verbatim to enable coding. Interviews that were conducted in Gujarati were first transcribed in Gujarati and later translated into English. In order to preserve important cultural concepts and meanings, certain indigenous terms and phrases were retained in the English transcripts; for example, terms like *punya* (virtue) and *paap* (sin).

Every moral reason that participants provided was analyzed using the Three Ethics coding manual (Jensen, 2008). In the coding manual, each of the Three Ethics includes thirteen to sixteen subethics. These subethics represent moral concepts that may be used in participants' reasoning about moral dilemmas. For instance, the Ethic of Autonomy includes subethics such as "Self's Psychological Well-Being," "Other Individual's Psychological Well-Being," "Conscience," and "Punishment Avoidance (to self)." Thus, each response given by participants was coded under one ethic and a specific subcode within the chosen ethic. Interrater reliability of 97.2 percent was obtained using Kappa calculations.

Next, we describe and elaborate on quantitative results for the Ethic of Divinity. Then, we provide a qualitative explication of the key divinity concepts used in children's moral discourse and their meaning within the broader Hindu Indian worldview pertaining to God and *karma*.

Quantitative results: age and SES differences

Participants used all three ethics in their moral reasoning. The Ethic of Autonomy was used frequently ($M = 3.51$, $SD = 2.22$), closely followed by the Ethic of Divinity ($M = 3.00$, $SD = 2.00$), and then the Ethic of Community ($M = 1.20$, $SD = 1.10$). Thus, the Ethic of Divinity was commonly used by participants across age and SES groups.

A 2(Age) × 2(SES) analysis of variance (ANOVA) test was conducted to examine whether there were any differences in the number of reasons provided by children across all five scenarios. Results showed that older children gave significantly more reasons ($M = 8.18$, $SD = 3.78$) than did younger children ($M = 6.73$, $SD = 2.80$), $F(1, 136) = 7.63$, $p < 0.01$. This finding supports past research that indicates that the number of moral reasons increases with age (Jensen, 2011; Walker, Pitts, Hennig, *et al.*, 1995). Additionally, children belonging to the higher SES group gave more reasons ($M = 8.54$, $SD = 3.47$) than did children in the lower SES group ($M = 6.37$, $SD = 2.91$), $F(1, 136) = 17.17$, $p < 0.001$.

In order to examine whether there were differences in the use of the Ethic of Divinity in the age and SES groups, 2(Age) × 2(SES) analysis of covariance (ANCOVA) tests were conducted with total number of reasons as the covariate. The total number of reasons was entered as a covariate to control for the significant differences in the total number of reasons given.

Results indicated a significant main effect for age, $F(1135) = 7.014$, $p < 0.05$, est. $\eta^2 = .049$, where younger children used significantly more Divinity ($M = 2.72$, $SD = 1.85$) than older children ($M = 2.66$, $SD = 2.14$). This finding did not support our hypothesis that older children are capable of using this ethic more compared with the younger group. We would argue that cultural socialization plays a major role in nurturing a sense of morality that includes divine and spiritual concepts in moral thought at a young age. Results show that children are capable of not only autonomy-oriented moral perspectives but also those that involve Divinity as a foundation. Additionally, as described in the qualitative section (below), children's moral understanding is not limited to concrete ideas but also extends to include transcendent aspects such as *karma*, *dharma*, and *moksha*.

A main effect was also obtained for SES, $F(1135) = 4.659$, $p < 0.05$, est. $\eta^2 = .03$, with the higher SES group reasoning more in terms of Divinity ($M = 2.87$, $SD = 2.24$) than the lower SES group ($M = 2.51$, $SD = 1.71$). One possible explanation for this finding is higher SES children have more access to monetary and other resources to organize and participate in elaborate forms of worshipping God and to enjoy affiliations with religious communities that also strengthen ritual-based practices. Moreover, by and large the higher SES group also represents the higher castes in the Indian social fabric, and therefore they are exposed to Brahminical rituals, values, and beliefs. Thus, affluence and the access to religious sources of moral learning may create a greater awareness of divine moral concepts in the Hindu worldview. However, these explanations are only speculations and need to be explored more through research.

Last, there was not a significant interaction effect between age and SES, $F(1136) = 0.181$, $p = 0.672$, est. $\eta^2 = 0.001$. Next, we present a qualitative explanation of concepts used by children in moral discourse. We include verbatim responses of participants. These responses accentuate the role of divinity concepts commonly used in children's moral judgments and reasoning, for instance, ideas about God, sin, divine authority, and *karma*.

Qualitative results

Paap: *sin and punishment from God*

A closer look at the subcodes used by children within the Ethic of Divinity informs us about moral concepts that children use while justifying their moral judgments. Punishment Avoidance was the most frequently used subcode for both age groups within the Ethic of Divinity. Children's reasoning reflected the belief that any wrongdoing will inevitably result in incurring *paap* from God. Children across the two age groups also indicated that the intensity of punishment from God depends on the nature of the transgression involved. More severe forms of *paap* were expected for transgressions involving disrespect for life and traditional practices as compared with transgressions such as lying or hurting another's feelings.

Children also spoke of consequences of *paap* on one's soul, by suggesting that our deeds (*karma*) in the present life influence our next life and that bad deeds would result in unpleasant consequences in our next birth. This view is illustrated in the following response given by a boy belonging to the higher SES group:

If we do good things in our present life, we will also get good things in our next life. But if we don't help the kitten even when we saw that she was in pain and that she was dying, then God will give us a lot of *paap*... he will make us an animal in our next life and will give us the life of an animal... an animal can't talk and tell others about problems or ask for help. As human beings we have a more developed brain, we have more capacities and we can live more comfortably.

Children of lower SES emphasized direct physical consequences of *paap*. These included accidents, physical injuries, poor health, illnesses, and direct physical disciplining from God. Illustrating this point, a third grader of lower SES explained that on committing sin, "God will beat us a lot when we go up [after death]. He will question us about times when we failed to make the right choice between right and wrong, if we would have harmed anyone, then God will beat us, too, he will make us walk on cinders, whip us, and punish us to make us realize our mistakes."

Children from the higher SES group perceived implications of *paap* in other respects, too, such as their academic performance. They talked about how incurring *paap* could make them perform poorly in exams even if they had prepared well or that the principal might suspend them from school and not give good grades because of bad moral conduct in school.

Children from across the two age and two SES groups also asserted that their moral conduct or misconduct could have consequences on their own well-being as well as the well-being of others closely related to them. For instance, a girl from the higher SES group said:

God will see what I did. I ate the *Prasad* before offering it to God. I will have to tell my mother. If I don't, then God will not give blessings to me or my family. He will punish me for what I have done and then God will think my parents haven't taught me what is right or wrong, so they may get punished too . . . our *sukh* (happiness) and *shanti* (peace) will be taken away.

This emphasis on punishment avoidance in the children's moral reasoning resonates somewhat with the structure of moral thought proposed by Piaget, in which he suggests that young children judge behaviors as right or wrong based solely on consequences rather than on intensions and that children are primarily motivated to follow rules because of the fear of punishment. However, qualitative analyses suggest that the moral understanding expressed in children's reasoning reflects more cultural leanings. For instance, the cultural meanings associated with transgressions and their consequences are seen in light of indigenous moral concepts of *karma*, *paap*, purity of the soul, rebirth, and so forth. Additionally, as discussed in the literature review, Piaget's theory does not adequately address moral concepts related to divinity, whereas children's reasoning in the present study shows consistent use of divinity concepts that are integral to the Indian moral worldview and value system. Most importantly, unlike Piaget's proposition, children as young as 8 years spoke of a wide range of divinity concepts, including abstract ones such as God's omnipotence and omnipresence and that one's moral conduct in the present life has consequences for one's next life.

God's authority

God's authority emerged as a frequently used subcode among the younger group of children. These children spoke of doing what pleases God and avoiding behaviors that make God angry. Additionally, younger children attributed emotions to God. The following response by an 8-year-old boy illustrates this:

If we do good for God, God will also do good for us. But if we have broken his idol by mistake and if we don't tell everyone, then God will be upset and angry. He will like for us to say the truth and to face the consequences. Even if we did it by mistake, he will be happy that we could let everyone know, he will feel less worried and will be so proud of us!

As exemplified in this response, children's ideas about God reflected an implicit conviction in God's existence. Children seem to understand what God would appreciate and, thus, are ready to face consequences of transgressions. God then becomes a medium to endorse morally appropriate behavior among children. Children also spoke about God as though they were connected to God through emotions and actions. Among older children this sense of connectedness seemed to extend into a sense of duty and obligation toward God. This sense of duty is expressed by an 11-year-old boy of lower SES: "We can't offer tasted food to God. We should first offer *prashad* to God and then taste it, so that fresh/pure food if offered to him. He is the one who gave us food and the life . . . and family that we have. How can we eat before him?"

Children's perception of God and God's characteristics

As evident from the verbatim responses in the previous sections, participants of both age and SES groups referred to God as omnipotent, omnipresent, and just. Children spoke of God's presence in everything and everyone. This belief in God as omnipotent was reflected in their reasoning when they talked about the sanctity of all forms of life. The following reasoning given by an 8-year-old girl from the lower SES group highlights a common response in favor of helping an injured kitten: "God has given life to the kitten, so her life is precious and we must save her. Like all animals and plants, God exists in the kitten too, and so, it is our duty to save her or at least do what we can to help her feel better."

Additionally, children frequently brought up the concept of purity and pollution. In the scenario involving the *prashad* being offered to God, children expressed the need to offer fresh food to God – the kind that is offered with clean hands, in a clean vessel, and with purity of heart. They spoke of the need to have a clear conscience before God and of the consequences of a polluted mind. As expressed by an 11-year-old girl from the higher SES group:

God is sacred and pure, we cannot offer tasted sweets to God or with dirty hands. We must offer sweets with clean hands. I think Neha should tell her mother that she has tasted the *prashad*. If we lie, we will not have peace in our mind. We will feel guilty, and our soul will be restless. That means that we are not doing right, we cannot steal or lie while we also worship God or pray for his blessings . . . it is just wrong to do that.

Furthermore, responses reflected the understanding that God exists across geographical borders and in living as well as nonliving worlds (such as books or nature). This understanding is reflected in the common Indian maxim of *kan kan mein bhagwan*, which asserts that God resides in every unit – in oneself, in others, in animals, in plants, in rocks, and in sand. This understanding of God as omnipresent is also expressed in the *Shanti Mantra* (peace invocation) mentioned in the Ishavasya Upanishad:

> *Om Poornam Adah Poornam Idam*
> *Poornaat Poornam Udachyate*
> *Poornasya Poornam Aadaay*
> *Poornam Evaa Vashishyate*

This Sanskrit *shloka* (verse) explains the nature of the cosmic order, as understood in the Hindu worldview. It implies that "this (*Brahmān*) is infinite, and this (universe) is infinite. The infinite proceeds from the infinite. (Then) taking the infinitude of the infinite (universe), it remains as the infinite (*Brahmān*) alone." Simply put, it emphasizes that God is the origin of all. God is the beginning and the end of all; all emanates from and converges into God. This *shloka* conveys a deep and abstract philosophical belief in the supremacy, infiniteness, and totality of *Brahmān* (universal order). Yet, qualitative findings from the present study show that this belief is very much a part of children's knowledge.

Responses that highlight this abstract nature of morality understood by children – at least in its basic form – pose a challenge to Piagetian theory, which assumes that children are capable of only concrete, anthropomorphic representations of God; that is, they attribute the human form to God. Several studies have explored people's understandings of divinity and God from Piaget's perspective. They provide evidence for a shift from concrete conceptualizations in childhood to abstract thinking in adolescence and adulthood (Elkind, 1970; Ladd, McIntosh, & Spilka, 1998). Yet others have provided evidence that suggests that people may talk in concrete as well as abstract terms through childhood and adolescence and that God may be "human-like" not only to children but also to adolescents and adults (Jensen, 2009). Additionally, research by Barrett and Richert (2003) suggests that young children are capable of thinking of God in terms of properties that are nonanthropomorphic. Similarly, children's moral reasoning in the present sample suggests that they perceive God as a supernatural entity who is formless, all-knowing, omnipresent, and all-powerful.

Children asserted that God is the ultimate moral authority. They expressed utmost faith in God and spoke of God as just and all-forgiving. Following is a response from an 11-year-old girl that reflects children's perception of God as just: "If we do wrong by mistake or unknowingly, then God will forgive us and give us a chance to make up for our wrong-doing, but if we purposely do wrong or harm others, then God will certainly give *paap*."

Furthermore, responses highlight a sense of mutual reciprocity and symbiotic dependence between oneself and God. Interestingly, this reciprocity is expressed in two forms. First, a direct form of reciprocity emerged in the reasoning. For example, "If I steal money from others, God will do the same to me. He will take away all our money and will ruin our life." Second, an indirect form of reciprocity was reflected wherein one's actions toward others would determine God's considerations for oneself. For instance, "I will rescue the injured kitten and take care of it. It must be hungry and her mother must be worried. I will help because if I help others, then God will always be with me and will help me when I am in need."

Early foundations of the karmic perspective and moral socialization

In the Indian worldview, *karma* is believed to be a moral order in which one's actions (right or wrong) have proportionate consequences (good or bad) for the self (Huebner & Garrod, 1991; Shweder & Much, 1991). In this study, children could relate to the concept of *karma* as the law of cause and effect (causality). For instance, if we steal money, we will ourselves be struck by poverty; overlooking the plight of an injured kitten will result in one's birth in the form of a kitten or animal and suffering in a similar way; the truth will reveal itself in some way, possibly with worse implications that are beyond our control.

Shweder (2003) challenges Piaget's universal claim that "immanent justice" is characteristic of young children and representative of an immature sense of morality. He suggests that it is unfair to assume that Hindus who believe in *karma* and other cultures that have faith in the supernatural or divine forces are intellectually immature. He explains that developmental standards or concepts developed by a culture need not be applied to other populations and that these standards are to be upheld by the cultural groups because they play a crucial role in allowing its people to "fit in" and develop self-identities that are well adjusted to and appreciated by their own people. We take this opportunity to highlight some of the differences in Piaget's ideas of immanent justice and Hindu beliefs regarding transgressions.

Unlike Piaget's understanding of immanent justice, moral discourse among children in the present study suggests that consequences of moral transgressions are not necessarily expected in the immediate present but may be experienced at any point in life or afterlife. This is possible because the soul is influenced by positive and negative *karma* and, thus, carries forward a record of sin and reward across the cycle of birth-death-rebirth. The possibility that one's actions have consequences on a broader time scale and across births becomes a motivational force for one to pursue a righteous path. This abstract understanding of divine justice needs to be acknowledged as a unique moral philosophy. It challenges

Piaget's understanding of ideas such as sin, transmigration of souls, and the sacred self as characteristic of primitive and superstitious thought.

Moreover, a common theme that emerges from children's responses is that human birth is superior to other forms of life and presents a continuous relationship between one's *karma* and the cycle of birth and rebirth. Hence, the course of one's present life is determined by one's *karma* in the previous life and is also an indicator of one's life in the next birth. Therefore, the pursuit of *moksha* (salvation) or the human form of life and happiness in the next birth guides righteous behavior. In the present study, children maintained that, as humans, they have a developed brain, speech functions, and the ability to distinguish between "right" and "wrong." These abilities make humans more developed and, hence, bestow upon them the onus of maintaining the natural order and being responsible toward all forms of life.

Additionally, children's reasoning emphasized the karmic connections between transgressions, *paap*, and reincarnation. Following is a response from an 8-year-old girl that illustrates this understanding: "If I see an injured kitten and choose to go for the match instead, then God will give me *paap*. He will make us a kitten in our next life, just like the dying kitten, and no one will help us. We will have to go through the same pain." As also seen in the words of an 11-year-old girl, "If we do good in this life and do good for others, then we will come closer to getting *moksha* [salvation] . . . we will not have to take birth in the form of a human being or a lesser being [*neechjeev*] in our next birth."

Importance was also given to Customary Traditional Authority, within the Ethic of Divinity. Children referred to traditional practices followed in their families (bathing, feeding, offering prayers to God, and other rituals) as major sources if moral knowledge. This emphasizes the influence of the cultural context and socialization through which moral concepts and meanings are implicitly conveyed to children through participation in daily activities and interactions with adults. These findings support the development of early foundations of the karmic perspective among children.

Conclusions and future directions

The existence and experience of God are central to the Hindu moral worldview and are reflected in multiple aspects of daily life – from traditional rituals to festivals, songs, stories, customs, and everyday practices. The present chapter gives considerable evidence that divinity emerges fairly early among children in India, highlighting the power of cultural socialization. Exactly how divinity develops over the course of childhood in India will require more research.

Children in India are continually assisted by adults to imbibe moral values conveyed in the context of routine practices and verbal exchanges, thereby facilitating greater continuity of cultural meanings and moral worldviews between generations. The use of karmic concepts in children's moral reasoning suggests that at an early age children are capable of learning not only concrete but also abstract concepts. On the one hand, children attribute human emotions to God and talk about reciprocity and a relationship of trust between themselves and God. On the other hand, they understand that God is formless and unseen and has powers that are beyond the scope of humans. Additionally, they are capable of explaining concepts such as sin (*paap*), *karma*, and rebirth as important considerations while making moral judgments and justifying them. It is interesting that such contrasting views regarding the concrete and the abstract are tacitly adopted by children and have implications of everyday moral decisions. Jensen (2011) rightly estimates that in some Hindu communities divinity concepts may emerge at an early age among children because these concepts find repeated use and expression in daily life and practices. Our findings lend support to this speculation and give evidence for the early use of divinity in children's moral discourse in India.

It is important to note that children used all three ethics in an integrated manner. For instance, preliminary aspects of children's reasoning, focusing on fulfillment of self-goals (Autonomy) and interpersonal obligations (Community), seemed to serve the means of attaining divine, karmic ends and avoiding moral degradation of the self. Participants talked about their beliefs regarding a sacred world and that divinity permeates the social order as well as the individual self. Thus, there is a continuous and rich exchange between the self, others, and the realms of divinity. Such a system offers a complex set of values, generating a distinct framework of morality. Given its intricacy, we think it would be not only difficult but also futile to conceptualize the Indian moral worldview without acknowledging the intersection of personal, social, and spiritual aspects of morality. Thus, our perspective differs from the traditional developmental accounts of morality that view these domains as distinct (e.g., Turiel). It further supports research that calls for the need to understand and appreciate the dynamics between the individual, social, and spiritual realms of morality (e.g., Kapadia & Bhangaokar, Chapter 4, this volume; Hickman & DiBianca Fasoli, Chapter 7, this volume).

The cultural-developmental approach offers tremendous scope to capture these cultural characteristics in moral development. Unlike early theories of morality, it acknowledges the legitimacy of multiple cultural worldviews and, most importantly, the role of divinity in moral reasoning. The Three Ethics manual is also helpful in capturing the diverse pool of moral concepts across cultures. We believe that the inclusion of indigenous concepts such as *dharma*, *karma*, and *paap* is necessary to make the manual more effective for Indian society. Additionally, there is a need to further explore the role of specific divinity concepts in moral reasoning and the different conceptualizations that may exist among cultural groups. An example would be the cultural understandings of reciprocity. In the Three Ethics manual, reciprocity falls under the Ethic of Autonomy, where it conveys the understanding that an individual helps another individual with the expectation of direct, immediate, and proportional reciprocity in return. However, in the qualitative section of this chapter we present an alternate view on reciprocity in which the consequences of reciprocal behavior go beyond the self to involve spiritual benefits. Thus, an individual does something for the other with the implicit understanding that the returns will be to the spiritual self (hence not necessarily immediate), as sanctioned by God. It would be fruitful for future research to study culturally grounded conceptualizations of specific moral concepts to understand the different cultural meanings associated with them.

We also feel the immense need for more developmental examinations of the Ethic of Divinity, which can inform us about developmental trajectories across the life span in India and other cultures. Our study shows that younger children use more Divinity in their reasoning than do older children. This finding has little support from previous studies largely based on cognitive theories. Kapadia and Bhangaokar (Chapter 4, this volume) show that in India adolescents use Autonomy significantly more than adults do, whereas adults use Divinity more than adolescents do. Shedding light on adolescents' agentic development, Trommsdorff (2015) asserts that developing an individual and social identity gains prominence during adolescence. Thus, the developmental trajectory in India may involve early emergence of Divinity in children's moral thought and reasoning, which seems to take a back seat during adolescence because their awareness about their autonomous and social selves takes center stage. Later, the use of Divinity seems to rise again during adulthood. However, this developmental trajectory of the Ethic of Divinity remains a speculation as a result of insufficient research focus and, thus, offers immense scope for future research. Longitudinal examinations, in particular, would yield a better understanding of how age interacts with this ethic in the context of moral reasoning.

Last, we wish to draw attention to the need for research involving different socioeconomic groups within a culture. Social class continues to be a major defining element of Indian society, especially in the contemporary times of globalization and change. In order to represent the Indian population, we think it is imperative to engage all sections of the society in research and to have their representation in the academic world. Our study is an attempt to do the same. We assert the need for more studies that focus on how economic conditions and resource availability influence moral orientations and the development of moral reasoning.

INTERVIEW SCHEDULE

Scenario 1

Rahul is one of the good players in his school's football team. There is an interschool match coming up and Rahul is looking forward to playing the match for his school. On the day of the match, everyone gets ready and leaves for the football ground. On the way, Rahul hears a strange sound coming from a nearby bush. He gets down from his cycle and goes towards the bush. He finds a little kitten whose leg is trapped in the fence adjoining the bush. Rahul feels sorry for the kitten and wants to help. But at the same time he realizes that he is getting late for the match. He knows that if he doesn't reach the football ground on time, someone else will take his place in the team. But he does not want to leave the kitten unattended.

Probe Questions:

What should Rahul do – help the kitten or proceed for the match?

Follow-up (Help the kitten)

- Why should Rahul help the kitten?
- What would you do if you were in Rahul's place? Why?
- What if you decide not to help the kitten and decide to go for the match instead?
- Would it be morally right or morally wrong to help the kitten? Why?

Follow-up (Go for the match)

- Why should Rahul go for the match?
- What would you do if you were in Rahul's place? Why?
- What if you decide not to go for your match and decide to help the kitten?
- Would it be morally right or morally wrong to proceed for the match? Why?

Scenario 2

One day, Preeti's mother gives her money to buy sweets for some guests who are going to visit them. Preeti goes to the shop on her cycle and buys the sweets. While returning home, she sees her friends in a nearby park, playing with a new toy. Preeti is curious and decides to go inside the park. She parks her cycle and forgets to take the bag of sweets with her. After some time when Preeti comes back to her cycle, she is surprised to find that her bag of sweets has disappeared. While she is thinking of what to do, she notices a wallet full of money which someone has left on a nearby cycle. Preeti is wondering if she should take the money from the wallet to buy a new packet of sweets.

Probe Questions:

What should Preeti do – take the money or not?

Follow-up (Take the money)

- Why should Preeti take the money?
- What would you do if you were in Preeti's place? Why?
- What if you don't take the money?
- Would it be morally right or morally wrong to take the money? Why?

Follow-up (Not take the money)

- Why should Preeti not take the money?
- What would you do if you were in Preeti's place? Why?
- What if you take the money?
- Would it be morally right or wrong to not take the money? Why?

Scenario 3

A group of children is playing soccer in their society garden. The festival of Ganesh Chaturthi is being celebrated and an idol of Lord Ganesha has been installed near the garden. While playing, one of the children – Nikhil – kicks the ball hard and it accidently hits the idol. As a result, the idol breaks and soon residents of the society come to know about it. They wonder who is responsible for this. None of the children speak up. Nikhil has to decide whether to tell everyone that he broke the idol by mistake or to stay quiet.

Probe Questions:

What should Nikhil do – tell everyone the truth or stay quiet?

Follow-up (Say the truth)

- Why should Nikhil say the truth to everyone?
- What would you do if you were in Nikhil's place? Why?

- What if you don't say the truth but stay quiet?
- Would it be morally right or morally wrong to say the truth? Why?

Follow-up (Stay quiet)

- Why should Nikhil stay quiet?
- What would you do if you were in Nikhil's place? Why?
- What if you don't stay quiet but say the truth to everyone?
- Would it be morally right or wrong to stay quiet? Why?

Scenario 4

Prachi studies in class IV. She and Seema are good friends. One day, the art teacher gives homework to the class which has to be done in the Diwali break and has to be submitted the day the school reopens. The teacher has asked everyone to make similar oil paintings. Prachi's parents cannot afford to buy paints for her and, so, she is unable to do the homework. When the school reopens and it is time to submit the homework, the teacher sees Seema's painting and is checking other children's work. Seema feels bad for Prachi. She wonders whether she should help her by giving her own homework to Prachi.

Probe Questions:

What should Seema do – give her own homework to Prachi or not?

Follow-up (Give homework)

- Why should Seema give her homework to Prachi?
- What would you do if you were in Seema's place and had a friend like Prachi? Why?
- What if you don't give your homework to your friend?
- Would it be morally right or morally wrong to help your friend in this way? Why?

Follow-up (Not give homework)

- Why should Seema not give her homework to Prachi?
- What would you have done if you were in Seema's place and had a friend like Prachi?
- What if you gave your homework to your friend?

- Would it be morally right or morally wrong to not help your friend in this way? Why?

Scenario 5

Neha's mother has organised a pooja (worship) at home. She makes sheera (sweet) as prashad (offering) to be offered to God and puts it on the table. Neha comes home after playing outside and sees the prashad on the table. She feels very tempted to taste the sheera. She looks around to ensure that no one sees her and eats a little bit of the prashad. At that point, her mother comes into the room and takes the prashad to offer it to God.

Probe Questions:

What should Neha do – should she tell her mother that she tasted the *prashad* or not?

Follow-up (tell the mother)

- Why should Neha tell her mother?
- What would you have done if you were in Neha's place? Why?
- What if you did not tell your mother that you had ate some of the prashad?
- Would it be morally right or morally wrong to tell your mother? Why?

Follow-up (not tell mother)

- Why should Neha not tell her mother?
- What would you have done if you were in Neha's place? Why?
- What if you tell your mother that you ate the prashad?
- Would it be morally right or morally wrong to stay quiet? Why?

REFERENCES

Barrett, J. L., & Richert, R. A. (2003). Anthropomorphism or preparedness? Exploring children's God concepts. *Review of Religious Research*, 44, 300–312.
Bhangaokar, R., & Kapadia, S. (2009). At the interface of "dharma" and "karma": Interpreting moral discourse in India. *Psychological Studies*, 54(2), 96–108.
Chatterjee, C. (1995). Values in the Indian ethos: An overview. *Journal of Human Values*, 1(1), 3–12.
Clooney, F. X. (1989). Evil, divine omnipotence and human freedom: Vedānta's theology of karma. *Journal of Religion*, 69(4), 530–548.

Edwards, C. P. (1987). Culture and the construction of moral values: A comparative ethnography of moral encounters in two cultural settings. In J. Kagan & S. Lamb (Eds.), *The emergence of morality in young children* (pp. 123–154). Chicago, IL: University of Chicago Press.

Elkind, D. (1970). The origins of religion in the child. *Review of Religious Research*, 12, 35–42.

Gandhi, M. K. (1951). *Satyagraha*. Ahmedabad, India: Navjivan Publishing House.

Haidt, J., Koller, S. H., & Dias, M. G. (1993). Affect, culture and morality, or is it wrong to eat your dog? *Journal of Personality and Social Psychology*, 65, 613–628.

Huebner, A., & Garrod, A. (1991). Moral reasoning in a karmic world. *Human Development*, 34, 341–352.

Jensen, L. A. (1998). Moral divisions within countries between orthodoxy and progressivism: India and the United States. *Journal for the Scientific Study of Religion*, 37, 90–107.

    (2008). Through two lenses: A cultural-developmental approach to moral psychology. *Developmental Review*, 28, 289–315.

    (2009). Conceptions of God and the Devil across the lifespan: A cultural-developmental study of religious liberals and conservatives. *Journal for the Scientific Study of Religion*, 48(1), 121–145.

    (2011). *Bridging cultural and developmental approaches to psychology: New synthesis in theory, research, and policy.* New York, NY: Oxford University Press.

Kohlberg, L. (1981). *The philosophy of moral development.* San Francisco, CA: Harper & Row.

Kohlberg, L., & Power, C. (1981). Moral development, religious thinking, and the question of a seventh stage. *Zygon*, 16(3), 203–259.

Kumari, A., & Pirta, R. S. (2009). Exploring human relationship with God as a secure base. *Journal of the Indian Academy of Applied Psychology*, 35, 119–124.

Krishnan, L., & Manoj, V. R. (2008). "Giving" as a theme in the Indian psychology of values. In K. R. Rao, A. C. Paranjpe, and A. K. Dalal (Eds.), *Handbook of Indian psychology* (pp. 361–382). New Delhi, India: Foundation Books.

Ladd, K. L., McIntosh, D. N., & Spilka, B. (1998). Children's God concepts: Influences of denomination, age, and gender. *International Journal for the Psychology of Religion*, 8(1), 49–56.

Menon, U. (2003). Morality and context: A study of Hindu understandings. In J. Valsiner & K. J. Connolly (Eds.), *Handbook of Developmental Psychology* (pp. 431–449). London, United Kingdom: Sage.

    (2013). The Hindu concept of self-refinement: Implicit yet meaningful. *Psychology & Developing Societies*, 25(1), 195–222.

Miller, J. G., & Bersoff, D. M. (1995). Development in the context of everyday family relationships: Culture, interpersonal morality, and adaptation. In M. Killen & D. Hart (Eds.), *Morality in everyday life: Developmental perspectives* (pp. 259–282). Cambridge, United Kingdom: Cambridge University Press.

Miller, J. G., & Luthar, S. (1989). Issues of interpersonal responsibility and accountability: A comparison of Indians' and Americans' moral judgments. *Social Cognition*, 7(3), 237–261.

Paranjpe, A. C. (1996). Some basic psychological concepts from the intellectual tradition of India. *Psychology & Developing Societies*, 8(1), 7–27.

(2013). The concept of *dharma*: Classical meaning, common misconceptions and implications for psychology. *Psychology & Developing Societies*, 25(1), 1–20.

Piaget, J. (1965). *The moral judgment of the child*. New York, NY: Free Press. (Original work published 1932)

Ramanujan, A. K. (1990). Is there an Indian way of thinking? An informal essay. In M. Marriott (Ed.), *India through Hindu categories* (pp. 1–40). New Delhi, India: Sage.

Saraswathi, T. S., Mistry, J., & Dutta, R. (2011). Reconceptualizing lifespan development through a Hindu perspective. In L. A. Jensen (Ed.), *Bridging cultural and developmental approaches to psychology: New syntheses in theory, research, and policy* (pp. 276–300). New York, NY: Oxford University Press.

Shariff, A. F., & Norenzayan, A. (2007). God is watching you: Priming God concepts increases prosocial behavior in an anonymous economic game. *Psychological Science*, 18(9), 803–809.

Sharma, A. (2000). *Classical Hindu thought: An introduction*. New Delhi, India: Oxford University Press.

Shweder, R. (2003). *Why do men barbecue? Recipes for cultural psychology*. Cambridge, MA: Harvard University Press.

Shweder, R. A., Mahapatra, M., & Miller, J. G. (1990). Culture and moral development. In J. W. Stigler, R. A. Shweder, & G. Herdt (Eds.), *Cultural psychology* (pp. 130–204). Cambridge, United Kingdom: Cambridge University Press.

Shweder, R. A., & Much, N. C. (1991). Determinants of meaning: Discourse and moral socialization. In R. Shweder (Ed.), *Thinking through cultures: Expeditions in cultural psychology* (pp. 186–240). Cambridge, MA: Harvard University Press.

Shweder, R. A., Much, N. C., Mahapatra, M., & Park, L. (1997). The "Big Three" of morality (Autonomy, Community, Divinity) and the "big three" explanations of suffering. In A. Brandt & P. Rozin (Eds.), *Morality and health* (pp. 119–159). New York, NY: Routledge.

Snarey, J. R., & Keljo, K. (1991). In a gemeinschaft voice: The cross-cultural expansion of moral development theory. In W. M. Kurtines & J. L. Gewirtz (Eds.), *Handbook of moral behavior and development: Theory* (Vol. 1; pp. 395–424). Hillsdale, NJ: Erlbaum.

Trommsdorff, G. (2015). Cultural roots of values, and moral and religious purposes in adolescent development. In L. A. Jensen (Ed.), *Oxford handbook of human development and culture: An interdisciplinary approach*. New York, NY: Oxford University Press.

Turiel, E. (2002). *The culture of morality: Social development, context, and conflict*. Cambridge, United Kingdom: Cambridge University Press.

Vainio, A. (2003). One morality – or multiple moralities? (Unpublished doctoral dissertation). University of Helsinki, Finland.

Vasquez, K., Keltner, D., Ebenbach, D. H., & Banaszynski, T. L. (2001). Cultural variation and similarities in moral rhetoric: Voices from Philippines and the United States. *Journal of Cross-Cultural Research*, 32, 93–120.

Vasudev, J. (1994). Ahimsa, justice, and the unity of life: Post conventional morality from an Indian perspective. In M. E. Miller & S. R. Cook-Greuter (Eds.), *Transcendence and mature thought in adulthood: The further reaches of adult development* (pp. 237–255). Lanham, MD: Rowman & Littlefield Publishers Incorporated.

Vasudev, J., & Hummel, R. C. (1987). Moral stage sequence and principled moral reasoning in an Indian sample. *Human Development*, 30, 105–118.

Walker, L. J., Pitts, R. C., Hennig, K. H., & Matsuba, M. K. (1995). Reasoning about morality and real-life moral problems. In M. Killen & D. Hart (Eds.), *Morality in everyday life: Developmental perspectives* (pp. 371–407). Cambridge, United Kingdom: Cambridge University Press.

Zimba, R. F. (1994). The understanding of morality, convention, and personal preference in an African setting: Findings from Zambia. *Journal of Cross-Cultural Psychology*, 25(3), 369–393.

3   Finnish moral landscapes: a comparison of nonreligious, liberal religious, and conservative religious adolescents

Annukka Vainio

To what extent do definitions of morality and moral reasoning depend on cultural and religious worldviews? Developmental psychology has been focused on uncovering a universal moral domain and moral reasons shared by all humans. This chapter, however, addresses the questions from a cultural-developmental vantage point. This chapter compares nonreligious, liberal religious, and conservative religious Finnish adolescents on how they define and reason about morality. The adolescents evaluated and reasoned about acts, such as stealing, that are generally regarded as morally wrong in Finland and that developmental theory has deemed to fall within the moral domain. They also evaluate "controversial" issues, such as cohabitation prior to marriage and keeping shops open on Sundays, that are characterized by differences of opinion in Finland and that developmental theory has typically deemed conventional rather than moral. The adolescents took part in in-depth interviews, and in this chapter I analyze and discuss their moral evaluations and reasoning in both quantitative and qualitative ways.

My focus is on adolescence because in many ways it is a significant phase in the development of moral reasoning. Adolescents often gain greater autonomy and responsibility in deciding about their lives. It is also a period when individuals begin forming personal ideologies and worldviews (Arnett, 1997; Arnett, Ramos, & Jensen, 2001), in part as a result of increasing awareness of the larger community, political institutions, and social issues (Flanagan & Levine, 2010). Furthermore, according to the cultural-developmental theory of moral reasoning (Jensen, 2008, 2011, and Chapters 1 and 8, this volume), adolescence constitutes a key developmental period in many cultures for the emergence of substantial and self-generated moral reasoning focused on religion and spirituality.

I start by reviewing the cultural and developmental literature that undergird my study. This includes attention to research specifically focused on the relation between religion and moral reasoning. Then, I provide a description of the cultural contexts of the present adolescents: how they all are coming of age within a Nordic welfare state and how they also differ markedly in terms of religious affiliation.

Culture and morality

The development of moral reasoning can take very different paths depending on cultural and religious environments (Guerra & Giner-Sorolla, Chapter 6, this volume; Jensen, Chapter 8, this volume; Trommsdorff, 2012, 2015). According to Shweder, Much, Mahapatra, and Park (1997), cultural explanations and daily practices modify in a fundamental way the development of individuals' moral reasoning. Specifically, they suggest that people in different cultures vary in the extent to which they reason in terms of the three Ethics of Autonomy, Community, and Divinity. They also suggest that each of these ethics is based on different definitions of personhood, humanity, and society (see also Shweder & Miller, 1985). The Ethic of Autonomy is based on the ideal of a free individual, and therefore the purpose of society is to promote individual autonomy and rights. The Ethic of Community is based on the concept of interdependence between people and is associated with a commitment to the harmony of the community. The Ethic of Divinity focuses on individuals as divine entities and seeks to maintain and protect this divine quality. The Ethics of Autonomy, Community, and Divinity are not mutually exclusive, and many individuals use a mixture of them. However, since the Ethics of Autonomy, Community, and Divinity promote different "goods," they can conflict with each other, and therefore individuals usually emphasize one ethic more than others.

Research has shown that people from different countries differ on their relative use of ethics. For example, people in the United States use the Ethic of Autonomy more than do people in Brazil, India, and the Philippines (Haidt, Koller, & Dias, 1993; Jensen, 1995; Kapadia & Bhangaokar, Chapter 4, this volume; Vasquez, Keltner, Ebenbach, et al., 2001). Moreover, research has demonstrated that the ethical orientation varies within countries. For example, a preference for the Ethic of Autonomy has been associated with emerging adulthood (Jensen, 2011), a liberal religious worldview (Jensen, 1997a, 1997b, 2006), a liberal or left-wing political orientation (Graham, Haidt, & Nosek, 2009), and higher socioeconomic status (Haidt, Koller, & Dias, 1993).

Apart from encompassing different kinds of moral reasons, the Ethics of Autonomy, Community, and Divinity are also characterized by different definitions of morality. Previous studies applying the "domain" model of sociomoral development (e.g., Nucci, 1985, 2001; Turiel, 1983) have examined how individuals distinguish between the domains of morality and social convention on the basis of criterion questions, namely, whether the extent to which an issue is regarded as right or wrong is perceived to be alterable by the relevant authorities, contingent on God's word, and generalizable to other countries. Moral issues are regarded as nonalterable by authorities, not contingent on

God's word, and generalizable to other countries, whereas social conventions are regarded as alterable by authorities, contingent on God's word, and not generalizable to other countries. Shweder, Mahapatra, and Miller (1987) found that individuals who predominantly use the Ethic of Autonomy make a distinction between universally binding and nonalterable moral issues, on one hand, and context-dependent and alterable social conventional issues, on the other. In other words, these individuals judge issues in accordance with domain theory. In contrast, however, individuals who use the Ethic of Community or Divinity do not make such a distinction. Instead, they differentiate between universal moral issues and context-dependent moral issues that are perceived as nonalterable but morally binding within one's own community (see also Vasquez, Keltner, & Ebenbach, *et al.*, 2001). Both issues, however, are regarded as moral.

Religion and morality

There is a dearth of research on moral development and religious socialization from a cultural perspective, including in adolescence, which may be a key time for the intersection of morality and religion in development (Trommsdorff, 2012). Previous research on the association between religious socialization and morality has focused on either moral reasoning or criterion judgments. Research pertaining to individuals' moral reasoning has demonstrated that religious socialization and the development of moral reasoning are closely intertwined. For example, we know that individuals' religious socialization is associated with their use of the Ethics of Autonomy, Community, and Divinity (Jensen, 1998; Padilla-Walker & Nelson, Chapter 5, this volume). This was found in a comparative study of conservative religious and liberal religious individuals' moral reasoning in India and the United States (Jensen, 1998). In both countries, the liberal religious individuals used the Ethic of Autonomy more than the conservative religious individuals, who in turn used the Ethic of Divinity more than liberal religious individuals. Conservative and liberal religious individuals in the two countries did not differ on their use of the Ethic of Community. Moreover, in both countries the conservative religious individuals focused on God as a creator of human beings and society, whereas the liberal religious individuals perceived society as a social system.

Research focusing on criterion judgments and religion has revealed that religious socialization shapes the conceptualization of the moral domain in many ways. First, it has been found that among the members of some religious communities, personal autonomy is perceived as part of – rather than separate from – the moral domain. Four studies conducted by Cohen and Rozin (2001) in the United States found that Protestant Christian adults made an intrinsic connection between believing in something and acting according to that belief, whereas Jewish adults did not. Although the Jewish and Protestant participants rated such things as dishonoring one's parents, having a sexual affair, and harming an animal as moral issues, these groups differed in the moral importance they attributed to thinking about engaging in these behaviors. Protestant participants rated a person having such thoughts more negatively than Jewish participants did. These differences were partially mediated by the Protestants' beliefs that individuals' thoughts are likely to lead to action. Among the Protestant participants, such beliefs predicted statements that thoughts about morally wrong behaviors are themselves morally wrong.

Research has also indicated that many religious communities evaluate their own religious rules as context-dependent moral obligations because they are perceived as not being alterable by authorities (moral criterion) and not generalizable outside their own community (social conventional criterion). Moreover, these studies suggest that many conservative religious persons perceive morality as contingent on God's word. For example, in a study conducted by Nucci (1985), members of the Amish community in the United States were found to consider their religious rules prohibiting abortion, homosexuality, and pornography as nonalterable by their religious authorities, and they did not generalize the evaluation of these religious rules outside their own religious community. Similarly, in a study by Nucci and Turiel (1993), Conservative and Orthodox Jewish participants did not perceive their religious rules such as those regulating the day of worship and work on the Sabbath as alterable by their religious authorities but only applicable to their own religious community. Glicksman (1997), in a study of Orthodox Jewish participants' evaluations of moral rules and religious rules such as prohibition against cooking on the Sabbath and eating pork, demonstrated that religious rules are conceptually different from nonreligious moral and conventional rules.

As a whole, previous studies have analyzed religious moral socialization from multiple perspectives. Those focusing on moral reasoning have found that liberal religious and conservative religious individuals give different degrees of emphasis to the Ethics of Autonomy, Community, and Divinity. Studies focusing on criterion judgments have found that, in religious contexts, individuals evaluate moral rules to be qualitatively different from nonreligious rules. In addition, these findings indicate that the perception of the moral domain is shaped by the religious context, such as the specific kind of interpretation of God's word endorsed in religious communities, the moral status of religious authorities, and the exclusive perception of one's own religious community. In other words, studies on religious contexts suggest that both aspects of morality – reasoning and criterion judgments – accommodate the specific cultural and religious contexts of individuals. Next, I discuss how the Finnish welfare state and Finnish religious cultures function as contexts for moral development.

The Finnish welfare state

Finland is one of the five Nordic countries (the others being Iceland, Denmark, Norway, and Sweden), which are small, relatively wealthy, and culturally homogenous states located in northern Europe. They are also characterized by the Nordic welfare state model. This model is morally relevant in many ways since the countries' social policies explicitly promote certain moral values (see Jensen, 2011), and exposure to such policies is likely to affect the moral attitudes and behaviors of individuals (Ervasti, Fridberg, Hjerm, *et al.*, 2008). According to Ervasti and colleagues, the Nordic model emphasizes collective welfare and the role of the state in maintaining it. The welfare state is usually defined as a political system where the state (and not the individual or the local community) assumes the primary responsibility for the individual and for the social welfare of citizens (Encyclopædia Britannica, 2012). Although the welfare state may take many forms, the Nordic model emphasizes both the reduction of socioeconomic differences and the enhancement of individual autonomy through extensive public care services (Esping-Andersen, 2002; Repo, 2004).

The Nordic countries are characterized by public policies that protect individuals from harm to self and others (Mäkelä & Österberg, 2009). For example, certain alcoholic beverages are sold only in state monopoly outlets in Sweden, Finland, Iceland, and Norway. Few studies have examined individuals' moral reasoning as shaped by the welfare state concept. Studies conducted by Arnett and Jensen (1994) in Denmark and by Scarr (1996) in Sweden suggest that individuals in the Nordic welfare states combine the notion of individual rights with the notion of collective responsibility.

The idea that the state is responsible for protecting the welfare of its citizens is a very recent historical occurrence (Jiggens, 1995). According to many scholars, modern welfare states should be interpreted as the heirs of religious values (Casanova, 1994; Opielka, 2008; Rokkan, 1999). Rozin (1997, 1999), for instance, has made a distinction between Protestant (e.g., Lutheran) and Catholic cultures. For example, from the perspective of morality, the values of self-discipline and self-control are regarded as moral virtues in Protestant, but not Catholic, cultures (Rozin, 1997, 1999). The connection between religious values and the welfare state also means that taking care of citizens' welfare is organized differently in Catholic and Protestant countries. Whereas earlier the welfare of individuals was tended to by the church in both Catholic and Protestant countries, in the Nordic countries this role has been assumed by the secular state. This Nordic model has been explained by the consensual relationship between the state and the Lutheran Church in these countries. For example, although the transition from religious to secular institutions taking care of the poor and sick was rather smooth in the Lutheran countries, in

Catholic countries it led to conflict between the state and the church (Kahl, 2005). Such a distinction exists even today.

Religion in Finland

As mentioned above, the adolescents in this study were nonreligious, religiously liberal, and religiously conservative. The nonreligious adolescents were not members of a religious community and described themselves as nonreligious. Such adolescents are common in Finland. According to Statistics Finland (2011), approximately 20 percent of the population identify themselves as having no religious affiliation.

The liberal religious adolescents identified themselves as Evangelical Lutheran. About 77 percent of Finns belong to the Evangelical Lutheran Church (Statistics Finland, 2011), one of the two state churches in the country, the other being the Finnish Orthodox Church. State church status means that the church has a significant influence on laws relating to marriage, divorce, and religious instruction in schools. However, at the level of personal beliefs, Finland is one of the most nonreligious countries in the world (Zuckerman, 2007). For example, in a study conducted with Finnish university students, religious believers associated God with omnipotence, whereas agnostics and "averagely religious" people associated God with nature (Lindeman, Pyysiäinen, & Saariluoma, 2002). Membership in the Evangelical Lutheran Church is granted soon after birth since the choice is made by the parents, not the children. At the age of 15 years, however, Finnish adolescents have the right to decide for themselves about their church membership. Yet despite the fact that for a long while it has been easy to withdraw from the church, very few do so. This pattern characterizes the religious life of not only Finns but also other Nordic populations (Heino, 1997).

The conservative religious adolescents were recruited from the Conservative Laestadian movement. This revivalist movement was founded in the 1840s within the Evangelical Lutheran Church. The Laestadian movement still exists within the Evangelical Lutheran Church, and many Evangelical Lutheran priests are from the Conservative Laestadian community. The community does not keep a register of its members, but it has been estimated that at least 2 percent of the Finnish population belong to this denomination (Evangelical Lutheran Church of Finland, 2013). Conservative Laestadians emphasize the unique and special status of their community in the eyes of God. Currently, they prohibit television watching, birth control, divorce, and alcohol and drugs (Larsen, 1993; Pyysiäinen, 2005). The Conservative Laestadian interpretation of the Bible is based on the Finnish translation by A. W. Ingman from the year 1859 (Nuorteva, 1992). For this reason, the authority of the Bible has a high moral status for Laestadians. Despite the exclusive nature of this religious community, the Conservative Laestadians are fully integrated into Finnish society in the sense that they study in the same schools and universities and work in occupations similar to those of other Finns (excluding the performing arts and professional sports). At the same time, the selective use of mass media, along with their choice of friends and active religious moral education within the community, keeps Conservative Laestadian adolescents well tied to their community.

The present study

Research hypotheses

On the basis of findings from previous studies, I tested three hypotheses. The first pertained to criterion judgments. I hypothesized that the groups would differ on the "controversial" issues, but not on the "typical" issues (Shweder, Mahapatra, & Miller, 1987; Vasquez, Keltner, Ebenbach, *et al.*, 2001).

The other two hypotheses addressed moral reasoning. One hypothesis was that nonreligious and liberal religious adolescents would reason more in terms of the Ethic of Autonomy and less in terms of the Ethic of Divinity as compared with conservative religious adolescents (Jensen, 1998). It was also hypothesized that because the Finnish welfare state policy emphasizes the state's responsibility for its citizens' well-being, the groups of adolescents would not differ on their use the Ethic of Community (Arnett & Jensen, 1994; Scarr, 1996).

Participants

Adolescents in their second year of higher secondary education who lived in the city of Oulu were recruited for interviews. The interviewees were from two schools, both mainstream. Written consent was given by the principals of the schools. As the adolescents were older than 15 years of age, their recruitment was based on their own informed consent, and parental consent was not needed.

The researcher contacted teachers, who agreed to announce the study in their classes in order to find volunteers who identified themselves as Evangelical Lutheran or Conservative Laestadian or who did not confess a religion, who were about 17 years of age, and who were studying in their second year of upper secondary school. The participants were selected at random from among these volunteers. The sample ($N = 30$) consisted of three groups of 10 participants. Each group included an equal number of both genders, and the mean age of the participants was 17.03 years ($SD = 0.18$). All participants were Finnish-speaking and of Finnish origin.

The participants completed a questionnaire measuring religiosity, designed for the purposes of the study. It included items about upholding religious beliefs, participating in activities organized by a religious community, and private religious behavior. They were asked to answer items on a five-point scale ranging from 1 to 5. The mean score of all 15 items had a satisfactory reliability ($\alpha = 0.97$). An ANOVA with planned contrasts (Helmert) indicated that the conservative religious adolescents ($M = 3.91$, $SD = 0.23$) were more religious than the other adolescents ($M = 1.80$, $SD = 0.68$), $F(1, 27) = 194.91$, $p = 0.000$. Moreover, liberal religious adolescents ($M = 2.31$, $SD = 0.31$) were more religious than nonreligious adolescents ($M = 1.30$, $SD = 0.55$), $F(1, 18) = 25.37$, $p = 0.000$.

Interviews

The interviews were semistructured. The participants were asked questions about three "typical" moral issues (stealing, religion-based discrimination, and gender-based discrimination) as well as seven "controversial" moral issues (making the current moral education in schools nonreligious, allowing the use and sale of marijuana, relaxing the censorship of TV and video programs, allowing shops to be open on Sundays, making the legal status of cohabitation equal to marriage, allowing the sale of wine in food shops, and making contraceptive pills prescription-free if their use does not involve health risks).

For each of these issues the interviewer asked two questions about alterability, one about contingency and one about generalizability. These *criterion questions* have also been used in previous studies examining individuals' criterion judgments of conventional and moral issues (e.g., Nucci, 1985, 2001; Nucci & Turiel, 1993; Shweder, Mahapatra, & Miller, 1987; Turiel, 1983). The criterion questions were as follows:

1. Alterability/government authority: "If the Finnish government removes the law about the issue, would this then be right or wrong?"
2. Alterability/religious authority: "If the Evangelical Lutheran Church [for the liberal religious and the nonreligious adolescents] or the religious leaders of the Conservative Laestadian community [for the conservative religious adolescents] remove the rule about the issue, would this then be right or wrong?"
3. Contingency on the perception of God's word: "If there was nothing written in the Bible about the issue, would this then be right or wrong?"
4. Generalizability: "If there is no law about the issue in another country, would this then be right or wrong?"

In addition, participants were asked to provide their *reasons* for their views on the issues. They were asked: "Why would the issue then be right or wrong?"

or "Why, in your opinion, is this criterion important when thinking about this issue?"

Because the interview questions about moral issues could potentially be stressful to the participants (see Miller, Goyal, & Wice, 2015), the researcher emphasized that if the participants did not want to continue the interview for any reason, they were free to stop and the tape was destroyed (this happened only once). At no point did the researcher ask the names of the participants, although the confessional group to which each participant belonged was known because some interview questions had to be adapted to apply to the participant's religious community. For purposes of debriefing, the researcher asked each participant about her or his feelings about the interview.

The interviews were carried out in empty classrooms or in the school library during school hours, and only the interviewer and interviewee were present. The same person (the author) conducted every interview, which ranged in length from 30 to 90 minutes. The researcher emphasized to the participants that there were no right or wrong answers to the interview questions. All interviews (except debriefings) were tape-recorded and transcribed.

Analyses

For the purposes of testing the hypotheses, ANOVAs with a priori Helmert contrasts were used for comparing religious conservatives to the other two groups combined and for comparing the nonreligious to liberal religious groups.

With respect to coding, participants' criterion judgments were coded as follows: a value of 1 was assigned to the response "the issue is right," a value of 2 indicated a judgment of both right and wrong, and a value of 3 indicated a judgment that "the issue is wrong."

Moral reasoning was coded following the coding manual developed by Jensen (2004). The manual consists of a description of the Ethics of Autonomy, Community, and Divinity, elaborated further into thirteen to sixteen subcodes (see Appendix A in this book). One code only was assigned to each reason. The participants could provide more than one reason, and each reason was assigned a code. Following the guidelines, the reasons were coded in terms of a subcode within one of the three ethics. Altogether 424 reasons were coded; on average, each participant provided 14 reasons (SD = 2.26).

Reliability coding was carried out by a trained coder familiar with the Ethics of Autonomy, Community, and Divinity model. Five randomly selected interviews were coded for the reliability. The selected interviews consisted of seventy-two reasons that were underlined by the author. The coding reliability was checked at the level of each ethic and the category "Other." (The number of categories was four.) The reliability between the coders was 78 percent. All disagreement was resolved through discussion.

The structure of the Ethics of Autonomy, Community, and Divinity was validated by means of a hierarchical cluster analysis using the Ward method, which usually provides a good fit with the real cluster structure of the data (StatSoft, 2013). The results can be said to be valid if a similar cluster structure emerges with another sample of individuals (Everitt, Landau, Leese, *et al.*, 2011). Each subcode belonging to the Ethics of Autonomy, Community, and Divinity ($N = 34$ in total) was entered as a variable in the analysis. The results produced a clear three-cluster structure and revealed clear "nested" differences between the initial and the final five levels of clusters. Three main clusters emerged within a short distance of each other, the next partitions taking place much later. According to Everitt and colleagues (2011), when deciding the appropriate numbers of clusters, large changes in fusion levels in the dendrogram indicate a particular number of clusters. The dendrogram here revealed that justifications reflecting autonomy and rights were grouped in the first cluster that corresponded to the Ethic of Autonomy. This cluster also included justifications emphasizing social order concerns, which could also have been grouped under the Ethic of Community. The second cluster corresponding to the Ethic of Community emphasized social duties, others' needs, and the maintenance of social stability, social relationships, authority, and tradition. The third cluster was religious in nature, including justifications referring to God's word, the Bible, and faith; it was named the Ethic of Divinity. In sum, the hierarchical cluster analysis supported the Three Ethics model.

How culture relates to adolescents' moral definitions and reasons

How religious culture relates to definitions of morality

The analysis of criterion judgments revealed that the three groups held similar definitions of the typical moral issues, but not of the controversial ones as hypothesized. The quantitative analysis of the three typical moral issues showed almost no differences between the groups. These issues were evaluated as not alterable by the government or church, as not contingent on God's word, and as generalizable to other countries (see Tables 3.1 and 3.2).

Some conservative religious adolescents, however, stated that women's and men's different treatment is legitimate because God created them as different, and therefore the criterion judgments associated with gender-based discrimination yielded some statistically significant differences between conservative religious and other participants (Table 3.2). Here is an example of a conservative religious adolescent explaining his view of the legitimacy of gender inequality:

Table 3.1 *Criterion judgments of nonreligious, liberal religious, and conservative religious adolescents*
The first line shows means, and the second line shows standard deviations (in italics).

Issue	Nonreligious				Liberal religious				Conservative religious			
	Government	Church	God's word	Other country	Government	Church	God's word	Other country	Government	Church	God's word	Other country
Stealing	2.90 *0.32*	2.90 *0.32*	2.90 *0.32*	2.70 *0.48*	3.00 *0.00*	2.90 *0.32*	2.80 *0.42*	2.70 *0.48*	3.00 *0.00*	3.00 *0.00*	2.50 *0.71*	2.80 *0.63*
Religion-based discrimination	3.00 *0.00*	3.00 *0.00*	3.00 *0.00*	2.80 *0.42*	3.00 *0.00*	3.00 *0.00*	3.00 *0.00*	2.90 *0.32*	3.00 *0.00*	3.00 *0.00*	2.60 *.052*	3.00 *0.00*
Gender-based discrimination	3.00 *0.00*	3.00 *0.00*	3.00 *0.00*	2.70 *0.68*	3.00 *0.00*	3.00 *0.00*	2.80 *0.63*	3.00 *0.00*	2.60 *0.84*	2.60 *0.84*	2.50 *0.85*	2.60 *0.84*
Nonreligious moral education	1.00 *0.00*	1.00 *0.00*	1.00 *0.00*	1.00 *0.00*	1.60 *0.70*	1.80 *0.79*	1.60 *0.70*	1.70 *0.82*	2.90 *0.32*	2.90 *0.32*	2.20 *0.79*	2.20 *0.63*
Censorship	1.50 *0.85*	1.50 *0.85*	1.50 *0.85*	1.10 *0.32*	1.70 *0.82*	2.00 *0.94*	1.80 *0.92*	1.60 *0.84*	2.90 *0.32*	2.90 *0.32*	2.30 *0.82*	2.60 *0.84*
Shops open on Sundays	1.50 *0.85*	1.60 *0.84*	1.50 *0.85*	1.20 *0.63*	1.60 *0.84*	2.10 *0.99*	1.70 *0.82*	1.20 *0.63*	3.00 *0.00*	3.00 *0.00*	1.70 *0.95*	2.20 *0.92*
Cohabitation	1.10 *0.32*	1.10 *0.32*	1.10 *0.32*	1.00 *0.00*	2.00 *0.94*	2.30 *0.95*	1.50 *0.85*	2.00 *0.94*	3.00 *0.00*	3.00 *0.00*	1.40 *0.84*	2.20 *0.92*
Wine sold in shops	1.20 *0.63*	1.40 *0.84*	1.20 *0.63*	1.20 *0.63*	1.80 *0.92*	1.80 *0.92*	1.80 *0.92*	1.70 *0.95*	2.90 *0.32*	3.00 *0.00*	1.90 *0.99*	2.30 *0.82*
Contraceptive pills	1.40 *0.70*	1.40 *0.70*	1.40 *0.70*	1.40 *0.70*	2.00 *1.05*	2.00 *1.05*	2.00 *1.05*	1.90 *0.99*	2.80 *0.63*	2.80 *0.63*	2.00 *0.82*	2.40 *0.84*
Marijuana	2.00 *0.94*	2.00 *0.94*	2.00 *0.94*	1.80 *0.92*	2.70 *0.68*	2.80 *0.63*	2.50 *0.85*	2.30 *0.95*	3.00 *0.00*	3.00 *0.00*	2.10 *0.74*	2.50 *0.85*

Table 3.2 *Results of planned contrasts (Helmert) on criterion judgments between conservative religious (CR) vs. other participants, F (1, 28), vs. liberal religious (NR) vs. liberal religious (LR) participants, F (1, 18), and nonreligious (NR) vs. liberal religious (LR) participants, F (1, 18)*

Issue	Contrast type	Government		Church		God's word		Other country	
		F	p	F	p	F	p	F	p
Stealing	CR vs. others	0.49	0.489	1.04	.317	3.24	0.082	0.24	0.629
	NR vs. LR	1.00	0.331	0.00	1.000	0.36	0.556	0.00	1.000
Religion-based discrimination	CR vs. others	0.00	1.000	0.00	1.000	12.44	0.001	1.65	0.21
	NR vs. LR	0.00	1.000	0.00	1.000	0.36	0.556	0.00	1.000
Gender-based discrimination	CR vs. others	4.67	0.039	4.67	0.039	2.90	0.100	1.07	0.311
	NR vs. LR	0.00	1.000	0.00	1.000	1.00	0.331	1.98	0.177
Nonreligious moral education	CR vs. others	67.31	0.000	43.30	0.000	12.81	0.001	11.10	0.002
	NR vs. LR	7.36	0.014	10.29	0.005	7.36	0.014	7.23	0.015
Censorship	CR vs. others	23.03	0.000	14.83	0.001	3.82	0.061	19.51	0.000
	NR vs. LR	0.29	0.600	1.55	0.229	0.57	0.458	3.08	0.096
Shops open on Sundays	CR vs. others	30.31	0.000	14.92	0.001	0.09	0.767	12.61	0.001
	NR vs. LR	0.07	0.795	1.47	0.241	0.29	0.600	0.00	1.000
Cohabitation	CR vs. others	30.31	0.000	19.47	0.000	0.13	0.723	4.44	0.044
	NR vs. LR	8.19	0.010	14.40	0.001	1.95	0.180	11.25	0.004
Wine sold in shops	CR vs. others	26.32	0.000	24.72	0.000	1.36	0.253	7.08	0.013
	NR vs. LR	2.89	0.106	1.03	0.324	2.89	0.106	1.92	0.182
Contraceptive pills	CR vs. others	11.41	0.002	11.41	0.002	0.76	0.392	5.01	0.033
	NR vs. LR	2.25	0.151	2.25	0.151	2.25	0.151	1.69	0.210
Marijuana	CR vs. others	5.42	0.027	4.54	0.042	0.20	0.655	1.61	0.215
	NR vs. LR	3.65	0.072	4.97	0.039	1.55	0.229	1.43	0.247

A: It is strange why men cannot give birth. In practice, equality is not possible in any way, because a man and a woman are different, so how could they be equal. How can a bear and a fox be equal when they have totally different skills, thoughts and instincts?

With respect to criterion judgments of the controversial issues, however, there were many statistically significant differences between the conservative groups and other two groups as expected (Table 3.2). Unlike the other adolescents, conservative religious adolescents evaluated these issues as not alterable by the government or church and generalizable to other countries. However, they perceived most controversial issues as contingent on God's word. Almost no significant differences between the nonreligious and liberal religious groups were found. These findings indicate that nonreligious and liberal religious groups considered controversial issues as social conventions, whereas conservative religious participants considered them as context-dependent moral issues. Moreover, this finding fits well with the notion by Shweder, Mahapatra, and Miller (1987) that culture is associated with the perception of controversial moral issues more than with the perception of typical moral issues.

How religious culture relates to moral reasoning: Ethic of Divinity

Conservative participants ($M = 8.90$, $SD = 3.80$ in the entire interview) used the Ethic of Divinity significantly more than the other groups ($M = 1.65$, $SD = 1.39$), $F(1, 28) = 145.47$, $p = 0.000$. On the other hand, there was essentially no difference in the use of Divinity between liberal religious ($M = 2.00$, $SD = 1.56$ in the entire interview) and nonreligious participants ($M = 1.30$, $SD = 1.16$), $F(1, 18) = 1.29$, $p = 0.270$. In fact, conservative religious adolescents used the Ethic of Divinity more than the other groups for every single issue, typical and controversial (see Tables 3.3 and 3.4).

The qualitative analysis of moral reasoning furthermore revealed that the Ethic of Divinity rhetoric used by conservative religious participants was different from liberal religious and nonreligious participants' Divinity rhetoric. When nonreligious participants used the Ethic of Divinity (which was quite rare), they referred to notions of what is "natural" as well as to the duty of the Evangelical Lutheran Church to follow the principles of Christianity.

Conservative religious participants instead focused on concepts such as "living according to God's word," "following one's God-given conscience," and "maintaining the moral purity of the soul." In addition, conservative religious adolescents emphasized the exclusive nature of their own religious community. In the following excerpt, a conservative religious adolescent explains why stealing is morally wrong, even if the government hypothetically did not prohibit it:

Table 3.3 *Nonreligious, liberal religious, and conservative religious adolescents' use of the Ethics of Autonomy, Community, and Divinity*

The first line shows means, and the second line shows standard deviations (in italics).

Issue	Nonreligious			Liberal religious			Conservative religious		
	Autonomy	Community	Divinity	Autonomy	Community	Divinity	Autonomy	Community	Divinity
Stealing	0.80	0.80	0.20	0.60	1.50	0.40	0.20	0.40	0.70
	0.63	*0.63*	*0.42*	*0.70*	*0.71*	*0.52*	*0.42*	*0.52*	*0.48*
Religion-based discrimination	1.00	0.40	0.20	1.10	0.40	0.10	0.70	0.00	0.60
	0.47	*0.52*	*0.42*	*0.57*	*0.52*	*0.32*	*0.48*	*0.00*	*0.52*
Gender-based discrimination	0.80	0.30	0.10	1.00	0.30	0.10	0.60	0.00	0.50
	0.32	*0.48*	*0.32*	*0.47*	*0.48*	*0.32*	*0.52*	*0.00*	*0.53*
Nonreligious moral education	0.90	0.30	0.00	0.60	0.40	0.20	0.00	0.50	0.90
	0.32	*0.48*	*0.00*	*0.52*	*0.52*	*0.42*	*0.00*	*0.53*	*0.32*
Censorship	0.80	0.40	0.00	0.90	0.40	0.00	0.10	0.30	1.20
	0.42	*0.52*	*0.00*	*0.57*	*0.70*	*0.00*	*0.32*	*0.48*	*0.42*
Shops open on Sundays	0.40	0.50	0.40	0.70	0.50	0.50	0.00	0.10	1.00
	0.52	*0.53*	*0.52*	*0.68*	*0.53*	*0.71*	*0.00*	*0.32*	*0.00*
Cohabitation	0.80	0.30	0.10	0.30	0.60	0.50	0.00	0.00	1.10
	0.42	*0.48*	*0.32*	*0.48*	*0.70*	*0.53*	*0.00*	*0.00*	*0.32*
Wine sold in shops	0.50	0.50	0.10	0.70	0.40	0.00	0.00	0.40	1.00
	0.53	*0.53*	*0.32*	*0.48*	*0.52*	*0.00*	*0.00*	*0.52*	*0.47*
Contraceptive pills	0.30	0.80	0.00	0.70	0.60	0.00	0.10	0.30	0.90
	0.48	*0.64*	*0.00*	*0.68*	*0.84*	*0.00*	*0.32*	*0.48*	*0.32*
Marijuana	0.30	1.10	0.20	0.30	1.10	0.20	0.10	0.30	1.00
	0.48	*0.74*	*0.42*	*0.48*	*0.88*	*0.42*	*0.32*	*0.48*	*0.47*

Table 3.4 *Results of planned contrasts (Helmert) on use of the Ethics of Autonomy, Community, and Divinity: conservative religious (CR) vs. other participants, F (1, 28), and nonreligious (NR) vs. liberal religious (LR) participants, F (1, 18)*

Issue	Contrast type	Ethic of Autonomy		Ethic of Community		Ethic of Divinity	
		F	p	F	p	F	p
Stealing	CR vs. others	4.76	0.038	8.11	0.008	4.74	0.038
	NR vs. LR	0.45	0.511	5.44	0.031	0.90	0.355
Religion-based discrimination	CR vs. others	3.24	0.082	6.22	0.019	7.64	0.010
	NR vs. LR	0.18	0.673	0.00	1.000	0.36	0.556
Gender-based discrimination	CR vs. others	2.71	0.111	4.00	0.055	6.95	0.014
	NR vs. LR	1.00	0.331	0.00	1.000	0.00	1.000
Nonreligious moral education	CR vs. others	28.00	0.000	0.60	0.447	44.25	0.000
	NR vs. LR	2.46	0.135	0.20	0.660	2.25	0.151
Censorship	CR vs. others	19.27	0.000	0.21	0.651	168.00	0.000
	NR vs. LR	0.20	0.660	0.00	1.000	0.00	1.000
Shops open on Sundays	CR vs. others	8.13	0.008	5.06	0.032	8.13	0.008
	NR vs. LR	1.25	0.279	0.00	1.000	0.13	0.722
Cohabitation	CR vs. others	11.41	0.002	5.44	0.027	23.43	0.000
	NR vs. LR	6.08	0.024	1.25	0.279	4.24	0.054
Wine sold to shops	CR vs. others	14.00	0.001	0.06	0.803	57.11	0.000
	NR vs. LR	0.78	0.388	0.18	0.673	1.00	0.331
Contraceptive pills	CR vs. others	3.78	0.062	2.43	0.130	168.00	0.000
	NR vs. LR	2.32	0.145	0.36	0.556	0.00	1.000
Marijuana	CR vs. others	1.46	0.236	8.60	0.007	22.97	0.000
	NR vs. LR	0.00	1.000	0.00	1.000	0.00	1.000

A: Conscience, I feel that it says that do the right thing, or when there is another voice that calms me down, saying "you can do it, it is not a bad thing."
Q: What is that other voice?
A: I don't know, could be maybe from Satan or Evil or the enemy of God or something like that?
Q: And what is conscience?
A: It's something like God's voice inside. If a human being does something wrong, God says that "now you've done wrong."
Q: What is the purpose of conscience?
A: To make a human being understand that he has committed a sin and that he should do the right thing.

In this excerpt, the conservative religious adolescent was referring to morality in general. He described how thoughts represent a conversation between two "voices": between one's conscience that represents "God's word" and an "other voice" that represents "the enemy of God."

For the conservative religious participants, God's word represented an important moral authority. Many of them said that God's word is binding on all human beings irrespective of their belief in God. In the following excerpt, a conservative religious adolescent using the Ethic of Divinity describes the basis of her moral reasoning:

Q: What would be the case if you hadn't heard of God's word?
A: I would have a totally different opinion of everything. If someone doesn't have faith, he uses his own brains and you know where you go when you do only that.

In this excerpt, a conservative religious adolescent explains that her moral reasoning is based on God's word. With the expression "you know where you go" (meaning hell), she implies that in order to be moral, people need faith and that people are not able to be moral by themselves.

The Ethic of Divinity used by conservative religious adolescents emphasized the concept of "providence." In the next excerpt, a conservative religious adolescent states that God is also responsible for global problems, such as overpopulation:

Q: What do you think about introducing prescription-free contraceptive pills in the developing countries?
A: I understand fully what they are doing and that overpopulation is a fact and has a purpose. But God reigns and we don't have to take care of it.
Q: Do you mean that overpopulation has a purpose?
A: Yes, he knows what he is doing. I don't have to care about it.

This conservative religious adolescent explained that because God has planned everything, people have limited responsibility with regard to solving global problems.

The conservative religious adolescents objected to some of the interviewer's questions that framed references to God as a contingency. For example, they expressed hesitance toward imagining that God had not said anything about stealing:

A: It would be a totally impossible idea that God had not said so. In my opinion it is very stupid to even think that God would change his own word. It is always the same.

In this excerpt, a conservative religious adolescent described that, although morality for her was contingent upon God's word, God's word was unchangeable. Some conservative religious participants expressed the view that God does not change his word because it is based on justice. Moreover, such thoughts appeared to have moral significance for these adolescents (see also Cohen & Rozin, 2001):

A: Because God has prohibited stealing, it means that he has prohibited it. In my view it is derogating to put oneself into this kind of situation to imagine what if he had not prohibited stealing because he is omniscient and does the right thing.

How religious culture relates to moral reasoning: *Ethic of Autonomy*

Nonreligious and liberal adolescents ($M = 6.75$, $SD = 2.07$) used the Ethic of Autonomy significantly more than conservative adolescents ($M = 1.80$, $SD = 1.03$), $F(1, 28) = 50.07$, $p = 0.000$. As shown in Tables 3.3 and 3.4, this difference in Autonomy reasoning was found for most of the controversial issues. There was no overall difference in the use of the Ethic of Autonomy between liberal religious ($M = 6.90$, $SD = 2.33$ in the entire interview) and nonreligious participants ($M = 6.60$, $SD = 1.90$), $F(1, 18) = 0.10$, $p = 0.756$, and essentially no significant differences on individual issues either (see Table 3.4). The qualitative analysis of the interviews suggested that all three groups emphasized individual rights, physical harm, psychological harm, and respect for individual property when speaking about the typical issues. For example, in the following excerpt a liberal religious adolescent describes why gender-based discrimination is wrong, not alterable by the government or church, not contingent on God's word, and generalizable to other countries:

A: Because in my opinion every human is equal and this also applies to both genders. Nobody can decide that someone is better than others because that person is a man or a woman.

In contrast to conservatives, nonreligious and liberal adolescents also spoke in terms of the Ethic of Autonomy to *support* the alterability, contingency, and context dependence of "controversial" moral issues. Here is an example of how a nonreligious adolescent explained why contraceptive pills should be sold without prescriptions as long as there is no risk of physical harm to individuals:

A: I do not see any reason why their use should be restricted. In my opinion the use of contraceptive pills belongs to individual freedoms. If they do not have negative health effects I do not see any moral reason why they should be prohibited.

How culture relates to moral reasoning: Ethic of Community

Although the Ethic of Community was quite commonly used by all participants (see Table 3.3), nonreligious and liberal religious adolescents ($M = 5.80$, $SD = 2.84$ in the entire interview) overall used this ethic more than conservative religious adolescents ($M = 2.30$, $SD = 1.83$), $F(1, 28) = 12.48$, $p = 0.001$, which was unexpected. Analyses for the individual issues showed that this was the case for a couple of the typical issues and a few of the controversial ones as well (see Table 3.4).

A qualitative examination of responses indicates that conservative religious adolescents to some extent combined the Ethics of Divinity and Community. In these cases, the Community concepts pertaining to social order and societal harmony were used, but society was defined as being based on religious values. As an example, in the following excerpt a conservative religious adolescent explains why moral education in Finnish schools should be based on Evangelical Lutheran religious instruction:

A: It provides a better foundation for the morality of the nation. Not all parents necessarily teach their children anything, they do not belong to any church and for this reason it leads to a moral decay.

Here a conservative religious adolescent presents his view that Evangelical Lutheran moral education in schools provides "morality for the nation," implying that morality should be based on religion (Ethic of Divinity), which in turn protects the nation from "moral decay" (Ethic of Community). In general, conservative religious adolescents emphasized the importance of the Evangelical Lutheran Church, as the state church of Finland, in maintaining societal stability and moral values.

The most common types of Community reasons used by nonreligious and liberal religious adolescents included common attitudes, habits, and majority opinion in the society, as in this example where a nonreligious adolescent explained why shops should be open on Sundays:

A: I must say that real, religious consecration of Sunday is so rare among people that it really does not make any difference nowadays.

Moreover, all groups of adolescents frequently used a discourse that reflected the moral ideals promoted by the Nordic welfare state. This discourse combined the Ethics of Community and Autonomy justifying why the state should limit the freedom of individuals to act in ways that are harmful to them. More specifically, the welfare state was depicted as responsible for protecting individuals from alcohol addiction, diseases, and the negative health effects of medicines (Table 3.3). In the following excerpt a liberal religious adolescent explains why contraceptive pills should not be sold without a doctor's prescription:

A: The Parliament would make a wrong decision because contraceptive pills have many risks so I do not see any sense in making them prescription-free.

Q: If they were proven to be safe?

A: It would lead to a situation where everybody would buy contraceptive pills. Anyway, when they don't protect themselves from those diseases it would become complicated and a girl would have to take more responsibility for it and that is not then good.

Conclusion: moral cultures in Finland

This chapter analyzed how the Finnish adolescents' definitions of morality and moral reasoning reflect the moral codes of a religious culture and of the Nordic welfare state. The results revealed that the moral rhetoric used by nonreligious and liberal religious adolescents combined the Ethics of Autonomy and Community, in other words, the values of individual autonomy and state responsibility for protecting individuals from self-harm. Similar findings have been obtained in Denmark (Arnett & Jensen, 1994) and Sweden (Scarr, 1996), suggesting that such moral rhetoric is characteristic of Nordic moral rhetoric.

In contrast, the conservative religious adolescents' reasoning emphasized the Ethic of Divinity. Their moral concepts focused on living according to God's word, following one's conscience and maintaining the moral purity of the soul. Such rhetoric has also been identified in previous studies examining conservative religious moral reasoning in countries such as India and the United States (Jensen, 1998). The conservative religious adolescents' reasoning according to the Ethic of Divinity revealed a broad scope of morality that extended into the domain of one's own thoughts (see also Cohen & Rozin, 2001).

Moreover, the definitions of morality given by nonreligious and liberal religious adolescents distinguished between nonalterable, noncontingent, universal moral issues and alterable, contingent, and context-dependent conventional social issues. In contrast, the moral criterion judgments and rhetoric of the conservative religious adolescents made no such distinction. Their constellation of morality was dependent on God's word and applied most strictly to one's own religious community.

The Finnish welfare state emphasizes the state's responsibility for the welfare of its citizens. However, the concepts of individual autonomy and state responsibility can conflict with each other: state responsibility can mean limited individual autonomy. The adolescents described the question of personal responsibility for one's own health as a controversial issue: those who supported the state control of alcohol, marijuana, and contraceptive pills described personal autonomy as something negative that threatened individuals' welfare, whereas those who opposed state regulation in such matters spoke in favor of increased personal autonomy and responsibility. Jensen, Arnett, Feldman, and Cauffman (2004) showed that during adolescence the perception of personal autonomy is heightened in cultures that endorse individualism, such as in the United States. Finnish adolescents' moral rhetoric that endorses limited personal autonomy reveals how the development of moral reasoning is influenced by national cultural values. The Finnish (or Nordic) welfare state can be said to provide a special kind of context for moral development, incorporating the moral ideas of personal autonomy, equality, and state (or shared) responsibility.

This study included only adolescents. Future studies comparing the moral reasoning of children, adolescents, and adults are needed to better understand how universal developmental patterns accommodate to the Nordic cultural context. For example, they could focus on the issues of how the moral concepts associated with the Nordic welfare state emerge and develop in individuals' thinking and how these are culturally transmitted and legitimized. They could also examine the legitimation of public services, such as those that aim at *increasing the autonomy* of individuals during different phases of life, such as old age, or those that aim at *promoting equality*, such as public day care facilitating women working outside the home (Repo, 2004).

Moreover, at least two important issues that can potentially affect the moral cultures of the Nordic welfare states need to be addressed in future research. The first is multiculturalism and increasing immigration in these countries. Since many individuals today are in contact with multiple moral cultures, such as ones that endorse (religious) conservatism and others that endorse (secular) liberalism, future research could examine how this is shaping the moral development of these individuals and how they resolve the apparent tensions between religious and secular moralities (see also Glicksman, 1997; Jensen, 2011). Second, research could examine how global environmental problems, such as climate change, are affecting the moral domains of individuals (Mäkiniemi & Vainio, 2013). It has been suggested that the resolution of environmental problems may fundamentally diminish the endorsement of individual freedoms (the Ethic of Autonomy), giving rise to a new ecological morality that emphasizes a collective sense of responsibility and self-control (the Ethics of Community and Divinity) (see Dobson, 2003).

Whereas for a long while research on morality has been a theoretically driven search for universal similarities, there is now a need for research that pays particular attention to difference, uniqueness, and exceptionality in our moral lives and development. The cultural-developmental template model aims at accommodating developmental trajectories to cultural differences. In this chapter,

I have provided an account of definitions of morality and moral reasoning of Finnish adolescents. It is a cultural landscape where adolescents come of age sharing a commitment to the welfare state, but where religiously conservative adolescents also differ markedly from nonreligious and liberal religious adolescents by encompassing a wider array of behaviors within the moral domain and by placing an Ethic of Divinity ahead of other ethics.

REFERENCES

Arnett, J. (1997). Young people's conceptions of the transition to adulthood. *Youth & Society*, 29, 1–23.

Arnett, J., & Jensen, L. A. (1994). Socialization and risk behavior in two countries: Denmark and the United States. *Youth and Society*, 26, 3–22.

Arnett, J., Ramos, K., & Jensen, L. A. (2001). Ideological views in emerging adulthood: Balancing autonomy and community. *Journal of Adult Development*, 8, 69–79.

Casanova, J. (1994). *Public religions in the modern world.* Chicago, IL: University of Chicago Press.

Cohen, A., & Rozin, P. (2001). Religion and the morality of mentality. *Journal of Personality and Social Psychology*, 81, 697–710.

Dobson, A. (2003) *Citizenship and the environment.* Oxford, United Kingdom: Oxford University Press.

Encyclopædia Britannica (2012). Welfare state *Encyclopædia Britannica Online Academic Edition.* Retrieved from www.britannica.com/EBchecked/topic/639266/welfare-state

Ervasti, H., Fridberg, T., Hjerm, M., Kangas, O., & Ringdal, K. (2008). The Nordic model. In H. Ervasti (Ed.), *Nordic social attitudes in a European perspective* (pp. 1–22). London, United Kingdom: Edward Elgar Publishing.

Esping-Andersen, G. (2002). Towards the good society, once again? In G. Esping-Andersen, D. Gallie, A. Hemerijck, & J. Myles (Eds.), *Why we need a new welfare state* (pp. 1–25). Oxford, United Kingdom: Oxford University Press.

Evangelical Lutheran Church of Finland. (2013). *Vanhoillislestadiolaisuus.* Retrieved from www.evl2.fi/sanasto/index.php/Vanhoillislestadiolaisuus

Everitt, B., Landau, S., & Leese, M., & Stahl, D. (2011). *Cluster analysis* (5th ed.). Chicester, West Sussex, United Kingdom: Wiley.

Flanagan, C., & Levine, P. (2010). Civic engagement and the transition to adulthood. *Future of Children*, 20, 159–179.

Glicksman, S. (1997). *The role of religion in the domain theory of moral development* (Unpublished doctoral dissertation). Yeshiva University, New York, NY.

Graham, J., Haidt, J., & Nosek, B. (2009). Liberals and conservatives rely on different sets of moral foundations. *Journal of Personality and Social Psychology*, 96, 1029–1046.

Haidt, J., Koller, S., & Diaz, M. (1993). Affect, culture, and morality, or is it wrong to eat your dog? *Journal of Personality and Social Psychology*, 65, 613–628.

Heino, H. (1997). *Mihin Suomi tänään uskoo.* Helsinki, Finland: WSOY.

Jensen, L. A. (1995). Habits of the heart revisited: Autonomy, Community, and Divinity in adults' moral language. *Qualitative Sociology*, 18, 71–86.

(1997a). Culture wars: American moral divisions across the adult lifespan. *Journal of Adult Development*, 4, 107–121.

(1997b). Different worldviews, different morals: America's culture war divide. *Human Development*, 40, 325–344.

(1998). Moral divisions within countries between orthodoxy and progressivism: India and the United States. *Journal for the Scientific Study of Religion*, 37, 90–107.

(2006). Liberal and conservative conceptions of family: A cultural-developmental study. *International Journal for the Psychology of Religion*, 16, 253–269.

(2008). Through two lenses: A cultural-developmental approach to moral psychology. *Developmental Review*, 28, 289–315. doi:10.1016/j.dr.2007.11.001

(2011). Autonomy, Community, and Divinity: The cultural development of three fundamental moral ethics. *Zygon*, 46, 150–167.

Jensen, L. A., Arnett, J., Feldman, S., & Cauffman, E. (2004). The right to do wrong: Lying to parents among adolescents and emerging adults. *Journal of Youth and Adolescence*, 33, 101–112.

Jiggens, J. (1995). Legislating morality: The war on cannabis. *Social Alternatives*, 14, 11–14.

Kahl, S. (2005). The religious roots of modern poverty policy: Catholic, Lutheran, and Reformed Protestant traditions compared. *European Journal of Sociology*, 46, 91–126.

Larsen, S. (1993). The origin of alcohol-related social norms in the Saami minority. *Addiction*, 88, 501–508.

Lindeman, M., Pyysiäinen, I., & Saariluoma, P. (2002). Representing God. *Papers on Social Representations*, 11, 1–13.

Mäkelä, P., & Österberg, E. (2009). Weakening of one more alcohol control pillar: A review of the effects of the alcohol tax cuts in Finland in 2004. *Addiction*, 104, 554–563.

Mäkiniemi, J.-P. & Vainio, A. (2013). Moral intensity and climate-friendly food choices. *Appetite*, 66, 54–61.

Miller, J. G., Goyal, N., & Wice, M. (2015). Ethical considerations in research on human development and culture. In L. A. Jensen (Ed.), *Oxford handbook of human development and culture: An interdisciplinary approach*. New York, NY: Oxford University Press.

Nucci, L. (1985). Children's conceptions of morality, societal convention, and religious prescription. In C. Harding (Ed.), *Moral dilemmas* (pp. 137–174). Chicago, IL: Precedent Publishing.

(2001). *Education in the moral domain*. New York, NY: Cambridge University Press.

Nucci, L., & Turiel, E. (1993). God's word, religious rules, and their relation to Christian and Jewish children's concepts of morality. *Child Development*, 64, 1475–1491.

Nuorteva, J. (1992). *Biblia 350: Suomalainen Raamattu 1642–1992*. Helsinki, Finland: Helsinki University Press.

Opielka, M. (2008). Christian foundations of the welfare state: Strong cultural values in comparative perspective. In W. Oorschot, M. Opielka, & B. Pfau-Effinger (Eds.), *Culture and welfare state: Values and social policy in comparative perspective* (pp. 89–116). London, United Kingdom: Edward Elgar Publishing.

Pyysiäinen, I. (2005). *Synti [Sin]*. Helsinki, Finland: WSOY.

Repo, K. (2004). Combining work and family in two welfare state contexts: A discourse analytical perspective. *Social Policy & Administration*, 38, 622–639.

Rokkan, S. (1999). *State formation, nation-building, and mass politics in Europe.* Oxford, United Kingdom: Oxford University Press.

Rozin, P. (1997). Moralization. In A. Brandt & P. Rozin (Eds.), *Health and morality* (pp. 379–401). New York, NY: Routledge.

(1999). The process of moralization. *Psychological Science*, 10, 218–221.

Scarr, S. (1996). Individuality and community: The contrasting role of the state in family life in the United States and Sweden. *Scandinavian Journal of Psychology*, 37, 93–102.

Shweder, R., Mahapatra, M., & Miller, J. (1987). Culture and moral development. In J. Kagan & S. Lamb (Eds.), *The emergence of morality in young children* (pp. 1–83). Chicago, IL: University of Chicago Press.

Shweder, R., & Miller, J. (1985). The social construction of the person: How is it possible? In K. Gergen & K. Davis (Eds.), *The social construction of the person* (pp. 41–69). New York, NY: Springer-Verlag.

Shweder, R., Much, N., Mahapatra, M., & Park, L. (1997). The "Big Three" of morality (Autonomy, Community, Divinity) and the "big three" explanations of suffering. In A. Brandt & P. Rozin (Eds.), *Health and morality* (pp. 119–169). New York, NY: Routledge.

Statistics Finland. (2011). *Official statistics of Finland (OSF): Population structure, annual review 2011.* Helsinki: Author. Retrieved from www.stat.fi/til/vaerak/2011/01/vaerak_2011_01_2012-11-30_tau_008_en.html

StatSoft, Inc. (2013). *Electronic statistics textbook.* Tulsa, OK: Author. Retrieved from www.statsoft.com/textbook/

Trommsdorff, G. (2012). Cultural perspectives on values and religion in adolescent development: A conceptual overview and synthesis. In G. Trommsdorff & X. Chen (Eds.), *Values, religion, and culture in adolescent development* (pp. 3–45). Cambridge, United Kingdom: Cambridge University Press.

(2015). Cultural roots of values, and moral and religious purposes in adolescent development. In L. A. Jensen (Ed.), *Oxford handbook of human development and culture: An interdisciplinary approach.* New York, NY: Oxford University Press.

Turiel, E. (1983). *The development of social knowledge: Morality and convention.* New York, NY: Cambridge University Press.

Vasquez, K., Keltner, D., Ebenbach, D., & Banaszynski, T. (2001). Cultural variation and similarity in moral rhetorics: Voices from the Philippines and the United States. *Journal of Cross-Cultural Psychology*, 32, 93–120.

Zuckerman, P. (2007). Atheism: Contemporary numbers and patterns. In M. Martin (Ed.), *The Cambridge companion to atheism* (pp. 47–65). Cambridge, United Kingdom: Cambridge University Press.

4 An Indian moral worldview: developmental patterns in adolescents and adults

Shagufa Kapadia and Rachana Bhangaokar

One should never do to another what one regards as injurious to oneself. This, in brief, is the law of dharma.

Mahabharata XVIII.113.8

The opening quote from the Mahabharata – India's Grand Epic – is a worthy contender for a universal moral "law of life" that should govern individual behavior in the social-moral realm. The Mahabharata is an all-encompassing treatise on morality, politics, society, and individual moral behavior. As a cultural template, it enjoys uncontested popularity and relevance in any given era. Stories, characters, and messages from the Mahabharata are evoked from time to time as guiding forces to resolve challenges in the individual as well as public domains. The concept of *dharma* has been recognized from time immemorial as a cornerstone of moral understanding in the Indian tradition. However, in A. K. Ramanujan's words (cited in Das, 2009, p. 293), "It is not *dharma* or right conduct that the Mahabharata seems to teach, but the 'subtle' nature of *dharma* – its infinite subtlety, its incalculable calculus of consequences, its endless delicacy." Though all pervasive, its characteristic subtlety makes *dharma* the most elusive and empirically understudied concept in Indian psychology. By anchoring to the concepts of truth and duty (also core concepts that constitute *dharma*) as they operate in everyday life, this chapter attempts to uncover some culture-specific aspects of morality in India. We aim to illuminate the development of morality in Indian thought across the two life stages of adolescence and adulthood. We also explore the role of gender, an important variable defining the duties and moral worldviews of individuals in Indian society.

Recently, Damon (2012) took stock of the field of moral psychology and wrote that it has "grown dreary from bloodless academic debates between over-intellectualized and narrowly-conceived theories." The push and pull between moral universals and relativism, between biological intuitions and cognitive reasoning remain unresolved, debatable issues in the field of moral development. In contemporary times, in our view, diverse voices from a variety of cultural contexts, especially non-Western ones, seem key to future directions

69

in the field. We begin the chapter by discussing the cultural approach to moral-ity. We focus on the Big Three Ethics framework (Shweder, 1990) and the cultural-developmental approach (Jensen, 2008). Next, we briefly review the-ory and research on gender and morality, including findings from India. We then turn specifically to the Indian context. We describe the core moral concepts of *dharma* and *truth* and present an account of empirical work on morality in India. Subsequently, we describe our study. Through quantitative analyses of interviews and a presentation of the voices of adolescents and adults, we argue that participants' moral reasoning and approaches to moral dilemmas are clearly culturally situated while also varying by age. We conclude with a discussion of the applicability of the cultural-developmental framework of morality in the Indian context and offer suggestions for future research directions.

A cultural approach to the development of morality

Developmental approaches to morality have for a long time aimed to uncover universal moral reasons and developmental sequences (for example, theories put forth by Piaget, Kohlberg, and Turiel). More recently, cultural psychology approaches have highlighted how moral reasons and concepts are culturally embedded and varied. Cultural psychology explains how cultural practices and traditions become a part of the human psyche and result not in the psychic unity of humankind but in various cultural divergences and local explanations of basic processes of human development (Shweder, 1990).

The Big Three Ethics framework (Jensen, 2004; Shweder, Much, Mahapatra, *et al.*, 1997) is useful to analyze moral reasoning to account for responses from the Indian context as it offers a broader conception of morality. Our study sheds additional light on the presence of each ethic and the interconnections of the ethics in the Indian context. The Ethic of Autonomy presupposes the concep-tualization of the self as an individual preference structure aimed at increasing choice and personal liberty. The Ethic of Community refers to concepts of duty, hierarchy, and interdependence and deals with various roles or stations of life that constitute a society or community. Here the self-conceptualization depends on one's roles and stations in life that are intrinsic to one's identity and also part of a larger interdependent social structure. This social structure is a "collective enterprise with a history and standing of its own" (Shweder, Much, Mahapatra, *et al.*, 1997, p. 99). Last, the Ethic of Divinity comprises concepts of souls or spirits and the religious-spiritual aspects of human agency. The self is conceptualized as a spiritual entity that is connected to some sacred and natural order of things. As much as possible, this spiritual self avoids moral transgression or sins of every kind and prefers gaining virtue to aid its journey toward spiritual purity. The authors claim that issues about morality and moral discourse can be accommodated within the three ethics across many cultures. The framework demonstrates an ability to accommodate many postconventional moralities or divergent rationalities found across cultures.

Jensen (2008, 2011) has expanded the Three Ethics framework to put forth a cultural-developmental approach integrating the cultural and developmental perspectives. This approach aims to address the intersection of culture and development by providing a developmental model of the three ethics given by Shweder to study the development of morality across diverse cultures. The cultural-developmental template suggests that while the Ethic of Autonomy emerges early, the degree to which individuals use this ethic stays relatively stable across adolescence and adulthood. However, the type of autonomy concepts used may differ with increasing age. For example, subcodes such as "Self's Interest" or "Punishment Avoidance" may be used more often by younger individuals as compared with the use of "Other's Psychological Well-Being" or "Others' Interest" by older individuals. In terms of the use of the Ethic of Community, both the degree of usage and diversity of types of concepts rise with age, for example, compared with younger children, older children and adolescents use more community concepts pertaining to social groups. The degree of use of Divinity proposed in the template is low among children but rises in adolescence and becomes similar to adult use of the ethic. This change can be attributed to the development of cognitive skills that allow more abstraction among adolescents as compared with young children. Although not much research is available on the Ethic of Divinity, Jensen proposes that in cultures such as India, where religious devotion finds expression in everyday activities (bathing, feeding, and dressing), and where certain people are attributed with godlike status and special powers to connect with God (e.g., *gurus, sadhus,* and priests), children may reason in terms of the Ethic of Divinity concepts from a fairly early age because these concepts exist in specific everyday activities. Overall, however, the increase in cognitive complexity that comes with age would enable the use of diverse moral concepts. Pandya and Bhangaokar (Chapter 2, this volume) found support for this when younger Indian children used the Ethic of Divinity significantly more than did older children in resolving moral dilemmas.

Gender, culture, and morality

Although culture has received significant attention in the study of moral development, the predominant theories of moral development have largely disregarded gender. Gilligan (1982) claimed to find a greater incidence of justice-oriented reasoning among men and care orientation among women. Studies from North America have not found support for Gilligan's claim (e.g., Haviv & Leman, 2002; Walker, Vries, & Trevethan, 1987).

In the Indian context, Sengupta, Saraswathi, and Konantambigi (1994) found that women predominantly used the care orientation, whereas men used a combination of the two orientations. They also found that, with increasing age, men used the justice orientation considerably more. Walker (2006) mentions that gender is becoming an increasingly significant social category that unravels multiple layers of meaning making for individuals and interacts with culture in significant ways. As a starting point, in our view, a study on the development of morality within the Indian cultural context that includes consideration of gender would be useful.

Dharma and truth in the Indian context

To further elucidate the present cultural context, we provide here an explication of key Hindu moral concepts of *dharma* and truth and how these operate in India. According to Hindu-Indian tradition, the self is mediated through an overarching framework of *dharma* that focuses on the performance of duties in diverse conditions and stimulates feelings of righteousness. *Dharma* is understood as a person's inner moral nature and consists of righteous action as well as the adherence to a natural and moral order. Kakar (1981) refers to *dharma* as the "social cement" (p. 40) that holds the individual and society together and, by defining tasks at each life stage, unfolds the ground plan for an ideal life cycle. *Dharma* in the Indian social-moral context is essentially understood as the performance of duties pertaining to one's station in life (Mascolo, Misra, & Rapisardi, 2004). Ramanujan's (1990) informal essay on an Indian way of thinking emphasizes contextual importance for the description of *dharma* as *asramadharma* (*dharma* to do with the stage of life), *svadharma* (conduct right with the *jati* [caste] or class or *svabhava*), and *apaddharma* (conduct necessary in times of distress or emergency). Thus, even if the concept of *dharma* seems broad and is understood as a universal order, its application is very context and situation specific. These context-sensitive and role-related understandings of *dharma* subtly influence self-conceptualizations in India. Kakar and Kakar (2007) explain the Indian emphasis on connection (over separation) in a person's life to nature, the divine, and all other living beings. This can be seen in many aspects of everyday life such as religious rituals, festival celebrations, and communal living, enabling Indians to underplay the importance of autonomy and independence, especially in the extended family.

Closely tied to the concept of self-realization is the pursuit of truth (*satya*). Not only is the realization of truth a coveted goal it also paves the way for *moksha*, or liberation of the soul (Rao, 2011). Following one's *dharma* includes truthfulness and being on the true side of a moral argument. Thus *dharma* is truth, and truth, *dharma*. Providing a vital analysis of truth as a concept, the Mahabharata – which we quoted at the outset – delineates thirteen attributes of truth, equating it to *dharma* (for details, see Gaur, 2011). But, in the same vein, stories from the epic drive home the point that in order to uphold *dharma*, truth must be spoken (or not) in correspondence to *desa* (place) and *kala* (time), contextualizing a universal idea. Modern India and the world witnessed Mahatma Gandhi's belief in *satyagraha* (holding to truth) and *ahimsa* (nonviolence) as the highest *dharma*, bridging the spiritual with the practical. The central principle of *satyagraha* is a spiritual commitment to the pursuit of truth and opposition to everything else that is contrary (Rao, 2011).

Both concepts, *dharma* and *satya*, hence reveal universal appeal as well as the context-specific nature of their application. Needless to say, many inherent contradictions in theoretical understanding and practical application of the concepts in everyday life remain unclear, making the empirical measurement of these concepts an interesting, if difficult, proposition for researchers. Both concepts also have significant implications for self-conceptualization in the Indian context. Kakar (1981) highlights the nature of *svadharma* in Indian society, where right action essentially means following the traditional, time-tested patterns based on caste, occupation, and gender rather than on personal initiative, to which individuals often attribute less wisdom and efficacy. Similarly, Saraswathi, Mistry, and Dutta's (2011) explanations of the Hindu worldview speak to the "individual-in-social-world" perspective (p. 202) in a context where *asramadharma* provides the script in which personal goals are made to align with social expectations. The understanding of the self as a spiritual and an embodied entity hence allows for an alternative view to the stark separation between individual and social worlds.

The use of the Ethics of Autonomy and Community individually and together, as well as in conjunction with the Ethic of Divinity, therefore seems to be of paramount importance in the Indian context. Our study tries to unravel some of the complexities through a developmental lens.

Studies on morality in India

We now turn to a more detailed overview of empirical research on morality in India and include a focus on the interface between morality and self-conceptualizations.

On the basis of many studies in India, Miller and her colleagues have found that a person's duties to others and obligation to serve the social whole are understood as fundamental moral commitments (Miller, Bersoff, & Harwood, 1990). Miller and Bersoff (1992) also found that Indians used a more contextually sensitive approach to moral judgments and relied more on external loci of control to regulate behavior than Americans did. Indians also prioritized beneficence prescriptions ahead of justice prescriptions. To explain the social and contextual nature of Indian morality, we look to Derne (1992), who emphasized the long-term effects of joint family living in Hindu households where awareness about social pressures is tremendous and gives rise to a "socially anchored self."

But even within a web of hierarchical family and group relationships, there is enough scope for individuals to develop individual identities and move toward the actualization of the real self – *Atman* (e.g., spiritual/actualized self) (Sinha & Tripathi, 2001; Tripathi, 2001). This remains a guiding philosophy in the Indian context, influencing everyday life beginning with early socialization practices. Self-discipline and self-control are emphasized as means to move toward a higher, more refined spiritual self, whereas the bodily self and materialistic pursuits are deemphasized(Saraswathi, Mistry, & Dutta, 2011).

Along with these goals, the development of individual interests and autonomy at different life stages is equally important (Mines, 1988; Shweder & Menon, 1998). Maintaining a balance between staying connected with family and community and moving closer to individual spiritual goals is an oft-reiterated template, and this is actualized when individuals align themselves to changing roles and corresponding responsibilities throughout the life span. Research on parent-adolescent conflicts in India (e.g., Kapadia & Miller, 2005) has revealed a balance between the need to explore personal autonomy and the need to seek parental support and guidance to resolve important matters at the family level. The parent-adolescent relationship emphasized mutual responsiveness on the basis of a common understanding that the adolescent stage was preparatory ground for adulthood and an acknowledgment of the respective duties of parents and children. Thus, while developmental shifts to self-related concerns and autonomy explorations predominantly occur in adolescence in most parts of the world, the very experience of personal autonomy and its expression may be culturally nuanced. Trommsdorff (2012, 2015) refers to the universally observed interaction between adolescents' agentic regulation of their own development and the ecological- and cultural-context influences on their worldviews, values, and morals.

In our study, we assessed the extent to which adolescents and adults discussed moral dilemmas in terms of both references to individual autonomy and collective community considerations. Adopting a cultural-developmental perspective, the present chapter seeks to understand how the three Ethics of Autonomy, Community, and Divinity interface with development. The study was conducted in the rapidly globalizing, urban Indian context in the state of Gujarat. Through five hypothetical dilemmas pertaining to everyday life events, we gathered in-depth interview data on how adolescents and adults reasoned about and resolved moral dilemmas. In line with the cultural-developmental approach (Jensen, 2008), we expected that adolescents would use more Autonomy than adults in an

Indian collectivistic context and that adults would use the Ethic of Community more than adolescents. Furthermore, based on previous research with Indian adults and the use of the three ethics (Kulkarni, 2007), we hypothesized that adults would make common use of both autonomy and community concepts.

In India, marriage and childbearing remain important cultural goals emphasizing the role of girls and women as caregivers. Numerous social practices reinforce the notion that the onus of maintaining harmonious social relationships within and outside the family is often on women. Yet, previous research remains inconclusive on the role of gender in moral reasoning. We tentatively hypothesized that cultural factors, such as the ones stated above, may lead adolescent girls and adult women to evoke the Ethic of Community more than boys and men do.

The study

Participants

Our study included 120 adolescents (ages 12 to 17 years) and 240 adults (ages 35 to 55 years). Each age group had even representation of female and male participants. All participants were of middle- to upper-middle-class backgrounds. The adolescents were recruited from a school. Some adults were recruited through the school where their children (not any of the adolescent participants) were enrolled, while others were identified through snowballing. Most of the adults had undergraduate or higher professional degrees. Most of the women were homemakers, whereas the men primarily worked in service jobs and business.

The interview

A semistructured, open-ended interview schedule consisting of five everyday social-moral hypothetical dilemmas was formulated. The dilemmas were situated in everyday life contexts such as the family, leisure, and workplace. The dilemmas focused on the broad themes of role-related obligations and personal goals as well as the concept of rights and duties in a variety of common interpersonal relationships. (The Interview Schedule at the end of this chapter provides a description of the dilemmas and interview questions.) The dilemmas were based on past research in this area with Hindu Maharashtrian families in Vadodara (Bhangaokar & Kapadia, 2009). The Interview Schedule was also content validated by experts in the field of human development and family studies, psychology, and sociology and revised based on their feedback. Pilot interviews were conducted to ensure that the interview was effective with participants of different age groups.

With respect to the administration of the interview, informed consent was obtained from all adult participants and from parents on behalf of the adolescents. Adolescents were interviewed individually at school during a specific class time (zero period, for example). Data from the adults were collected at their homes. Interviews were conducted in Hindi or English, depending upon the preference of the participant. The interviews were transcribed verbatim, and Hindi interviews were translated to English. Key Hindi terms such as *dharma, satya,* and *karma* were retained in the English translations.

Data analysis

Data were coded using the *Coding Manual: Ethics of Autonomy, Community, and Divinity* (Jensen, 2004). The manual includes coding guidelines as well as definitions of the three ethics and subcodes within each ethic (see Appendix A in this volume). Intercoder reliability was established by calculating the composite reliability coefficient between three pairs of coders. An agreement of 87 percent was reached (Cohen's kappa).

Next, a two-way MANCOVA was computed with age and gender as independent variables. Total number of reasons was entered as a covariate because adolescents had provided significantly more reasons than adults did (F [1, 359] = 43.20, $p < 0.001$).[1] We also engaged in a qualitative analysis that involved creating decision models and concept clusters for key moral concepts such as truth. We considered it important to include this qualitative section in order to further elaborate on the quantitative findings in a way that would be sensitive to the Indian context.

Quantitative results: age differences

Table 4.1 shows the use of the three ethics by adolescents and parents.

The Ethics of Autonomy and Community were commonly used. The Ethic of Divinity was rarely used. With reference to gender, men and women used all three ethics almost equally (Table 4.2).

The MANCOVA showed main effects of age. As hypothesized, adolescents used the Ethic of Autonomy significantly more than adults did ($F[1359] = 358.01, p < 0.001$). Adults, as expected, used the Ethic of Community ($F[1, 359] = 305.39, p < 0.001$) and the Ethic of Divinity ($F[1, 359] = 28.40, p < 0.001$) significantly more than adolescents did. There were no significant main effects for gender and no interactions. The hypothesis that girls and women use the Ethic of Community more was thus not supported.

---

[1] The F statistic for total number of reasons is available on request.

Table 4.1 *Mean ethic use across age (N = 360)*

Groups	Mean ethic use (SD)		
	Autonomy	Community	Divinity
Adolescents	5.09 (1.79)	0.97 (0.85)	0.08 (0.32)
Adults	1.62 (2.64)	1.28 (2.21)	0.15 (0.49)
Total	2.78 (2.90)	1.18 (1.87)	0.13 (0.44)

Table 4.2 *Mean ethic use across gender (N = 360)*

Groups	Mean ethic use (SD)		
	Autonomy	Community	Divinity
Men	2.76 (2.80)	1.08 (1.81)	0.13 (0.47)
Women	2.80 (3.00)	1.28 (1.94)	0.12 (0.41)

Qualitative elaboration: the meaning of age differences

In this section we elaborate on the ways that adolescents and adults framed their resolutions to the hypothetical dilemmas and specific ways in which they spoke in terms of the Ethics of Autonomy and Community. For the adolescents, we argue that they focused on reaching a decision for dilemmas, and they emphasized a variety of Ethic of Autonomy justifications in doing so. In contrast, adults framed the dilemmas as requiring interpersonal and longer-term processes of resolution among the people involved, and consequently they often combined the Ethics of Autonomy and Community in their moral reasoning. We illustrate our argument with the help of detailed excerpts from one of the five hypothetical dilemmas, the dilemma in which respondents were asked whether a wife who wants to learn to dance should lie to her disapproving husband in order to attend classes (see dilemma 4 in the Interview Schedule).

Adolescents: decisions about truth, trust, and personal autonomy

Figure 4.1 depicts the decision model and the most common, specific Ethic of Autonomy reasons used by adolescents. A majority of adolescents believed that the wife should pursue her hobby (59 percent). They were, however, divided about the means to achieve this end.

Twenty-five percent of adolescents believed that it was all right if the wife lied to the husband to attend dance classes. These adolescents often spoke in terms of autonomy considerations pertaining to individual rights and spousal equality. Thirty-four percent of adolescents argued that the wife should not lie

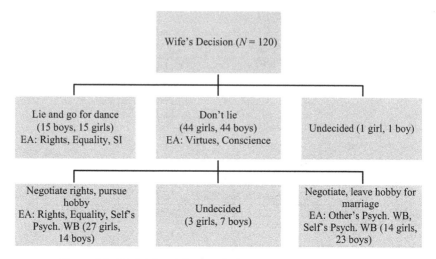

Figure 4.1 Model for adolescent decision making and reasoning

to her husband but rather inform and negotiate with him in order to attend dance classes. These adolescents typically reasoned in terms of virtues, conscience, rights, equality, and self-interest. Finally, 31 percent of adolescents wanted to convince the husband about the wife's interest but would comply with his wishes even if he remained unconvinced. These adolescents reasoned in terms of virtues of trust in a relationship and the psychological well-being of the wife and the husband. Thus, although the adolescents reasoned within the Ethic of Autonomy (EA), their responses were concentrated on maintaining a harmonious marital relationship. Ten percent of adolescents remained undecided on the matter.

The following response from a 12-year-old girl illustrates the argument for lying in order to pursue the interest in dancing:

A: She should go [for the dance class]. It is important to do something you like. There has to be some time for yourself. So she should lie and go.
Q: Is it OK to lie?
A: Yes.
Q: What would you do if you were in her place?
A: I would do the same. You should take your own decisions. If you are doing something bad, only then you should think about it [implying that pursuing a hobby was not something bad]. [EA: Rights]

A 16-year-old boy also believed that the issue is not about the hobby as much as it is about living life on one's own terms. He said, "She should lie and go because it is her life, she should follow her dreams. It is not about our hobby, it is about what you have to do. You should be the most important person

in your life; it should not be that you are living your life for someone else."
(EA: Self's Interest, Rights)

In contrast to the above responses, many adolescents mentioned trust and truthfulness to be important factors that contribute to stability in a spousal relationship. For them, lying was not acceptable. A 15-year-old girl, who is herself a dancer, expressed the view that the wife should not lie but should have the courage of her convictions to negotiate with the husband in order to pursue dancing.

A: Morally, she should not lie because once you are married, you have a commitment of sharing all your thoughts, all your wishes with each other.
Q: What would you do in her place?
A: I am actually a dancer and I would not like to give up dancing for someone else.
Q: Why is lying wrong?
A: If you are lying to someone, it means you are not close to that person . . . but if you are married, then you have to be close and committed to your spouse. I might have a fight with my husband that even if you say no, I am going. If I love him, I should have the guts to say I am going for my personal development . . . and if I don't go, I will not be happy and it will also lead to your unhappiness, which I don't want.
Q: So, you would go even if he was not convinced?
A: Yes . . . , she should go. Over a period of few years, he will be convinced, because he will see her grow. [EA: Virtues, Self's Psychological Well-Being, Other Individual's Psychological Well-Being]

Some adolescents favored not lying and accommodating to the husband's wishes. According to a 16-year-old girl:

A: She should not lie because the husband is more important. She has to stay with this person for the whole life and for [upholding] one lie, she may have to continue lying.
Q: What would you do in her place?
A: I would not have lied.
Q: Why?
A: Because with one lie, there are many lies. And one day he will come to know . . . and relations basically get worse because of lying . . . lying creates misunderstanding. If she lies and goes, she won't be comfortable in dancing; she will think what if my husband comes to know. Her conscience will be constantly biting her . . . so it is better to give up dancing.
Q: What about her hobby?
A: She can practice at home also. [EA: Conscience]

Adults: truth, trust, and negotiating autonomy with family harmony

In contrast to the adolescents, most adults focused less on reaching a decision in the moment and more on the conditions over time that could lead to the

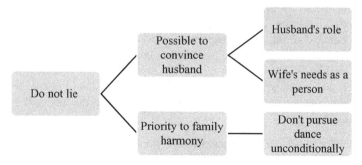

Figure 4.2   Model for process view of adults

resolution of letting the wife pursue dancing. However, priority was given to the maintenance of family harmony and an amicable agreement between the spouses rather than to letting the wife pursue her interest unconditionally. This process is illustrated in Figure 4.2.

For example, some spoke in terms of the Ethic of Autonomy in describing how over time they could convince the husband. For example, a 40-year-old woman said:

A: I will not lie to my husband and go for dance class, because I am confident I will be able to convince him in my own way. If he is not getting convinced, then I have to tell him that I have never stopped him from doing what he wants, so he is not supposed to stop me from doing things my way. It is important to maintain your identity. When I have a fear of something, then I will lie . . . but when I don't have any fear, why will I lie? It may take time to convince him, but he should also understand my views. [EA: Fairness and Reciprocity, Self's Interest]

Many men responded from the husband's perspective and also did not see any reason why the husband would not be convinced to let the wife pursue her interest. Speaking in terms of both Ethic of Autonomy and Ethic of Community (EC) considerations, a 45-year-old man explained:

A: She should not lie . . . because if she lies once, she will have to lie every time, and somewhere . . . at some point, the truth will be revealed. Due to this, the husband-wife relationship gets into problems, now if the next time she does not lie. . . . even then the husband will not believe her. The husband also needs to understand that it is wrong not to allow her to do what she wishes. Also, it is the husband's first duty (*kartavya*) to encourage her in that activity and he should discuss the possibilities with her. Being a life partner, emotions have to be secured in a relationship, till that time there will be no problems in our life. But if a small emotion can lead to telling lies in a relationship, then it is a selfish attitude where only personal gain is important . . . this will lead to the individual taking wrong steps. [EA: Virtues; EC: Duty]

In contrast to these responses, some respondents (both men and women alike) believed that the wife should give up her hobby in the interest of family harmony if her attempts to convince the husband were not successful. The following responses illustrate these opinions. A 43-year-old man said:

A: She should give up the hobby ... she should definitely not lie to join the dance class ... but her husband is not ready to understand. So ... if her decision is not going to disturb their family life, then it is OK ... but if you want to continue with your family life, then you have to sacrifice something. Either you can have your professional life or your personal life ... sometimes, having both is not possible. [EC: Virtues; Social Order or Harmony Goals]

A similar response from a woman, 39 years, highlights the woman's role in maintaining harmony in the family, evoking all three ethics:

A: According to Hindu beliefs, even today, husband is considered as equivalent to God ... so she should not hide anything from him. Sooner or later if he comes to know about the lie, then because of his male ego he may get angry or their relationship may get spoilt. She can try other means to convince him ... friends, family relatives ... Even after all this, if he disagrees, then ... if she wants to maintain her married life, then she should listen to her husband; otherwise, there will be a dispute between them. [Ethic of Dvinity (ED): Important Spiritually Defined Person's Authority; EA: Punishment Avoidance; EC: Social Order or Harmony Goals]

Overall, from the adult responses, it is clear that an "either-or" approach to resolving the dilemma was not preferred. The use of the Ethic of Autonomy often along with the Ethic of Community (and occasionally the Ethic of Divinity) also reflects the adults' role-related concerns that exist alongside an understanding of the need for autonomy or the pursuit of personal goals. Here is one last example of the interweaving of autonomy and community characteristic of many adults:

A: She should not lie to her husband, but convince him ... that she loves dancing ... She should take care of her family time, her responsibilities as a mother, wife and duty of a homemaker (*gruhini dharma*), then she should join the dance institute because a few hours there will give her a lot of happiness. And if she is happy, the whole family is going to be happy, that is the center of it. If he does not agree, she should wait till he agrees, but she should [sooner or later] go.

In contrast to the adolescent decision model, we would argue that parents' responses are better depicted as a process with many components, as illustrated in Figure 4.2. Maintaining harmony in the spousal relationship was of utmost importance to all the respondents, irrespective of their gender. In consonance with this, decisions about pursuing dance depended on how and whether the husband would be convinced. For adults, the concepts of duty and maintenance of social harmony (in a marriage) existed alongside the concern for the psychological well-being of self and spouse under the Ethic of Autonomy. This kind of a situation is, by and large, representative of an Indian adult mind-set that struggles to strike a balance between personal goals and demands of social roles, both important facets of self-conceptualization. In the course of the interview, adolescents and adults mentioned a number of beliefs about the nature of truth, the pitfalls of lying, and the significance of trust as the most important factor to sustain the spousal relationship.

Discussion and conclusions

The cultural-developmental approach

The cultural-developmental approach proposed by Lene Jensen (2008) integrates the cultural and developmental perspectives. This approach addresses the intersection of culture and development by providing a developmental model of the three ethics put forth by Shweder to study the development of morality across diverse cultures. In the present study, the use of the Ethic of Autonomy was higher among adolescents than among adults, whereas the use of the Ethic of Community was higher among adults than among adolescents. These findings support Jensen's contention that Autonomy may go down somewhat from adolescence into adulthood in cultures such as India where familism and collectivity are emphasized, and meanwhile Community is likely to continue to rise into adulthood.

With respect to adults, the simultaneous use of the Ethics of Autonomy and Community to resolve the dilemmas was indicative of an overlap in the two ethics in the Indian psyche. Role-related responsibility, within the boundaries of specific social-familial roles such as those of a parent, child, wife, husband, friend, and colleague, mediated respondents' decisions and was an inseparable part of their mentalities. At the same time, respondents understood personal autonomy not independently but vis-à-vis these important interpersonal relationships. This creates the necessary foreground to discuss the close association between the Ethics of Autonomy (self) and Community (self-in-society) in adult respondents' psyches.

Overall, we can conclude that the results support the utility of the cultural-developmental approach in understanding the developmental differences in moral reasoning within the Indian context, both in terms of moral reasoning and processes of decision making. As the ethics and moral reasoning relate to research on self-conceptualization (Shweder & Miller, 1985), it becomes necessary to turn now to the nature of the Indian self.

Self-conceptualization in the Indian context

Roland (1988) denoted that the Indian self is a contextual "we" self rather than an "I" self. The highly contextual nature of the Indian self is expressed through many social roles, and the self finds its identity through the relationships it maintains with the larger group (family, caste, society). Unlike the Western self, which has fixed boundaries for the self and the group, the Indian self has variable boundaries and is situated within the group (Tripathi, 2001). Comparing self-conceptualizations in India with those in the United States, Mascolo, Misra, and Rapisardi (2004) have put forth the model of an encompassing self in India, wherein the boundaries of the self are not blurred, but the self is always embedded in relationships and subsumed by others. Like the roles, even the responsibilities represent hierarchy and asymmetry. Because of this trait, it is not surprising to find that individuals identify with their roles in relation to others rather than only as autonomous units or persons. Within this cultural framework, a person expresses his/her moral self in relation to others through the appropriate execution of duty, which is always in correspondence to one's station and roles in life. Any decision that prioritizes self-goals over the fulfillment of corresponding duties is considered ethically and culturally inappropriate. A person who makes such decisions not only will run the risk of moving closer to moral-spiritual degradation but also will be socially criticized. The "either me – or others" model is not viable in the Indian context because the Indian self finds it very difficult to justify the separation of the individual from the roles he/she is executing.

Interestingly, adolescence as a life stage involves both an active exploration of one's self and initiation into the various roles of family and society. Adolescence thus marks the beginning of independent interpretation of one's own self against the backdrop of culturally grounded social and spiritual underpinnings of the self. These reflective, internal processes take place in the dynamic context of globalization and affluence, especially in the middle and upper-middle classes of Indian society. Many adolescents, like the ones who participated in the study, thus grow up in a family context where the cultural script of family connectedness is adapted to encourage and encompass autonomy so as to facilitate adjustment to the changing context (Kapadia, 2011).

In regard to marriage in Indian families, the spousal relationship is con-ceptualized within a framework of identity and complementarity rather than of equality (Misra & Gergen, 2002). Duties of a husband and of a wife are clearly spelled out within this broad framework of cultural understanding so that the marital relationship of complementarity becomes the foundation of all family and social life. Thus, the nonfulfillment of duty (*kartavya* or *dharma* in a marital relationship) has moral implications for the self. Any achievement of self-goals is morally justified only if the corresponding duties are taken care of.

If the duties are not discounted in the process of achieving one's personal goals, it is the best possible condition or state of mind. Again, it is important to reiterate that in many cases the duties are not prioritized over self-goals, but one tries to take on both challenges simultaneously, not one at the cost of another. Developmentally, these navigations were evident more among adults.

Ethic of Divinity and gender differences in moral reasoning: conspicuous by absence?

Overall, the Ethic of Divinity was used least by the present set of adolescents. However, in comparison with the adolescents, adults evoked the Ethic of Divinity more. An understanding of the nature and meaning of *dharma*, an overarching moral framework guiding the Indian psyche, may help explain this finding. Paranjpe (2013) described *dharma* as a concept that encompasses faith and forms of worship and that also includes right conduct and duty in the social-familial sphere. Tripathi and Ghildyal (2013) also argued that oneness with God seamlessly permeates all other facets of life in the Indian psyche. We think that it is possible, then, that the Ethic of Divinity within the *dharmic* framework was present but unspoken and hence invisible. Even if religious dilemmas had been used (Kapadia & Bhangaokar, 2012), divinity considerations might have remained understood but unspoken. The pervasive nature of divinity in the Indian context undercuts many events such as incidents of illness and accidents that are attributed to bad *karma*. Indian respondents may find it difficult to neatly separate personal autonomy, communal/social living, and faith in the divine in everyday life or people's reasoning about events and relationships. Possibilities of Divinity shaping other ethics, especially the concept of self (Autonomy) and the social order (Community), cannot be denied. However, more systematic exploration is required to explain how the Ethic of Divinity functions in India and to know its subtle yet significant role as well as its relative influence on other ethics.

Gender was not found to be a significant variable. Empirical evidence from Vasudev and Hummel (1987) and Sengupta, Saraswathi, and Konantambigi (1994) supports the lack of significant gender differences in moral understanding in India. Our finding could well be indicative of the gradually changing mind-sets of urban, educated families with "modernizing" outlooks that emphasize women's assertion of their identities. A number of quotations from our participants show this focus on women's happiness, equality with men or husbands, and rights.

Another plausible explanation may be sought from the understanding of *dharma* and its constituent elements. Moral understanding in India, by virtue of a *dharmic* framework, is inherently contextual, accounting for gender, class, caste, and status in all social transactions. Virtues of truth, sacrifice, and compassion are all interpreted vis-à-vis the context and the roles one plays. This makes gender a "natural" part of the context rather than a specially imposed category. Further, the understanding of virtues and generalized morality is closely associated with the idea of *sanskaar* (values), which is unanimously upheld in Indian families. Truth (as also other virtues), as mentioned earlier in the chapter, is also intrinsically a part of *dharma*. While the execution of *dharma* and duties, in particular, depends strongly on one's life stage, social roles, and gender, the acquisition of an understanding of *dharma* may be more generic and pervasive in nature. Both men and women from a very young age are exposed to concepts of duty and other virtues through socialization practices, myths, stories, and social feedback on their behaviors. Sensitivity to the needs and expectations of others, right conduct, and the upholding of family and social harmony is hence generalized and not different for men and women.

The need to add indigenous Indian moral reasons

While the three ethics coding manual is extremely useful in capturing a variety of moral concepts across cultures, analyses of moral reasoning in the Indian context need to add culture-specific concepts such as *karma, paap,* and *dharma/kartavya* (Kapadia & Bhangaokar, 2012). In the study, adults used these concepts much more than adolescents did. Pandya and Bhangaokar (Chapter 2, this volume) also refer to the prominent use of culturally grounded divinity concepts such as *paap* and *karma* by younger Indian children, also from Vadodara city, indicative of a developmental trend.

Many responses brought to light the concept of reciprocity (responses such as, if we help others, others will help us; as human beings, we must help others), indicating a pattern of generalized reciprocity that emphasizes communal norms characterized by need-based responsiveness and comfort with long-term reciprocation that is characteristic of Indians (Miller, Akiyama, & Kapadia, 2012). Currently, reciprocity is coded as an Ethic of Autonomy subcode because the focus is on an individual doing something for another individual with an eye to future reciprocation.

In the Indian context, however, reciprocity was mentioned in light of individuals' conception of a hierarchical society and of human beings living in civil society. Reciprocity is understood in a way so that behaviors need not translate into immediate and measured return of help or favors in interpersonal relationships (Kapadia, Miller, & Akiyama, 2012). Thus we suggest that in the Indian context there is a need to consider reasoning in terms of reciprocity as reflecting an Ethic of Community rather than an Ethic of Autonomy.

In sum, it would be worthwhile to include indigenous concepts such as *dharma* and communal reciprocity in a three ethics manual for India. Such a merger of indigenous psychology and a cultural-developmental perspective would contribute to the much required creation of a "global" theory of moral development. To align with the arguments made by Miller, Goyal, and Wice (2015), these efforts in research on moral development would enable sensitivity to both cultural concepts and constructs as they actually operate in varied cultures.

Future directions

This study used hypothetical dilemmas to elicit social-moral reasoning from respondents. The limitations of using hypothetical dilemmas are many, and linkages between moral reasoning and action are not clearly predictable. Instead, real-life dilemmas and experiences of resolving them might better capture actual applications of social-moral reasoning. We think that the study of reasoning processes in which individuals reconcile with unfair situations and take a retrospective view on past life events can be a good starting point to overcome the methodological limitations of hypothetical dilemmas.

We used a cross-sectional design and were able to examine age-related reasoning processes in different groups of individuals. However, we cannot know the extent to which the age group differences that we observed between adolescents and adults are developmental or generational shifts. Future longitudinal follow-up studies would be helpful.

This study provides substantial information about the cultural grounding of moral reasoning. There is enough scope to pursue cross-cultural comparisons on this topic, especially with respect to differences or similarities in the use of ethics. Importantly, cross-cultural studies would have more potential to highlight the influences of concepts such as *dharma, karma,* and belief in fate or destiny. More multisite studies from different contexts within and across cultures would also lead to the diversification and expansion of the coding manual.

Conclusion

Studies that illuminate understanding of the concepts of *karma* and *dharma* and their influence on social-moral development are necessary for the Indian context. One should not be surprised if these overarching concepts transcend or engulf all three ethics in India. The history of Indian thought reveals that most psychological concepts in the Indian tradition are deeply interconnected with the pursuit of spiritual self-development and self-realization. Very often, indigenous, non-Western concepts like *karma* and *dharma* are discarded at the doorstep of "scientific psychological inquiry" because of their intricate connections with religiosity and spirituality (Paranjpe, 2003), thereby precluding adequate understanding of the development of an Indian psyche. An understanding of developmental patterns or progression in the use of the three ethics will shed light on the age-related foci in the Indian psyche, indicating commonalities in moral reasoning across culturally diverse groups. Such research efforts eventually would meet the goal of the cultural-developmental approach, which is to bring forth both universal and culture-specific aspects of moral reasoning.

APPENDIX INTERVIEW SCHEDULE

1 "Promise"

Sonal/Abhi and Gargi/Chintan are best friends. Sonal/Abhi has been borrowing money from Gargi/Chintan for a long time. One day Gargi/Chintan confides to Sonal/Abhi that she/he has cheated her/his family in their business and asks her to keep it a secret. Sonal/Abhi promises Gargi/Chintan that she/he would not tell anyone. Later, Sonal/Abhi comes to know that Gargi/Chintan's manager has been accused by the family and he would be handed over to the police. Sonal/Abhi pleads with Gargi/Chintan to confess the crime. She/he refuses and reminds Sonal/Abhi of the promise made. Abhi/Sonal thinks of informing the police about the main culprit but remembers that she/he owes money to Gargi/Chintan. **What should Sonal/Abhi do?**

2 "Stealing"

Aditi/Rohit is studying engineering and is in the third year of her/his college in Baroda. She/he is simultaneously also preparing for a competitive exam. The date of the exam has been announced and the centre of the examination has been finalized as Mumbai. Aditi/Rohit has booked the ticket well in advance. On the day of departure, Aditi/Rohit is at the station and after a while she/he realizes that her/his wallet is stolen and along with it the ticket. She/he then enquires at the counters, approaches the railway officials but no one helps her/him. She/he has to reach Mumbai at a specified time; there is no other train available that would leave soon. A distressed Aditi/Rohit sits on the bench thinking of what to do. The person sitting next to her gets up and leaves. After a while Aditi/Rohit notices that the person's ticket has been left behind and when Aditi/Rohit looks carefully at the ticket, she sees that the ticket is of the same train which Aditi/Rohit was to board. The person's age too is the same as Aditi's/Rohit's. **What should Aditi/Rohit do?**

3 "Helping"

Ravi/Swati and Aakash/Avni are good friends. Both of them are working in different companies which are competitors of each other. Both of them have been working in their respective companies for a few years. Ravi/Swati has been promoted to a higher post and is satisfied with himself/herself. Aakash/Avni is badly in need of a promotion as he/she knows that he/she deserves it and he/she also needs a hike in salary for personal reasons. He/she tries his/her best to impress the boss with his/her work but to no avail. Ravi/Swati knows of Aakash's/Avni's problem and feels bad for him/her. One day Ravi/Swati comes across important information which is vital to his/her company and also to herself/himself. He/she also knows that if this information reaches into Aakash's/Avni's hands, it will benefit his/her company and he/she will also get the much desired promotion. Ravi/Swati wants to help Aakash/Avni. **What should Ravi/Swati do?**

4 "Unfairness"

Ria and Anup is a married couple. They both work in different companies. Ria is an excellent dancer. She had to discontinue her hobby after her marriage. However, now Ria comes home early from work and she has ample time to practice dancing. She considers dance as a divine form of art and wants to join a dancing institute to pursue her hobby. Anup does not approve of her interest in dance and disapproves her idea of joining the dance institute. The only way she can pursue her hobby is by lying to her husband. **What should Ria do?**

5 "Duty"

There are 2 sons. One of the sons is settled abroad while the other is working in India and living with his parents in a rural area. One of his parents is bed ridden. One day the son's company decides to send him abroad for better career opportunity. However, there is no one to look after his parents, no relatives. **What should the son do?**

REFERENCES

Bhangaokar, R., & Kapadia, S. (2009). At the interface of "*dharma*" and "*karma*": Interpreting moral discourse in India. *Psychological Studies*, 54(2), 96–108.

Damon, W. (2012). Why can't we all just get along? A review of Jonathan Haidt's *The Righteous Mind: Why Good People Are Divided by Politics and Religion*. Retrieved from www.hoover.org/research/why-we-cant-all-just-get-along

Das, G. (2009). *The difficulty of being good: On the subtle art of dharma*. New Delhi, India: Penguin, Allen Lane.

Derne, S. (1992). Beyond institutional and impulsive conceptions of self: Family structure and the socially anchored self. *Ethos*, 20(3), 259–288.

Gaur, S. D. (2011). Why am I here? Implications of self and identity for conceptualizing motivation. In R. M. Matthijs Cornelissen, G. Misra, & S. Varma (Eds.), *Foundations of Indian psychology: Concepts and theories* (Vol. 1; pp. 401–414). Delhi, India: Pearson.

Gilligan, C. (1982). *In a different voice: Psychological theory and women's development.* Cambridge, MA: Harvard University Press.

Haviv, S., & Leman, P. J. (2002). Moral decision-making in real life. Factors affecting moral orientation and behavior justification. *Journal of Moral Education*, 31(2), 373–391.

Jensen, L. (2004). *Coding manual: Ethics of Autonomy, Community, and Divinity (Revised).* Retrieved from www.lenearnettjensen.com.

Jensen, L. A. (2008). Through two lenses: A cultural-developmental approach to moral psychology. *Developmental Review*, 28, 289–315.

(2011). The cultural-developmental theory of moral psychology: A new synthesis. In L. A. Jensen (Ed.), *Bridging cultural and developmental approaches to psychology: New synthesis in theory, research, and policy* (pp. 3–25). New York, NY: Oxford University Press.

Kakar, S. (1981). *The inner world: A psycho-analytic study of childhood and society in India.* New Delhi, India: Oxford University Press.

Kakar, S., & Kakar, K. (2007). *The Indians: Portrait of a people.* New Delhi, India: Penguin Press.

Kapadia, S. (2011, February). Intersections among culture, context and development: Exemplars from studies with youth. Paper presented at the National Seminar on Childhood, Culture and Development, Lady Irwin College, New Delhi, India.

Kapadia, S., & Bhangaokar, R. (2012). *Social-moral development in the Indian context: A cultural analysis using the "Big Three" ethics (Autonomy, Community, and Divinity) framework: A report.* Vadodara, India: The Maharaja Sayajirao University of Baroda.

Kapadia, S., & Miller, J. (2005). Parent-adolescent relationships in the context of interpersonal disagreements: View from a collectivist culture. *Psychology and Developing Societies*, 17(1), 33–50.

Kapadia, S., Miller, J., & Akiyama, H. (2012, December 10–12). When should I reciprocate, to whom? Cultural norms of reciprocity in India, *United States, and Japan.* Paper presented at the XXIIth Conference of the National Academy of Psychology, Christ College, Bangalore, India.

Kulkarni, R. (2007). Understanding social-moral development in Hindu, Maharashtrian families of Vadodara city: Insights from a cultural psychological perspective (Unpublished doctoral dissertation). The Maharaja Sayajirao University of Baroda, Vadodara, India.

Mascolo, M. F., Misra, G., & Rapisardi, C. (2004). Individual and relational conceptions of self in India and the United States. *New Directions for Child and Adolescent Development*, 104, 9–26.

Miller, J., Akiyama, H., & Kapadia, S. (2012, July 9–11). Role of reciprocity and relationship considerations in cultural variation in social support. Paper presented at the Understanding Cultural Dimensions of Responsiveness to Need: Moral Emotions and Norms of Support Provision symposium at the 22nd Biennial Meeting of the International Society for the Study of Behavioral Development (ISSBD), Edmonton, Alberta, Canada.

Miller, J. G., & Bersoff, D. M. (1992). Culture and moral judgment: How are conflicts between justice and interpersonal responsibilities resolved? *Journal of Personality and Social Psychology*, 62(4), 541–554.

Miller, J. G., Bersoff, D. M., & Harwood, R. L. (1990). Perceptions of social responsibility in India and in the United States: Moral imperatives or personal decisions? *Journal of Personality and Social Personality*, 58, 33–47.

Miller, J. G., Goyal, N., & Wice, M. (2015). Ethical considerations in research on human development and culture. In L. A. Jensen (Ed.), *Oxford handbook of human development and culture: An interdisciplinary approach.* New York, NY: Oxford University Press.

Mines, M. (1988). Conceptualizing the person: Hierarchical society and individual autonomy. *American Anthropologist*, 90(3), 568–579.

Misra, G., & Gergen, K. (2002). On the place of culture in psychological science. In A. K. Dalal & G. Misra (Eds.), *New directions in Indian psychology: Social psychology* (pp. 405–424). New Delhi, India: Sage.

Paranjpe, A. (2003). Contemporary psychology and the mutual understanding of India and Europe. In J. W. Berry, R. C. Misra, & R. C. Tripathi (Eds.), *Psychology in social and human development: Lessons from diverse cultures – A festschrift for Durganand Sinha* (pp. 18–30). New Delhi, India: Sage.

(2013). The concept of *dharma*: Classical meaning, common misconceptions and implications for psychology. *Psychology and Developing Societies*, 25(1), 1–20.

Ramanujan, A. K. (1990). Is there an Indian way of thinking? An informal essay. In M. Marriott (Ed.), *Indian through Hindu categories* (pp.1–40). New Delhi, India: Sage.

Rao, K. R. (2011). Indian psychology: Implications and applications. In R. M. Matthijs Cornelissen, G. Misra, & S. Varma (Eds.), *Foundations of Indian psychology: Concepts and theories* (Vol. 1; pp. 7–26). Delhi, India: Pearson.

Roland, A. (1988). *In search of self in India and Japan.* Princeton, NJ: Princeton University Press.

Saraswathi, T. S., Mistry, J., & Dutta, R. (2011). Reconceptualizing lifespan development through a Hindu perspective. In L. A. Jensen (Ed.), *Bridging cultural and developmental approaches to psychology: New synthesis in theory, research, and policy* (pp. 276–300). New York, NY: Oxford University Press.

Sengupta, J., Saraswathi, T. S., & Konantambigi, R. (1994). Gender differences in moral orientations: How different is the voice? (Unpublished manuscript). The Maharaja Sayajirao University of Baroda, Vadodara, Gujarat, India.

Shweder, R. (1990). In defense of moral realism: Reply to Gabennesch. *Child Development*, 61, 2060–2067.

Shweder, R. A., & Menon, U. (1998). The return of the "white man's burden": The moral discourse of anthropology and the domestic life of Hindu women. In R. A. Shweder (Ed.), *Welcome to middle age! (And other cultural fictions).* Chicago, IL: University of Chicago Press.

Shweder, R. A., & Miller, J. G. (1985). The social construction of the person: How is it possible? In K. J. Gergen & K. E. Davis (Eds.), *The social construction of the person* (pp. 41–69). New York, NY: Springer-Verlag.

Shweder, R. A., Much, N. C., Mahapatra, M., & Park, L. (1997). The "Big Three" of morality (Autonomy, Community, Divinity) and the "big three" explanations of suffering. In A. M. Brandt & P. Rozin (Eds.), *Morality and health: Interdisciplinary perspectives* (pp. 119–169). New York, NY: Routledge.

Sinha, D., & Tripathi, R. (2001). Individualism in a collectivistic culture: A case of coexistence of opposites. In A. Dalal & G. Misra (Eds.), *New directions in*

Indian psychology: Vol. 1. Social psychology (pp. 241–258). New Delhi, India: Sage.

Tripathi, R. C. (2001). Aligning development to values in India. In A. K. Dalal & G. Misra (Eds.), *New directions in Indian psychology* (pp. 307–325). New Delhi, India: Sage.

Tripathi, R. C., & Ghildyal, P. (2013). Selfhood in search of Godhood. *Psychology and Developing Societies*, 25(1), 43–76.

Trommsdorff, G. (2012). Development of "agentic" regulation in cultural context: The role of self and worldviews. *Child Development Perspectives*, 6, 19–26.

(2015). Cultural roots of values, and moral and religious purposes in adolescent development. In L. A. Jensen (Ed.), *Oxford handbook of human development and culture: An interdisciplinary approach.* New York, NY: Oxford University Press.

Vasudev, J., & Hummel, R. C. (1987). Moral stage sequence and principled reasoning in an Indian sample. *Human Development*, 30, 105–118.

Walker, L. J. (2006). Gender and morality. In M. Killen & J. Smetana (Eds.), *Handbook of moral development* (pp. 93–115). Mahwah, NJ: Erlbaum.

Walker, L. J., Vries, B., & Trevethan, S. D. (1987). Moral stages and moral orientations in real-life and hypothetical dilemmas. *Child Development*, 58, 842–858.

5 Moral worldviews of American religious emerging adults: three patterns of negotiation between development and culture

Laura M. Padilla-Walker and Larry J. Nelson

The cultural-developmental approach to morality suggests that the process of moral development cannot be accurately understood without examining both the developmental life period of the individual and the cultural context in which morality is socialized. This theoretical framework draws on the Three Ethics approach and suggests that individuals' moral reasoning may be influenced or shaped by one of three broad ethics that are indicative of one's moral worldview, two of which are considered in the present chapter, the Ethic of Autonomy and the Ethic of Divinity (Jensen, 2008, 2011, 2012; Shweder, Much, Mahapatra, *et al.*, 1997). The *Ethic of Autonomy* is characteristic of Western society and is primarily focused on justice and the rights of the individual (Jensen, 2008; Shweder, Much, Mahapatra, *et al.*, 1997). Autonomy is based on equality, promotes the self-esteem and independence of individuals, and recognizes that individuals are free to pursue their desires and preferences as long as they do not infringe upon the rights of others. The *Ethic of Divinity* is a focus on deity or a motivation born from spiritual or religious tenets, with goals of making oneself pure and worthy so as to strengthen connection with the divine. Being faithful and humble is valued, and learning and morality are often based on information from sacred texts or tenets held by Deity. There is a general attempt to avoid sin and spiritual impurity. The Ethic of Divinity may be seen as a gradual process wherein an individual becomes "increasingly connected" (Jensen, 2011, p. 5) over time to the divine, which may be seen by some faiths as something one must strive for throughout one's life.

Examining these two ethics using a cultural-developmental template, the present chapter addresses how individuals negotiate their moral worldviews when they may hold strongly to two potentially competing ethics, one that is dominant as a function of their developmental period and another that is dominant in their culture. It is important to note that one's worldview has often been defined broadly as how one defines humanness and approaches broad questions of who and where he or she is as well as explanations of suffering and solutions to that suffering (Jensen, 1997; Walsh & Middleton, 1984).

In the present chapter the term *moral worldview* is used to place specific emphasis on the way one thinks about moral issues in particular (as opposed to broader notions of humanness), including cultural values and tenets that provide guidelines for moral reasoning and behavior (Snarey, 1985). Thus, one's moral worldview as presently conceptualized may be just one aspect of a broader worldview, and though the two would most likely be interrelated, our focus is on the moral aspect of one's worldview in particular. Taking this into consideration, the present chapter examines the developmental age of emerging adulthood (ages 18 years through the mid- to late twenties) and the culture of highly religiously conservative individuals (members of the Church of Jesus Christ of Latter-day Saints; Latter-day Saints; LDS; Mormons) in an attempt to examine how individuals negotiate these two ethics that may produce qualitatively different worldviews in regard to morality.

Developmentally, emerging adulthood in the United States (and other industrialized countries) is a time of fairly significant developmental change (Arnett, 2000), which makes this a key time period for examination and possible modification of one's approach to morality (Jensen, 2011). Research has found that emerging adult college students with high socioeconomic status (SES) primarily report using an Ethic of Autonomy regardless of culture (Haidt, Koller, & Dias, 1993), or they use relatively comparable proportions of the Ethics of Autonomy and Community (Arnett, Ramos, & Jensen, 2001), and they rarely report using an Ethic of Divinity. Thus, given the nature of emerging adulthood in the United States, it would be expected that emerging adults would favor an Ethic of Autonomy when approaching moral issues. Culturally, an Ethic of Divinity has most commonly been observed in Hindu (Shweder, Much, Mahapatra, *et al.*, 1997) and other highly conservative religions (Jensen, 2008; see also Vainio, Chapter 3, this volume) and is rarely used by liberal Christians in the United States (Jensen, 1997, 2011). However, it has been found that religiously conservative Christians tend to reason using an Ethic of Divinity and discourage somewhat an Ethic of Autonomy (Jensen, 1997, 2011, and Chapter 8, this volume). Although research on conservative Christians is somewhat limited, we would expect that highly religiously conservative individuals would favor an Ethic of Divinity when approaching moral issues.

Taken together, these findings raise the question of the relative roles in one's moral decision making that are played by development and culture among highly religiously conservative emerging adults. Research suggests that for the average religiously conservative American, the Ethic of Autonomy is relatively stable over time, whereas the Ethic of Divinity may increase sharply in adolescence, primarily as a result of gains in the cognitive ability needed to understand abstract concepts of the divine. However, the cultural-developmental *template* allows for different degrees of each ethic as a function of culture (Jensen, 2011), making it possible that, in a religious culture in which lessons of deity are taught to young children in a developmentally appropriate (i.e., nonabstract, tangible, recurrent) way, the template may look quite different from that of a nonreligious or even a religiously liberal culture (see Hickman & DiBianca Fasoli, Chapter 7, this volume).

Thus, given the specific religious culture examined in this chapter (Latter-day Saints), and the extensive teachings beginning at a very young age that suggest that moral reasoning and moral behavior are primarily issues of divinity or spirituality, it is possible that these highly religious individuals will have been negotiating these ethics for most of their formative years and, by emerging adulthood, may have clearly settled on one dominant ethic or will have found a meaningful way to balance the two. Indeed, given the complexity of one's moral actions, it might be necessary and even more effective to draw from multiple ethics depending on the moral issue, either relying on a single ethic as it is most appropriate or taking a multidimensional approach and drawing from several ethics in order to consider multiple solutions (Shweder, Much, Mahapatra, *et al.*, 1997). However, drawing in a nonsystematic manner from all ethics at once may create confusion and incoherence, especially if each worldview or multiple worldviews present conflicting messages regarding a moral behavior (Shweder & Sullivan, 1993). Thus, for Latter-day Saints culturally, the Ethic of Divinity may be taught and expected to increase from a very young age, while the Ethic of Autonomy may be expected to decrease somewhat over time (Jensen, 2011) or to be "absorbed" into the Ethic of Divinity, wherein Autonomy would not be unimportant but would remain somewhat in the background of moral decision making (Shweder, Much, Mahapatra, *et al.*, 1997, p. 141). However, given the strong focus on identity and autonomy during the developmental period of emerging adulthood, we expect that the Ethic of Autonomy will also be high among Latter-day Saint college students, potentially resulting in conflict between these two ethics that are both highly valued.

Therefore, we first discuss the period of emerging adulthood and the unique developmental issues of this age that are relevant for the development of morality. Second, we discuss the Latter-day Saint religious culture, explicating the ways in which morality is taught in the culture and the emphasis that is placed on the role of the divine in one's sense of morality. We then discuss the results of data collected from a sample of 500 highly religious emerging adults using a new measure of the three ethics, the Ethical Values Assessment (EVA; Jensen & Padilla-Walker, Appendix C in this volume; see also Table 5.1).We conclude with a discussion of what we envision as fruitful avenues for future research in this area.

Development: emerging adulthood

Arnett (2000, 2004) characterized emerging adulthood as including five important features. First, it is an *age of feeling in-between*, as most emerging adults

Table 5.1 *Ethical Value Assessment (EVA)*

Autonomy items	
1.	I should take responsibility for myself
2.	I should take good care of my body
3.	I should feel good about myself
4.	I should try to achieve my personal goals
5.	I should be fair to other individuals
6.	I should respect other individuals' rights
7.	I should keep myself out of trouble
Divinity items	
1.	I should aim for spiritual salvation
2.	I should take good care of my soul
3.	I should have a spiritual compass
4.	I should aim to live a holy life
5.	I should follow God's law
6.	I should strive for spiritual purity
7.	I should respect my ancestors

do not see themselves as either an adolescent or an adult. Second, emerging adulthood is an *age of possibilities*, as most young people are extremely optimistic and have high hopes for the future. Third, this period of development is an *age of instability* because it tends to be marked by instability in work, relationships, education, and residential status. Next, emerging adulthood is characterized as an *age of identity exploration* because many emerging adults are free to explore identities in the areas of education, work, love, and worldviews. Finally, emerging adulthood is a *self-focused age of life*. This is not meant to suggest that emerging adults are necessarily self-centered but are rather free from social obligations and other responsibilities that allow for a productive focus on the self.

It should be noted from the outset that in calling emerging adulthood a period in the life stage, both Arnett (2000) and we acknowledge that there is a historical and cultural component to these features. Indeed, the features of emerging adulthood tend to exist more among the economically advantaged within industrialized cultures and are heavily influenced by cultural beliefs and attitudes. In other contexts, the features of emerging adulthood may be condensed or take on different forms. As a result, there are many emerging adulthoods within and between countries and cultures (Arnett, 2011). This, however, is not unique to emerging adulthood in that multiple paths through infancy, adolescence, and late adulthood also exist. In each of these stages, though, there are "common features across contexts that justify conceptualizing it as a life stage" (Arnett, 2012, p. 242). It is from this perspective (i.e., that these features of emerging adulthood do in fact capture the life experiences of a large portion of emerging adults) that we approach emerging adulthood as the developmental lens for this chapter.

Indeed, the theoretical features mentioned above capture some of the actual behaviors of many emerging adults in the United States. As part of the exploration, instability, experimentation, and self-focus that are typical for this age, a number of trends are now prevalent during emerging adulthood. More and more young people are engaging in premarital intercourse (see Regnerus & Uecker, 2011), and cohabitation is preceding more than half of all marriages in the United States (Whitehead & Popenoe, 2001). It is taking longer for emerging adults to finish their education (Arnett, 2000). Emerging adulthood is the peak period for risk behaviors such as binge drinking, experimentation with drugs, and unprotected sex (e.g., Bachman, Johnston, O'Malley, *et al.*, 1996; Leftkowitz & Gillen, 2006; Schulenberg & Maggs, 2001). Finally, many emerging adults hold pessimistic views about marriage (Bachman, Johnston, & O'Malley, 2009) and desire to postpone marriage until the late twenties or even thirties (e.g., Carroll, Willoughby, Badger, *et al.*, 2007). In sum, these behaviors represent a belief by many emerging adults that they should behave as though they are only young once and therefore should engage in as many "now-or-never" (Ravert, 2009) behaviors as possible.

Indeed, the features, behaviors, and beliefs typical of emerging adulthood reflect a prevailing emphasis on the individual. This is not meant to suggest that this age of self-focus is one of complete negativity (e.g., narcissism), as many young people engage in endeavors that are beneficial to others (e.g., Peace Corps, Teach for America), but even these behaviors are done with the view of self-growth and self-improvement (e.g., Arnett, 2000) and that emerging adulthood is the time to do them or there will never be another opportunity (Ravert, 2009). This is why it has been hypothesized that this period of life would be characterized substantially by an Ethic of Autonomy (Jensen, 2011). However, cultural beliefs for some emerging adults may compete with the developmental beliefs and values of the time period.

Culture: highly religious individuals

Although culture may be conceptualized by some as reference to a specific ethnicity or individuals from a specific country, the present chapter treats culture as a group of individuals who are members of a community and who share a set of core beliefs and behaviors (Jensen, 2011). Thus, when referring to culture, we will consider one specific religious denomination, or members of the Church of Jesus Christ of Latter-day Saints (i.e., Latter-day Saints, LDS, Mormons).

Like many religiously conservative groups, Latter-day Saints are expected to engage in a number of religious practices, including personal and family prayer, reading of sacred texts, and regular attendance at religious services (see *Articles of Faith*, 1985). Furthermore, Latter-day Saints value the family and serving others, especially those less fortunate, emphasize the importance of obeying God's commandments, and revere life. Finally, like many groups who focus on the purity of the body, Latter-day Saints' reverence for the body is reflected in teachings regarding dress (e.g., clothing that is modest rather than revealing), grooming (e.g., no body piercings for men), substance prohibition (e.g., abstaining from alcohol, tobacco, and illegal drugs), and behavior (e.g., no premarital or extramarital sexual intimacy, no pornography). Taken together, these core beliefs and behaviors make up a culture within which a set of worldviews may develop that are potentially at odds with the developmental period of emerging adulthood within the United States.

Indeed, in this brief description of Latter-day Saint culture, five tenets, or features, stand out as being in stark contrast to the views and behaviors typical of the developmental context of emerging adulthood, which may be why devout Latter-day Saint emerging adults have been shown to differ from their peers in the majority culture in the United States in a number of important areas (e.g. Barry & Nelson, 2005; Nelson, 2003). One of the first areas in which highly religious emerging adults such as Latter-day Saints may differ is a marked emphasis on *service* to and concern for others. In both of their sacred texts (The Holy Bible and The Book of Mormon), Latter-day Saints are taught that rendering service to others is how one worships God. For example, two passages of scripture known to nearly every devout Latter-day Saint are "Inasmuch as ye have done it unto one of the least of these my brethren, ye have done it unto me" (Matthew 25:40) and "When ye are in the service of your fellow beings ye are only in the service of your God" (Mosiah 2:17). Unique from the experience of most emerging adults, young Latter-day Saints are given a variety of roles and responsibilities centered on service to others during the emerging adulthood years.

For example, missionary service is a 2-year commitment required of all physically capable men beginning at age 18 years and an optional 18-month commitment for women beginning at age 19 years. Although much of this time is spent in proselytizing, which might not be seen as service by those outside the culture, those within the culture see it as time spent focused on others rather than the self. Furthermore, missionaries are expected to spend four hours a week engaged in community service that should come from a sincere desire to help others rather than as a means of proselyting or gaining publicity for the Church (Florence, 1991). Similarly, before and after missionary service (and for those who do not serve missions) Latter-day Saint emerging adults receive assignments to attend to the spiritual and temporal needs of two to four specific members of their wards (i.e., congregations). Thus, the specific emphasis on service to others in both teaching and practice within Latter-day Saint culture may not align with the self-focused values and practices of the developmental period of emerging adulthood.

Another aspect of the developmental period of emerging adulthood that may be at odds with that of Mormon culture is identity development, especially in regard to *religiousness.*

Emerging adulthood is a period for exploration of one's beliefs (Arnett, 2004). Indeed, studies have shown that between adolescence and emerging adulthood, nearly half of emerging adults change their religious affiliation (Smith, 2009), suggesting a rather large amount of exploration and change. In that same study, however, Smith found that far fewer Latter-day Saints in his sample of American emerging adults changed their religious affiliation. Furthermore, other studies have reported that Latter-day Saint emerging adults report higher levels of religious faith than both their nonreligious *and* religious peers (Barry & Nelson, 2005). The lack of exploration of and change in beliefs for Latter-day Saints during emerging adulthood may be the result of the fact that in Mormon culture young people are encouraged to settle on their religious convictions well *before* emerging adulthood. Indeed, a common message conveyed to young people, starting at very young ages, is that they cannot live on "borrowed light" (Whitney, 1967, p. 450) from their parents or anybody else. Because of the emphasis placed on settling on one's own religious faith before emerging adulthood, that period of life for many Latter-day Saints, unlike the majority of their peers, is no longer a period of exploration in regard to religiousness.

Next, individual happiness and *well-being* are aspects of Mormon culture that are heavily emphasized. In general, religiosity and spirituality have been related to numerous positive life outcomes for emerging adults, such as personal-emotional adjustment, healthy attitudes and behaviors, as well as high self-esteem (e.g., Gilliam, Barry, & Bacchus, 2008; Knox, Langehough, & Walters, 1998; Rew & Wong, 2006; although see also Trommsdorff, 2015). The important distinction to be made, however, is that Mormon culture does not just view positive adjustment as stemming from being religious, but Mormons believe it is a spiritual imperative to be happy, positive, and, in general, well adjusted. Mormon scripture reads "Adam fell that men might be; and men are, that they might have joy" (2 Nephi 2:25). Therefore, there is reason to expect that one's worldviews stemming from cultural beliefs and values would be associated with personal well-being.

Another set of features that stand out as being in contrast to the views and behaviors typical of the developmental context of emerging adulthood revolves around *self-regulation.* For example, as mentioned previously, emerging adulthood is the peak period in the life span for risk behaviors such as heavy drinking, alcohol-related problems, drug use, and risky sexual behaviors and a period in which behaviors such as alcohol and pornography use are considered normative (e.g., Carroll, Padilla-Walker, Nelson, *et al.*, 2008). In contrast, Mormon culture counsels against all of these behaviors. For example, to adolescents and young adults, the cultural expectation is "Never do anything that could lead to sexual transgression . . . Before marriage, do not participate in passionate kissing, lie on top of another person, or touch the private, sacred parts of another person's body, with or without clothing. Do not do anything else that arouses sexual feelings. Do not arouse those emotions in your own body" (The Church of Jesus Christ of Latter-day Saints, 2001, p. 36). Hence, Latter-day Saint proscriptions against drug and alcohol use, premarital intercourse, and other sexual behaviors (e.g., pornography use, masturbation) seem to run counter to the views of typical emerging adults.

Finally, there is a marked difference between Mormon culture and development during emerging adulthood regarding *views about family*. Although approximately 92 percent of emerging adults report that they are both planning for and expecting to marry in the future (Thornton & Young-DeMarco, 2001; Whitehead & Popenoe, 2001), emerging adulthood is not the time, on average, during which that actually happens (median age of marriage in the United States is 28 years for males and 26 years for females; U.S. Census Bureau, 2010). Likewise, rises in nonmarital cohabitation, delays in fertility, and the pursuit of greater independence from parents all point toward emerging adulthood being a time of individual centeredness rather than family centeredness.

Mormon culture, on the other hand, places heavy emphasis on the role of the family, and the effects of that can be seen in the demographic differences showing that the median ages of marriage and first childbirth are as much as 4 years earlier among Mormons than among the American population as a whole (McClendon & Chadwick, 2005). Oft-repeated teachings to Latter-day Saints are "no success can compensate for failure in the home" (McKay, 1935) and "the most important of the Lord's work you and I will ever do will be within the walls of our own homes" (Lee, 1974, p. 225). These teaching are not just directed toward adults; rather, the emphasis on marrying and having children is directed toward emerging adults in particular. Church leaders have taught that "the most important decision of life is the decision concerning your companion" (Hinckley, 1999) and young people need to "pay careful attention to finding your [spouse]" (Ballard, 2012, p. 100) and have as many children as they can reasonably care for (Oaks, 1993). Hence, emerging adults in the Mormon culture are still taught to put family responsibilities first, even during a time that may be a developmental period focused on the individual.

In sum, there are numerous tenets, or teachings, within the Latter-day Saint culture that may compete with what is characteristic of the developmental period of emerging adulthood, thus requiring a process of negotiation between development and culture. Five of the most obvious include Latter-day Saints' emphasis on *service to others*, commitment (rather than exploration) of *religious beliefs*, the connection between spirituality and *well-being*, *self-regulation*, and *family centeredness*.

Present study

In order to more carefully examine how religiously conservative emerging adults negotiate the Ethics of Autonomy and Divinity, we obtained a sample of 500 Latter-day Saint emerging adults from Brigham Young University using an online questionnaire. The mean age of those participating in the study was approximately 20 years, 70 percent of the participants were female, and 91 percent of them were Caucasian. Nearly 80 percent of participants reported being conservative or highly conservative, with only 1 percent reporting being liberal. The ethics were assessed using a new instrument developed to measure the *degree* each ethic is endorsed by the individual (EVA; Jensen & Padilla-Walker, Appendix C in this volume; see Table 5.1). For these analyses only the Autonomy and Divinity subscales were used, each of which consisted of 7 items tapping an Autonomy worldview (e.g., "I should take responsibility for myself," "I should feel good about myself") and 7 items tapping a Divinity worldview (e.g., "I should follow God's law," "I should take good care of my soul"). We conducted exploratory factor analysis on the 14 items, and these analyses revealed two factors, with all Autonomy items loading on one factor and all Divinity items on another, with no items cross-loading above acceptable levels (specific factor loadings available upon request). Internal reliability estimates were also above acceptable standards (Autonomy, $\alpha = 0.82$; Divinity, $\alpha = 0.86$).

To examine the five tenets of the LDS faith discussed above that tend to stand in contrast to the developmental features of emerging adulthood, we used nine measures, including measures of service (prosocial behavior and empathic concern), religiosity, well-being (depression and self-worth), self-regulation (sexual and emotional impulsivity), and family centeredness (cohabitation and family centeredness). More specifically, we measured service using a 5-item measure of prosocial behavior toward strangers (e.g., "I volunteer in programs to help others in need"; Peterson & Seligman, 2004; $\alpha = 0.75$) and a 5-item measure of empathic concern (e.g., "I often have tender, concerned feelings for those less fortunate than I am"; Davis, 1983; $\alpha = 0.82$). We measured religiosity using a 4-item measure of religious faith (e.g., "My relationship with God is extremely important to me"; Lewis, Shevlin, McGuckin, *et al.*, 2001; $\alpha = 0$ .93). We measured well-being using a 7-item measure of depression (e.g., "I felt everything was an effort"; CES-D, Radloff, 1977; $\alpha = 0.75$) and a 5-item measure of self-worth (e.g., "I like the kind of person I am"; Neeman & Harter, 1986; $\alpha = 0.86$). We measured self-regulation by combining two items assessing sexual behavior that are relevant measures of sexual impulsivity for this sample ("Masturbate/stimulate yourself sexually" and "View pornography"; $\alpha = 0.78$) and by using a 5-item measure of emotional impulsivity (e.g., "I get so frustrated I am ready to explode"; Novak & Clayton, 2001; $\alpha = 0.79$).

Finally, we measured family centeredness using a 7-item measure of attitudes in favor of cohabitation (e.g., "It is all right for a couple to live together without planning to get married"; $\alpha = 0.91$) and a 4-item measure of attitudes regarding family centeredness (e.g., "Having children is a very important goal for me"; $\alpha = 0.86$).

In the following analyses we sought to answer two main questions. First, how do highly religious emerging adults negotiate developmental and cultural worldviews? We addressed this question by first examining to what degree participants valued the Ethics of Autonomy and Divinity, the strength and direction of the correlation between the ethics, and participants' ratings of the most important items from the list of ethics. We then conducted a number of regression analyses to determine how both ethics were associated with outcomes that are salient to individuals of the LDS faith. The second question addressed in these analyses was whether additional values held by highly religious emerging adults were not covered in the new quantitative measure. To address this question we examined qualitative responses from a subset of participants, which also provided additional information into the types of each ethic that were used by this sample.

Analyses with the Ethics of Autonomy and Divinity

First we examined preliminary descriptive statistics and found that the Ethics of Autonomy and Divinity were strongly positively correlated ($r = 0.69$), but the Ethic of Divinity was rated as significantly more important for this group of emerging adults than was the Ethic of Autonomy (Divinity: $M = 4.62$, $SD = 0.44$; Autonomy: $M = 4.52$, $SD = 0.43$; $F[1, 499] = 43.14, p < 0.001$; partial eta^2 = 0.08). Emerging adults were also asked to choose the three most important values from the list they were given. Nearly 70 percent chose an Ethic of Divinity item ("I should aim for spiritual salvation" was most common) compared with only 24 percent who chose an Ethic of Autonomy item ("I should take responsibility for myself" was most common) as their most important item. Given research suggesting a negative correlation between multiple highly endorsed ethics (Arnett, Ramos, & Jensen, 2001), it is notable that there was a strong, positive correlation between the Ethics of Autonomy and Divinity in this sample, which suggests that LDS emerging adults do not see the two ethics as incompatible despite the mixed messages they may send. These analyses also suggest that although highly religious emerging adults believe both ethics are important, the Ethic of Divinity was identified as more important when making moral decisions.

To further examine how highly religiously conservative emerging adults negotiate the Ethics of Autonomy and Divinity, we conducted nine hierarchical regression analyses on five broad outcomes, including service (prosocial behaviors and empathy), religious faith, well-being (depression and self-worth), self-regulation (sexual impulsivity and emotional impulsivity), and family centeredness (cohabitation and family centeredness). Statistical details are available upon request. For each regression, gender was entered at step 1, followed by the Ethic of Autonomy and Ethic of Divinity subscales at step 2, and the two-way interactions between gender and each of the two ethics at step 3 (mean centered). Three-way interactions between gender and the two ethics were not statistically significant in any of the analyses, so were not explored further. See Table 5.2 for all regression analyses.

Congruent ethics. The analyses dealing with service and well-being revealed that both the Ethics of Autonomy and Divinity were related to prosocial behavior, empathy, and self-worth at roughly comparable levels. The similarities in the findings for both ethics present a picture of congruence in that both culture and development appear to play a similar role in the display of a behavior. Indeed, these findings suggest that despite a reported preference of their cultural moral worldview, this group of highly religious emerging adults is drawing from *both* ethics when it comes to behaviors that emphasize helping others and feelings of self-worth. Indeed, although emerging adulthood has been characterized as a self-focused time of life (Arnett, 2000), research has found that prosocial behavior and values tend to be reported at consistently high levels among emerging adults, perhaps partly as a reflection of helping behavior being socially desirable in nature (Bardi & Shwartz, 2003) but also because the freedom of emerging adulthood is used by some as a means of reaching out and helping others (Padilla-Walker, Barry, Carroll, *et al.*, 2008). In addition, individualistic cultures such as the United States place premium value on self-esteem, especially during emerging adulthood (Arnett, 2000). Prosocial behavior and self-worth are also pursuits that are highly valued in the LDS culture, as stated above, which would allow individuals to approach prosocial behavior and self-esteem from either worldview and find congruence between values and behavior.

In sum, an important contribution of these results is the identification of areas in which reconciliation of two potentially competing worldviews is apparent. However, it is unclear whether these specific moral behaviors would be approached using congruent ethics at any developmental age period or whether this is unique to emerging adulthood because heightened levels of autonomy require reconciliation rather than the reduction of an Autonomy ethic. This will be an important avenue of future research. It will also be important to examine additional moral outcomes that may be motivated by congruent ethics, such as outcomes related to taking care of one's body, being just and fair, and taking responsibility for one's choices, which may be seen as important from both an Autonomy and a Divinity worldview.

Table 5.2 *Regression analyses of Autonomy and Divinity predicting emerging adult outcomes*

	Prosocial	Empathy	Religious faith	Self-worth	Depression	Emotional impulsivity	Sexual impulsivity	Cohabitation	Family centeredness
1. Gender (A)	0.08	0.30***	0.10*	0.02	0.14***	0.12*	-0.33***	-0.04	0.02
2. Autonomy (B)	0.17**	0.24***	-0.13**	0.15*	-0.19***	-0.14*	0.18**	-0.03	0.09
Divinity (C)	0.23***	0.15**	0.68***	0.13*	-0.01	-0.01	-0.35***	-0.49***	0.44***
3. A × B	0.02	0.03	0.20*	0.14	-0.01	0.01	-0.30***	-0.02	0.03
A × C	0.03	0.02	-0.24***	0.06	-0.11	-0.08	0.32***	-0.01	-0.08
B × C	-0.07	-0.04	-0.14**	-0.04	0.02	0.01	-0.01	0.08	-0.20***
R^2	0.15***	0.22***	0.40***	0.08***	0.07***	0.04**	0.20***	0.26***	0.29***

Note. Values represent standardized beta coefficients.
* $p < 0.05$, ** $p < 0.01$, *** $p < 0.001$.

Dominant ethic. A second pattern emerged in which one ethic played a more dominant role than the other in areas that included depression, emotional impulsivity, and family outcomes. In the case of emotional impulsivity and depression, the Ethic of Autonomy (but not Divinity) was negatively associated with both of these outcomes. In turn, the Ethic of Divinity (but not Autonomy) was negatively associated with attitudes in favor of cohabitation and was positively associated with attitudes of family centeredness. Taken together with the above analyses, it seems that there are moral behaviors for which highly religious emerging adults clearly favor a cultural *or* developmental ethic rather than drawing from both. It is possible that during this time period some issues are more salient developmentally to emerging adults, while others are cultural issues that have seemingly been part of the individual's worldview since childhood and will likely continue to be important given the strong and consistent teachings of the LDS culture.

Findings suggested that emotional impulsivity and depression were negatively associated with an Ethic of Autonomy. It was not surprising that the Ethic of Autonomy, with a focus on taking care of oneself and achieving personal goals, was somewhat protective against depression. However, the lack of significant association between Divinity and depression was somewhat perplexing because a central tenet of the LDS culture is that one of the purposes of life is to find joy. One possibility is that depression is more salient to emerging adults at this particular developmental time point given the focus on fun and enjoyment coupled with the challenges they may be facing, and it may therefore feel like an issue influenced primarily by oneself and one's situation rather than one's cultural values.

It was also somewhat perplexing that only an Ethic of Autonomy (and not Divinity) was associated with lower levels of emotional impulsivity (e.g., "I get so frustrated I am ready to explode"), as one of the central tenets of most religions is self-regulation and research has found religiosity to be linked to the promotion of self-control and self-regulatory behaviors (McCullough & Willoughby, 2009). Similar to the argument above, it is possible that Latter-day Saints approach emotional impulsivity from an autonomous worldview because they see emotional regulation as a salient developmental issue (e.g., taking responsibility for oneself and one's actions) during emerging adulthood, and this may overshadow any cultural teachings regarding this behavior. Indeed, many emerging adults are away from home for the first time and are trying to learn to balance their autonomy with their continued need for guidance from parents, which often calls for heavy regulatory demands, both emotionally and cognitively. Furthermore, although the LDS faith clearly teaches the importance of emotional regulation ("He that is slow to anger is better than the mighty"; Proverbs 16:32), much more cultural emphasis is placed on behavioral regulation (e.g., prohibition against use of alcohol and premarital sexual behaviors), especially during adolescence and emerging adulthood. Thus, it is possible that in this case the developmental ethic presents a stronger value message than does the cultural ethic regarding emotional regulation. In sum, it appears that as long as there is not a strong and consistent cultural (i.e., spiritual) message regarding a behavior, highly religious young people may focus on the developmental importance of a value or behavior.

However, results also suggest that, if there is a clear cultural message, then the Ethic of Divinity is the dominant basis for moral behavior. Indeed, there is extensive emphasis placed on the centrality of the family within Mormon culture, which would explain why the Ethic of Divinity was the dominant ethic associated with family-related issues. Because family formation values are clearly taught culturally but are not emphasized (or clearly discouraged) developmentally, there is likely little contradiction between the two ethics, allowing one's dominant cultural ethic to shape one's moral worldview on this outcome.

Taken together, results suggest that there are some areas in which highly religious emerging adults rely predominantly on one moral ethic. Specifically, it appears that if there is a clear cultural message with no competing developmental value, then the Ethic of Divinity is the dominant worldview, but in the absence of a clear cultural message, the Ethic of Autonomy may become more significant. Although negotiation resulting in the use of a dominant ethic exists for emerging adults on some issues, it is possible that a similar pattern could be found at any developmental age and that this pattern may be seen even more frequently in adults. Indeed, as other research suggests (Jensen, 2008; Shweder, Much, Mahapatra, *et al.*, 1997), it is possible that the moral worldview of highly religious individuals becomes more and more saturated by the Ethic of Divinity over time as the exploration of emerging adulthood decreases, roles change, and one becomes increasingly connected to the divine.

Conflicting ethics. Finally, a third pattern emerged in how highly religious emerging adults negotiate worldviews, suggesting there are some areas in which one's developmental and cultural worldviews are in conflict. For example, an Ethic of Autonomy was negatively related to religious faith (for young men), while an Ethic of Divinity was positively related to religious faith. A similar pattern was seen in relation to sexual impulsivity in that an Ethic of Autonomy was positively related to sexual behavior (for young men), while an Ethic of Divinity was negatively associated with sexual behavior. In addition, when individuals (both males and females) noted high levels of both the Ethic of Divinity *and* the Ethic of Autonomy, religious faith was lower.

These findings suggest that in terms of behaviors that have very different meanings when approached from one's dominant cultural ethic and the ethic that is central to one's developmental time period, highly religious emerging adults (especially men) may struggle to make sense of these conflicting messages, and this struggle may be reflected in behavior that is inconsistent with one's dominant cultural values. For example, the average emerging adult may be interested in exploring spirituality but has less interest in religious practices in the traditional sense (Arnett & Jensen, 2002), while an individual who holds to the Ethic of Divinity values religious faith (beliefs *and* behaviors) as an issue of primary importance. Similarly, sexual behaviors are seen as quite normative to the average emerging adult college student (especially males; Carroll, Padilla-Walker, Nelson, *et al.*, 2008) and are not seen as moral violations according to an Ethic of Autonomy. However, Latter-day Saint emerging adults report using pornography considerably less than do non-LDS emerging adults (86 percent of non-LDS males report use vs. 35 percent of LDS males) and place great value on sexual purity, perceiving acts of masturbation and pornography use as violations of this purity (Nelson, Padilla-Walker, & Carroll, 2010). This is also true of religiously conservative cultures in general, as research has found that religiousness is associated with later age of sexual debut among adolescents (Hardy & Raffaelli, 2003) and with abstinence, lower number of lifetime partners, and more conservative attitudes regarding sexuality among emerging adults (Lefkowitz, Gillen, Shearer, *et al.*, 2004).

Taken together, the analyses regarding religious faith and sexual outcomes suggest that for an individual whose culture teaches a strong moral value on a given behavior, but who has entered a period of life that is dominated by a strong moral value that is conflicting, the individual may struggle to negotiate both worldviews, and this moral dilemma may be reflected in behavior. Because the issue of conflicting ethics seems particularly relevant to developmental periods in which there is a great deal of developmental change (e.g., adolescence and emerging adulthood), this may be a pattern that is somewhat unique to this time period and may be particularly relevant from a cultural-developmental standpoint. Thus, we discuss conflicting ethics in more detail below as we propose fruitful ideas for future research.

Additional moral values

In addition to assessing the degree to which each ethic was valued using the questionnaire items, we also asked participants an open-ended question to try and tap any moral values we might have missed. More specifically, we asked, "In your own words, indicate if there are moral values that you consider *completely important* to pass on to the next generation which are *not* mentioned on the list above." Of the 500 participants, 329 (66 percent) added an open-ended response to this question, and these responses were coded for the type of ethic they referenced. The analysis for this qualitative item was conducted using NVivo, and all answers were coded (by two independent coders; kappa = 0.805, standard error = 0.027, $p < 0.001$) using "focused coding" that involved breaking down the comments into conceptually distinct categories. Analyses revealed that of those who responded, 34 percent responded with a moral value that could be coded as an Autonomy ethic and 25 percent responded with a moral value that could be coded as a Divinity ethic. A number of emerging adults endorsed the Ethic of Autonomy in reference to the importance of valuing education (e.g., 19-year-old female said that it was important to value an "Active approach to education and finding my place in the world"), being financially independent (e.g., a 19-year-old female said, "I believe it is completely important for me to maintain a financial budget at this time in my life and be cognizant of how I am spending my money"), always trying to be one's very best and continually improving (e.g., a 23-year-old male said, "I should strive to do better with each new moment than I did in my past"), and standing up for their individual beliefs (e.g., a 21-year-old male said, "Standing up for what you believe in is completely important").

In terms of responses that could be coded as Divinity, emerging adults made references to the importance of chastity both before and after marriage (e.g., a 21-year-old male said, "Complete fidelity in marriage"), the importance of spiritual progression (e.g., a 21-year-old female said, "Strive to reach your divine potential in all things"), the importance of keeping the commandments (e.g., a 22-year-old male said, "How much I adhere to the rules of God is of critical importance because it determines my eternal salvation"), and the importance of valuing religious practices (e.g., a 19-year-old female said, "At this time of my life I believe that attending the temple regularly, reading my scriptures, writing in my journal, and saying my daily prayers are completely important").

Taken together, it is interesting to note that several of the most common values added by emerging adults that were classified as an Ethic of Autonomy may not be considered moral issues in a traditional religious sense. More specifically, these issues do not deal with harm to others or one's purity and are therefore not taught as moral issues by the LDS culture, although they are clearly important issues that are developmentally salient during this time period (e.g., education and financial independence). In turn, in cases in which clear cultural values surround an issue (e.g., prohibitions against certain sexual behaviors) and the issue is clearly framed as a moral issue, there was a resounding use of the Ethic of Divinity. It could be that it is more difficult for highly religious young people to frame moral issues from an autonomous worldview because they have been socialized to think about most moral issues from a Divinity perspective. Indeed, the free responses that were categorized as representing an Ethic of Divinity were values that could all be considered moral values, suggesting that perhaps highly religious emerging adults strongly identify with an Ethic of Autonomy and may hold to this worldview when considering nonmoral issues or issues for which there is not a strong cultural value, but they still consistently draw from an Ethic of Divinity when moral dilemmas arise. This is purely speculative and will be an interesting avenue for future research.

Conceptual issues and future directions

The present analyses raise a number of important conceptual issues for the cultural-developmental template and provide fruitful avenues for future research in this area. First, we discuss the process of negotiating multiple moral worldviews and speculate about possible explanations for the various patterns found in our analyses as well as the implications for cognitive and behavioral outcomes. Second, we discuss gender differences, specifically during the developmental period of emerging adulthood, and the importance of considering moral development as a function of gender. Finally, we discuss the methodological issues raised by the present analyses and the need for future research to examine not only the degree of each ethic but also the type or quality of each ethical value statement.

Negotiating the Ethics of Autonomy and Divinity

The cognitive developmental template allows for individuals to endorse a central dominant worldview at certain developmental periods (e.g., Autonomy may dominate in childhood) or in certain cultures (e.g., Divinity may dominate in religiously conservative cultures; Jensen, 2008, 2011); the template also allows for the use of multiple different ethics at any given developmental time period. Indeed, all three ethics are seen as promoting moral behaviors and often work together for the greater good of individuals and in the promotion of human dignity (Shweder, Much, Mahapatra, *et al.*, 1997). However, the present chapter adds to existing research by suggesting that when culture and development are considered together, worldviews may not always be in agreement with one another, especially during developmental periods that are characterized by heightened exploration and change.

The emerging adults in the present sample clearly placed greater importance on a cultural worldview (Ethic of Divinity), but further analyses revealed a more complicated process. Indeed, we found three patterns of negotiation that varied largely as a function of the clarity and consistency of the cultural emphasis placed on the particular behavior. Namely, when both culture and development presented a similar moral value regarding the behavior (e.g., service, self-worth), the Ethics of Autonomy and Divinity were both associated with the behavior (congruent ethics), but when one's culture presented a strong value regarding a behavior or when development presented a strong value and the cultural value was weak or nebulous, the ethic that presented the clearest message was most strongly related to the behavior (dominant ethic).

A final pattern, and perhaps the most unique to this developmental time period, was when both cultural and developmental worldviews presented a strong, clear ethic regarding a behavior, but in conflicting directions. Although cultural and cognitive research suggests that the "moral dilemmas" created by two worldviews presenting competing value messages may actually encourage deeper refection and lead to moral and spiritual growth (Shweder, Much, Mahapatra, et al., 1997; Walker, Hennig, & Krettanauer, 2000), it appears from the present analyses that this may, at least temporarily, be associated with behavior that is not consistent with one's self-reported dominant cultural ethic. This may result in ethical dissonance, which is the discomfort that comes from the disconnect between one's moral values and one's behaviors (Barkan, Ayal, Gino, et al., 2012), and has been associated with other negative outcomes among highly religious emerging adults such as low self-worth and higher rates of depression (Nelson, Padilla-Walker, & Carroll, 2010).

However, a developmental approach would suggest that this pattern of conflicting ethics being reflected in behavior is a largely developmental issue made more salient by the period of emerging adulthood, when one's identity formation and search for ideology are at a peak (Arnett, 2000). Some qualitative research on religiously conservative cultures highlights the use of a dominant ethic in one's moral decision making (Jensen, 2008) and suggests that some moral issues may be "saturated" by an Ethic of Divinity (Shweder, Much, Mahapatra, et al., 1997, p. 138). However, studies have also found that both college students (Arnett, Ramos, & Jensen, 2001) and highly religious individuals (Shweder, Much, Mahapatra, et al., 1997) are able to find a way to balance or reconcile two or more ethics (e.g., Divinity and Community). Indeed, for highly religiously conservative emerging adults it is possible that, over time, as individuals settle into a more consistent sense of self and beliefs, they may gradually form a worldview that consists of multiple ethics that are compatible with one another when considering moral issues (congruent ethics). Alternatively, it is possible that for highly religious individuals, an Ethic of Autonomy peaks during emerging adulthood, and once adult roles are adopted and the focus on self and independence that is central to emerging adulthood is lessened, the Ethic of Autonomy may no longer be as salient and the Ethic of Divinity would dominate moral decision making (dominant ethic). Taken together, this approach would suggest that highly religious emerging adults will "grow out of" the occasional conflict that may occur between developmental and cultural worldviews. These findings highlight important avenues for future research in the area of culture and development as they relate to morality, especially longitudinal work that follows the developmental process of negotiating moral worldviews to determine whether congruent, dominant, and competing ethics exist at all ages or only during adolescence and emerging adulthood.

The importance of gender

Gender is a salient cultural issue as well as an important developmental variable to consider in all developmental periods but seems to be particularly important to consider during emerging adulthood. Although gender intensification begins in adolescence (Hill & Lynch, 1983), it seems to continue into the third decade of life as well, with some research suggesting there are arguably two different emerging adulthoods, one for males and one for females. In a recent paper examining patterns of behavior for emerging adults, Nelson and Padilla-Walker (2013) found that there was a large group of emerging adults who were flourishing in many ways (low levels of risk behaviors, high levels of positive behaviors) and two groups of emerging adults who seemed to be floundering (high levels of both externalizing and internalizing outcomes). It was interesting to note that the flourishing group (64 percent of all participants) consisted largely of young women (80 percent) and both floundering groups consisted almost entirely of young men (83 percent and 77 percent). This adds to a growing literature that suggests consistent gender differences on multiple behaviors during emerging adulthood. More specifically, during emerging adulthood young women report higher levels of prosocial behavior and internalized values (Padilla-Walker, Barry, Carroll, *et al.*, 2008), higher levels of disclosure and companionship with mothers (Barry, Padilla-Walker, Madsen, *et al.*, 2008), and higher levels of religious faith (Nelson & Padilla-Walker, 2013) than do young men. In turn, young men report higher levels of drinking (Peralta, Steele, Nofziger, *et al.*, 2010), drug use (McCabe, Morales, Cranford, *et al.*, 2007), delinquency (Langhinrichsen-Rohling, Arata, Bowers, *et al.*, 2004), pornography use (Carroll, Padilla-Walker, Nelson, *et al.*, 2008), and violent video game use (Padilla-Walker, Nelson, Carroll, *et al.*, 2010) than do young women.

Our findings contribute to this growing literature by suggesting that perhaps balancing cultural and developmental worldviews is also an issue that is more difficult for males, even those who are highly religious and therefore may not be engaging in the risk behaviors that are indicative of floundering during emerging adulthood (Nelson & Walker, 2013). In terms of the present findings, Mormon culture emphasizes to young men that the most important roles they will have in the future will be to provide for and protect their families. The combination of emphasizing the role of provider with the directives to not delay marriage and parenthood, as well as expectations to serve a 2-year mission, leads many Latter-day Saint young men to feeling a sense of urgency to decide on a career and finish their education in order to be prepared to provide for their families. Indeed, for Latter-day Saint young men, viewing emerging adulthood as a time to engage in now-or-never behaviors (Ravert, 2009) seems to be in direct conflict with the cultural messages and expectations conveyed to them, which may account for their heightened struggle with conflicting moral worldviews.

That being said, high levels of Autonomy and Divinity were associated with lower levels of religious faith for both males and females, suggesting Latter-day Saint females were not immune to this dissonance. In regard to sexual impulsivity, these findings may have been more salient for males merely because females are much less likely to engage in such behaviors (Carroll, Padilla-Walker, Nelson, *et al.*, 2008). Indeed, future research should examine a wider variety of moral behaviors that are more relevant for females (e.g., modesty, taking care of one's body). Although we are only speculating about the processes behind the present findings, these are all important questions for future research as we seek to determine how highly religiously conservative males and females may approach morality differently during emerging adulthood, especially when developmental and cultural worldviews conflict.

Measurement considerations

Finally, the present analyses raise a number of issues regarding the measurement of moral worldviews. More specifically, when examining how moral worldviews differ developmentally, Jensen (2008) points out that one must consider the degree or frequency with which each ethic is used and the different types or kinds of moral justifications individuals use at different developmental periods (e.g., do emerging adults reason using different kinds of Divinity statements than those of adults?). A quantitative approach tells us relatively little about the type or quality of ethical justification highly religiously conservative emerging adults may use and how this is impacted by the intersection of culture and development. Indeed, qualitative research may more clearly identify a dominant ethic, while quantitative statements requesting participants to report whether or not they "value" a certain behavior may lead to a tendency for somewhat of a ceiling effect on multiple ethics. This suggests utility in using a mixed-method approach when examining moral worldviews (see Jensen, Chapter 8, this volume).

Further, it will be valuable to use a mixed-method approach to examine how the type of ethic used might differ for the three different patterns of negotiation found in our analyses (congruent, dominant, conflicting). When individuals endorse high levels of both the Ethics of Autonomy and Divinity, but have found a way to reconcile the two, perhaps the specific type of ethic used is more sophisticated or represents a higher level of moral reasoning than the type used by those who are still grappling to reconcile the two ethics or who have adopted a dominant ethic without considering multiple moral worldviews. For Latter-day Saint emerging adults, who clearly reported favoring an Ethic of Divinity but who also strongly valued an Ethic of Autonomy, it may be necessary to think more carefully and deeply about issues of morality, and this may lead to a more internalized understanding of one's values and more principled reasoning about moral issues. The present findings provide no evidence to support this idea, but given research suggesting that the challenging of one's moral beliefs may actually result in deeper contemplation of those beliefs and subsequently higher levels of moral reasoning (Shweder, Much, Mahapatra, *et al.*, 1997; Walker, Hennig, & Krettanauer, 2000), this question is certainly worthy of future attention.

Limitations and conclusions

The present study was not without limitations. Indeed, it will be important for future research to examine these questions longitudinally, with multimethod designs, and with more socioeconomically diverse samples. It will also be important to examine additional periods of development as well as a wider variety of cultures in order to determine whether the three patterns of negotiation found in the present study are generalizable. However, the present chapter is an important contribution to the growing literature using a cultural-developmental template and raises a number of avenues for future research. It is clear that how one formulates a moral worldview is a complex process, especially when considering development and culture simultaneously. These findings have implications for others who study highly religious cultures but also highlight broader issues regarding the potential interplay between development and culture that should continue to be considered. Namely, it will be fascinating to see whether the three patterns of negotiation found in the current study hold for other cultures and at other ages or if additional patterns can be identified. In short, the present chapter highlights the complex process of moral development, with particular emphasis placed on how individuals negotiate their moral worldview. Future research should continue to examine how this process of negotiation is associated with moral behavior during emerging adulthood and throughout the life course, as findings may have important implications for a variety of healthy outcomes.

REFERENCES

Arnett, J. J. (2000). Emerging adulthood: A theory of development from the late teens through the twenties. *American Psychologist*, 55, 469–480.
   (2004). *Emerging adulthood: The winding road from the late teens through the twenties*. New York, NY: Oxford University Press.
   (2011). Emerging adulthood(s): The cultural psychology of a new life stage. In L. A. Jensen (Ed.), *Bridging cultural and developmental psychology: New syntheses*

in theory, research, and policy (pp. 255–275). New York, NY: Oxford University Press.

(2012). New horizons in emerging and young adulthood. In A. Booth & N. Crouter (Eds.), *Early adulthood in a family context* (pp. 231–244). New York, NY: Springer.

Arnett, J. J., & Jensen, L. A. (2002). A congregation of one: Individual religious beliefs among emerging adults. *Journal of Adolescent Research*, 17, 451–467.

Arnett, J. J., Ramos, K. D., & Jensen, L. A. (2001). Ideological views in emerging adulthood: Balancing autonomy and community. *Journal of Adult Development*, 8, 69–79.

Articles of faith. (1985). Salt Lake City, UT: The Church of Jesus Christ of Latter-day Saints.

Bachman, J. G., Johnston, L. D., & O'Malley, P. M. (2009). *Monitoring the future: Questionnaire responses from the nation's high school seniors, 2008*. Ann Arbor, MI: Institute for Social Research.

Bachman, J. G., Johnston, L. D., O'Malley, P. M., & Schulenberg, J. (1996). Transitions in drug use during late adolescence and young adulthood. In J. A. Graber, J. Brooks-Gunn, & A. C. Petersen (Eds.), *Transitions through adolescence: Interpersonal domains and context* (pp. 111–140). Mahwah, NJ: Erlbaum.

Ballard, M. R. (2012, May). That the lost may be found. *Ensign*, 42.

Bardi, A., & Schwartz, S. H. (2003). Values and behavior: Strength and structure of relations. *Personality and Social Psychology Bulletin*, 29, 1207–1220.

Barkan, R., Ayal, S., Gino, F., & Ariely, D. (2012). The pot calling the kettle black: Distancing response to ethical dissonance. *Journal of Experimental Psychology: General*, 141(4), 757–773.

Barry, C. M., & Nelson, L. J. (2005). The role of religion in the transition to adulthood for young emerging adults. *Journal of Youth and Adolescence*, 34, 245–255. doi:10.1007/s10964-005-4308-1

Barry, C. M., Padilla-Walker, L. M., Madsen, S. D., & Nelson, L. J. (2008). The impact of maternal relationship quality on emerging adults' prosocial tendencies: Indirect effects via regulation of prosocial values. *Journal of Youth and Adolescence*, 37, 581–591.

Carroll, J. S., Padilla-Walker, L. M., Nelson, L. J., Olsen, C., Barry, C. M., & Madsen, S. D. (2008). Generation XXX: Pornography acceptance and use among emerging adults. *Journal of Adolescent Research*, 23, 6–30.

Carroll, J. S., Willoughby, B., Badger, S., Nelson, L. J., Barry, M., & Madsen, S. D. (2007). So close, yet so far away: The impact of varying marital horizons on emerging adulthood. *Journal of Adolescent Research*, 22, 219–247.

The Church of Jesus Christ of Latter-day Saints. (2001). *For the strength of youth* [pamphlet]. Salt Lake City, UT: Author. Retrieved from http://www.lds.org/bc/content/shared/content/english/pdf/ForTheStrengthOfYouth-eng.pdf?lang%20=%20eng

Davis, M. H. (1983). The effects of dispositional empathy on emotional reactions and helping: A multidimensional approach. *Journal of Personality*, 51, 167–184.

Florence, G. H., Jr. (1991, September). Called to serve. *Ensign*, 21.

Gilliam, A. K., Barry, C. M., & Bacchus, N. A. (2008). The relation between stress and college adjustment: The moderating role of spirituality. *Modern Psychological Studies*, 13, 84–101.

Haidt, J., Koller, S. H., & Dias, M. G. (1993). Affect, culture, and morality, or is it wrong to eat your dog? *Journal of Personality and Social Psychology*, 65, 613–628.

Hardy, S. A., & Raffaelli, M. (2003). Adolescent religiosity and sexuality: An investigation of reciprocal influences. *Journal of Adolescence*, 26, 731–739.

Hill, J. P., & Lynch, M. E. (1983). The intensification of gender-related role expectations during early adolescence. In J. Brooks-Gunn & A. Petersen (Eds.), *Girls at puberty: Biological and psychosocial perspectives* (pp. 201–228). New York, NY: Plenum.

Hinckley, G. B. (1999, February). Life's obligations. *Ensign*, 29.

Jensen, L. A. (1997). Different worldviews, different morals: America's culture war divide. *Human Development*, 40, 325–344.

Jensen, L. A. (2008). Through two lenses: A cultural-developmental approach to moral psychology. *Developmental Review*, 28, 289–315.

Jensen, L. A. (2011). The cultural-developmental theory of moral psychology: A new synthesis. In L. A. Jensen (Ed.), *Bridging cultural and developmental approaches to psychology: New syntheses in theory, research, and policy* (pp. 3–25). New York, NY: Oxford University Press.

Jensen, L. A. (2012). Bridging universal and cultural perspectives: A vision for developmental psychology in a global world. *Child Development Perspectives*, 6(1), 98–104.

Knox, D., Langehough, S. O., & Walters, C. (1998). Religiosity and spirituality among college students. *College Student Journal*, 32, 430–432.

Langhinrichsen-Rohling, J., Arata, C., Bowers, D., O'Brien, N., & Morgan, A. (2004). Suicidal behavior, negative affect, gender, and self-reported delinquency in college students. *Suicide and Life-Threatening Behavior*, 34(3), 255–266.

Lee, H. B. (1974). *Stand ye in holy places*. Salt Lake City, UT: Deseret Book.

Lefkowitz, E. S., & Gillen, M. M. (2006). "Sex is just a normal part of life": Sexuality in emerging adulthood. In J. J. Arnett & J. L. Tanner (Eds.), Emerging adults in America: Coming of age in the 21st century (pp. 235–255). Washington, DC: American Psychological Association. doi:10.1037/11381-010.

Lefkowitz, E. S., Gillen, M. M., Shearer, C. L., & Boone, T. L. (2004). Religiosity, sexual behaviors, and sexual attitudes during emerging adulthood. *Journal of Sex Research*, 41(2), 150–159.

Lewis, C. A., Shevlin, M., McGuckin, C., & Navrtil, M. (2001). The Santa Clara Strength of Religious Faith Questionnaire: Confirmatory factor analysis. *Pastoral Psychology*, 49, 379–384.

McCabe, S., Morales, M., Cranford, J. A., Delva, J., McPherson, M. D., & Boyd, C. J. (2007). Race/ethnicity and gender differences in drug use and abuse among college students. *Journal of Ethnicity in Substance Abuse*, 6(2), 75–95.

McClendon, R., & Chadwick, B. A. (2005). Latter-day Saint families at the dawn of the twenty-first century. In C. H. Hart, L. D. Newell, E. Walton, & D. C. Dollahite (Eds.), *Helping and healing our families* (pp. 32–43). Salt Lake City, UT: Deseret Book.

McCullough, M. E., & Willoughby, B. B. (2009). Religion, self-regulation, and self-control: Associations, explanations, and implications. *Psychological Bulletin*, 135(1), 69–93.

McKay, D. O. (1935, April). *Conference Report*, no. 116.

Neeman, J., & Harter, S. (1986). Manual for the self-perception profile for college students (Unpublished manuscript). University of Denver, Denver, CO.

Nelson, L. J. (2003). Rites of passage in emerging adulthood: Perspectives of young Mormons. *New Directions for Child and Adolescent Development*, 100, 33–49.

Nelson, L. J., & Padilla-Walker, L. M. (2013). Flourishing and floundering in emerging-adult college students. *Emerging Adulthood*, 1, 67–78.

Nelson, L. J., Padilla-Walker, L. M., & Carroll, J. S. (2010). "I believe it is wrong but I still do it": A comparison of religious young men who do versus do not use pornography. *Psychology of Religion and Spirituality*, 2, 136–147.

Novak, S. P., & Clayton, R. R. (2001). The influence of school environment and self-regulation on transitions between stages of cigarette smoking: A multilevel analysis. *Health Psychology*, 20, 196–207.

NVivo [Computer software]. Doncaster, Victoria, Australia: QSR International Pty Ltd.

Oaks, D. H. (1993, November). The great plan of happiness, *Ensign*, 23, 72–75.

Padilla-Walker, L. M., Barry, C. M., Carroll, J. S., Madsen, S., & Nelson, L. J. (2008). Looking on the bright side: The role of identity status and gender on positive orientations during emerging adulthood. *Journal of Adolescence*, 31, 451–467.

Padilla-Walker, L. M., Nelson, L. J., Carroll, J. S., & Jensen, A. C. (2010). More than just a game: Video game and Internet use during emerging adulthood. *Journal of Youth and Adolescence*, 39, 103–113.

Peralta, R. L., Steele, J. L., Nofziger, S., & Rickles, M. (2010). The impact of gender on binge drinking behavior among U.S. College students attending a Midwestern university: An analysis of two gender measures. *Feminist Criminology*, 5(4), 355–379.

Peterson, C., & Seligman, M. E. P. (2004). *Character strengths and virtues: A handbook and classification*. Washington, DC: Oxford University Press.

Radloff, L. S. (1977). The CES-D scale: A self-report depression scale for research in the general population. *Applied Psychological Measurement*, 1, 385–401.

Ravert, R. D. (2009). "You're only young once": Things college students report doing now before it is too late. *Journal of Adolescent Research*, 24(3), 376–396.

Regnerus, M., & Uecker, J. (2011). *Premarital sex in America: How young Americans meet, mate, and think about marrying*. New York, NY: Oxford University Press.

Rew, L., & Wong, Y. J. (2006). A systematic review of associations among religiosity/spirituality and adolescent health attitudes and behaviors. *Journal of Adolescent Health*, 38, 433–442.

Schulenberg, J., & Maggs, J. L. (2001). *A developmental perspective on alcohol use and heavy drinking during adolescence and the transition to adulthood*. Washington, DC: National Institute on Alcohol Abuse and Alcoholism.

Shweder, R. A., Much, N. C., Mahapatra, M., & Park, L. (1997). The "Big Three" of morality (Autonomy, Community, Divinity), and the "big three" explanations of suffering. In A. Brandt & P. Rozin (Eds.), *Morality and health* (pp. 119–172). New York, NY: Routledge.

Shweder, R. A., & Sullivan, M. A. (1993). Cultural psychology: Who needs it? *Annual Review of Psychology*, 44, 497–523.

Smith, C. (with Snell, P.). (2009). *Souls in transition: The religious and spiritual lives of emerging adults*. New York, NY: Oxford University Press.

Snarey, J. R. (1985). Cross-cultural universality of socio-moral development: A critical review of Kohlbergian research. *Psychological Bulletin*, 97, 202–232.

Thornton, A., & Young-DeMarco, L. (2001). Four decades of trends in attitudes toward family issues in the United States: The 1960s through the 1990s. *Journal of Marriage and the Family*, 63, 1009–1037.

Trommsdorff, G. (2015). Cultural roots of values and moral and religious purposes in adolescent development. In L. A. Jensen (Ed.), *The Oxford handbook of human development and culture: An interdisciplinary perspective*. New York, NY: Oxford University Press.

U.S. Census Bureau. (2010). U.S. Decennial Census (1890–2000): figure 1. Median age at first marriage by sex: 1890 to 2010. *American Community Survey*. Retrieved from www.census.gov/hhes/socdemo/marriage/data/acs/ElliottetalPAA2012figs .pdf

Walker, L. J., Hennig, K., & Krettanauer, T. (2000). Parent and peer contexts for children's moral reasoning development. *Child Development*, 71, 1033–1048.

Walsh, B. J., & Middleton, J. R. (1984). *The transforming vision. Shaping a Christian world view*. Downers Grove, IL: InterVarsityPress.

Whitehead, B. D., & Popenoe, D. (2001). Who wants to marry a soul mate? In *The state of our unions 2001* (pp. 6–16). New Brunswick, NJ: National Marriage Project.

Whitney, O. F. (1967). *Life of Heber C. Kimball*. Salt Lake City, UT: Bookcraft.

6   Investigating the three ethics in emerging adulthood: a study in five countries

Valeschka M. Guerra and Roger S. Giner-Sorolla

In this chapter we report a study of moral ethics endorsement comparing younger and older emerging adults across five different countries. Emerging adulthood – the time period between adolescence and settling down – has not been studied as intensively from a developmental perspective as childhood or adolescence has. Yet, theoretical and research perspectives give reason to believe that emerging adulthood is a time of meaningful change in moral, religious, and social worldviews (e.g., Padilla-Walker & Nelson, Chapter 5, this volume). Complicating these matters is further evidence that emerging adulthood has different meanings in different cultures. Transition to adulthood is defined more strongly by the adoption of social roles in less individualistic cultures. Therefore, we conducted this study to see whether, when comparing early (18–20 years old) to late (21–23 years old) emerging adults, patterns of change and stability in different moral ethics were themselves variable across five meaningfully different cultures – two English-speaking countries, Brazil, Israel, and Japan.

Development: emerging adulthood

Around one-seventh of the world's population is between 19 and 29 years old (United Nations, 2011). This group of approximately one billion people has been called many names: "youth," "young adults," and "emerging adults," for example (Arnett, 2007b). Currently, life for this group in developed societies is marked by ready adoption of technological advances, tolerance toward different types of interpersonal relationships, late entry into the labor market, and postponement of marriage and children (Groppo, 2000). As they still do not have established identities, emerging adults tend to pursue different experiences, in a continuous search for the elements that will help them build an identity (Calligaris, 2000).

Developmental approaches often see each life stage as a series of tasks that should be fulfilled or events that should happen (Greenfield, Keller, Fuligni, *et al.*, 2003). In the transition from childhood to full adult responsibility, the main task has been characterized as learning how to be an autonomous person.

117

These transition events, as named by sociologists Buchmann and Kriesi (2011), have been defined as including "completion of initial schooling, labor market entry, leaving the parental home, forming a first union, and finally, entry into parenthood" (p. 482). In their view, all these events involve a mature process of decision making and moral judgment considered essential to become an adult. However, according to Smetana, Campione-Barr, and Metzger (2006), "mature decision making does not emerge until the middle twenties" (p. 258) because the brain cannot be considered fully mature until this age.

Although emerging adults may be considered adults in most biological terms, Carrano (2000) suggested that to achieve adulthood in the contemporary world is not only a biological condition but essentially a cultural definition. According to Smetana and colleagues (2006), "Adolescence begins in biology and ends in culture, because the transition into adolescence is marked by the dramatic biological changes of puberty, while the transition to adulthood is less clearly marked" (p. 258).

According to Arnett (2007a, 2007b), several historical developments have changed the transition to adulthood in industrialized countries. For example, the contraceptive pill in the 1960s changed the way people perceived premarital sex. Another important change is observed regarding technological advances, which have increased the years of schooling necessary for working in specific areas, consequently increasing the need for higher education as well as postgraduate courses. Likewise, emerging adults are getting married at a later stage in their lives, usually around the thirties, bringing a reduction in the number of children per woman and an older age of mothers at first birth.

Based on these socioeconomic and cultural changes, adult commitments have been delayed for most individuals in their twenties, creating a new life cycle termed *emerging adulthood* (Arnett, 2000). According to Arnett (2000), this period

> is neither adolescence nor young adulthood but is theoretically and empirically distinct from them both. Emerging adulthood is distinguished by relative independence from social roles and from normative expectations. Having left the dependency of childhood and adolescence, and having not yet entered the enduring responsibilities that are normative in adulthood, emerging adults often explore a variety of possible life directions in love, work, and worldviews. (p. 469)

Because this new developmental stage proposed by Arnett (2000) is characterized by a delay in specific adult commitments, it risks creating an image of emerging adults as undecided, selfish, or lazy. However, in the more positive evaluation of Arnett (2007c), these individuals are, in fact, exploring possible identities (Smetana, Campione-Barr, & Metzger, 2006), becoming less oriented toward the self when compared to adolescents, and deciding the type of relationship and job that would be meaningful (Arnett, 2007a, 2007b).

Given that emerging adulthood is culturally and historically situated (Arnett, 2011), it makes sense that cultural variations may influence the way individuals in their twenties make decisions, judge actions as right or wrong, or pursue selfish experiences versus interpersonal relationships and economic stability (Arnett, 2000, 2003). In order to test this assumption that different cultural or social contexts influence their conceptions of adulthood during this life cycle, Arnett (2003) interviewed 574 emerging adults in the United States between 18 and 29 years of age of different ethnic backgrounds (White Americans, African Americans, Latinos, and Asian Americans). The strongest finding was that non-Whites compared to Whites defined adulthood more in terms of social roles. As compared to Whites, the ethnic minority samples also more strongly endorsed the idea that starting and supporting a family, complying with social norms, and having a full-time job are necessary conditions for a person to be considered an adult. These results suggest stronger support for collectivistic norms and values among the ethnic minority groups because they emphasized duties toward others instead of individual rights. However, all emerging adults also showed cross-ethnic similarities. They agreed that in order to become an adult, a person needs to take responsibility for self, decide upon key values, obtain financial independence, and relate to parents on equal terms (Arnett, 2003).

One unanswered question, however, is whether there are any changes occurring in moral values and reasoning in the course of emerging adulthood. Another unanswered question is the role of culture in regard to the moral values and reasoning among emerging adults. These are questions that we aimed to address in the present study. Before we turn to the details of our study, however, we review literature on culture and development in regard to moral values and reasoning.

Cultural lines of research on ethics and moral values

Research in different countries has shown that moral reasoning varies across cultural contexts (e.g., Haidt, Koller, & Dias, 1993; Jensen, 2009; Rozin, Lowery, Imada, *et al.*, 1999; Shweder, Much, Mahapatra, *et al.*, 1997; Vasquez, Keltner, Ebenbach, *et al.*, 2001). These studies have examined moral reasoning in terms of Shweder and colleagues' (1997) differentiation among three ethics: the Ethics of Community, Autonomy, and Divinity. The Ethic of Community emphasizes social rules and norms, the importance of family and in-group ties, as well as membership in social groups as essential for one to judge what is right and wrong. Society, family, and one's social group are the main moral authorities, and moral reasoning is usually related to duties and obligations toward others and the welfare of the group and the group's interests, customs, and objectives (Guerra & Giner-Sorolla, 2010; Jensen, 2009; Shweder,

Much, Mahapatra, *et al.*, 1997). The Ethic of Autonomy emphasizes individual rights and one's own conscience as moral authority. Moral reasoning based on autonomy often draws on concepts of justice, fairness, and harm to individual interests. The Ethic of Divinity emphasizes nature and spiritual or religious entities as moral authorities. Conceptions of the divine, natural law, concerns for how specific actions could affect one's soul, and religious rules are present in moral reasoning based on this ethic (Guerra & Giner-Sorolla, 2010; Jensen, 2009; Shweder *et al.*, 1997).

Guerra (2009) has proposed that differences in the importance of the three ethics on individual and cultural levels are related to differences in the importance of values on individual and cultural levels. In our view, it is useful to also draw on findings from the cross-cultural literature on values (Trommsdorff, 2015). According to Wan, Chiu, Peng, and Tam (2007), the hierarchy of values of a culture reflects the normative preferences regarding moral ideas, life principles, personal and shared beliefs, and what is considered desirable for its citizens. Although cultural values have been studied as the average endorsement of personal values shared by individuals from a cultural community, Schwartz (2004; see also Schwartz & Ros, 1995) proposed that they can present a structure of their own (Wan, Chui, Peng, *et al.*, 2007). Three cultural dimensions were proposed: (1) *embeddedness* versus *intellectual or affective autonomy*, which distinguishes the relationship people establish with their groups, whether the self is considered embedded in the collectivity or autonomous; (2) *hierarchy* versus *egalitarianism*, which distinguishes the way people recognize themselves as moral and responsible individuals, whether the behavior is employed by using hierarchy and roles or by encouraging personal responsibility; and (3) *mastery* versus *harmony*, which distinguishes the relationships between people and the natural and social world, whether the individuals are legitimate to change and exploit nature or to preserve and protect it (Fischer, 2006; Schwartz, 2004).

Distinguishing among cultural dimensions has proven useful in cross-cultural research examining other constructs (Allen, Ng, Ikeda, *et al.*, 2007; Fischer, Smith, Richey, *et al.*, 2007; Wong, Bond, & Rodriguez Mosquera, 2008). For example, in a study by Leong and Ward (2006) on racism and xenophobia among nine European nations, the nation-level value of mastery was associated with opposition to policies intended to bring immigrants and native-born people together and pessimistic attitudes toward multiculturalism. Wong, Bond, and Rodriguez-Mosquera (2008) conducted an investigation of 25 cultural groups and showed that the cultural dimensions of hierarchy, mastery, and embeddedness are negatively associated with nonverbal expressions of shame, guilt, and fear. Could cultural values also explain differences in endorsement of ethics?

Bringing these cultural dimensions together with the three ethics, a cross-cultural study by Guerra (2009) in six countries (Brazil, Japan, New Zealand, Spain, United Kingdom, and United States) showed that countries that are characterized as emphasizing embeddedness over autonomy (such as Brazil) presented higher endorsement of the Ethics of Community and Divinity. Also, English-speaking nations, characterized as emphasizing egalitarianism over hierarchy, presented higher endorsement of the Ethic of Autonomy.

Schwartz (2007) also differentiated between narrow and broad moral universes. He proposed that people from cultures with a narrow moral universe apply moral values (e.g., universalism, benevolence) only to their in-groups, whereas people from cultures with a broad moral universe apply the same moral values to other groups as well and ultimately to all humankind. These results suggest an additional association between culture and morality: not just which values are endorsed but how wide is their scope may vary across cultures.

The cultural-developmental template model

Shweder, Much, Mahapatra, *et al.* (1997) have not proposed a developmental theory but rather emphasized that all three ethics can vary cross-culturally in their level of endorsement. No proposition was made by these authors regarding how these codes emerge, how they develop throughout an individual's life, or whether there are identifiable patterns of endorsement in specific life cycles. To address these questions, Jensen (2008, 2011a, 2011b) proposed a template for the association between morality and development in different cultures (Jensen, 2011a, 2011b). Figure 6.1 shows the template for degree of use of the three ethics during childhood, adolescence, and adulthood.

According to Jensen (2011a), two main issues should be addressed when investigating the development of the three ethics: "(1) the *degree* to which an ethic is used at different ages ... and (2) the specific *types* of moral concepts that persons of various ages use within an ethic" (p. 157). The proposal is that degree of use of the Ethic of Autonomy remains relatively stable throughout the individual's life, even as types change. For example, a focus on individual interest will emerge early, whereas consideration of rights and equity will emerge only later. The Ethic of Community increases in usage from childhood into adulthood, with children giving consideration to family roles and norms and other types of community concepts being added with age, such as the in-group and the society as moral authorities. With respect to the Ethic of Divinity, Jensen (2011b) proposes a significant increase in divinity ethics during adolescence – in cultures that emphasize religion and spirituality and where the divine is conceptualized in abstract terms, such as Brazil.

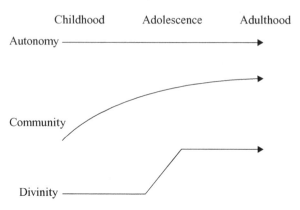

Figure 6.1   Cultural-developmental template (From Jensen, L. A. [2011].
The cultural-developmental theory of moral psychology: A new synthesis.
In L. A. Jensen (Ed.), *Bridging cultural and developmental psychology:
New syntheses in theory, research, and policy* [pp. 3–25]. New York, NY:
Oxford University Press.)
Note. Each line is considered as being on a separate vertical scale.

It is important to emphasize that the model proposed by Jensen (2008, 2011a,
2011b) should not be interpreted as a universal. The idea is that it is a template
that accommodates to culture. It allows for variation in the development of the
three ethics across the life span, and it can be used for cultural comparison.

With respect to emerging adulthood and cultural variation, Jensen (2011b)
notes:

Emerging adulthood is not a period of life that is present in all cultures. Researchers see
it as a period that has come notable in societies where educational training has become
extended and marriage and family obligations often are postponed . . . In cultures where
there is an emerging adulthood phase, one might expect this phase to be characterized
by substantial Ethic of Autonomy reasoning. (p. 16)

The three ethics during emerging adulthood in five countries

In this chapter, we focus on the degree of use of each ethic during emerging
adulthood across diverse countries. Samples from five countries took part in
this research. In each sample, only participants who reported having been born
in the country of the sample and who were between 18 and 23 years old were
retained for analysis.

Participants from five different nations were invited to take part in the study:
two English-speaking countries (New Zealand and United Kingdom), Japan and
Israel, representing industrialized nations, and Brazil, as a developing country.

When choosing these countries, the aim was to collect data from at least one country on each continent. Unfortunately, no data collection was conducted in Africa to fulfill this aim, but the samples were varied according to previously established research partnerships. Each of these nations has specific cultural characteristics that we highlight below.

Brazil

According to the most recent census (Instituto Brasileiro de Geografia e Estatística – IBGE, 2010), Brazil's population is constituted of 193 million people, with 10.5 percent of this total belonging to the age group between 18 and 23 years. Eighty-five percent of these 20 million emerging adults live in urban areas.

This is the only Portuguese-speaking country in South America, historically influenced by several immigrant groups (Rabinovich, 2008). Previous research on moral codes has shown that Brazilian university participants tended to use more divinity and community-based discourse than did American university participants (Haidt, Koller, & Dias, 1993; see also Guerra & Giner-Sorolla, 2010). Religiosity and spirituality, in general, are extremely important for Brazilians, and a sense of community and family is still strong, even in big cities. Brazil is also considered a collectivistic culture, presenting higher scores in hierarchy (e.g., authority, social power) and embeddedness (e.g., respect for tradition, social order) (Schwartz, 2004). In terms of moral inclusiveness, Brazil presents a low score of 1.5 on a scale of 0 to 4 (Schwartz, 2007), which suggests the importance of the participants' social groups to their moral judgments. This narrow moral universe suggests that Brazilians consider that the moral values and rules they endorse apply first and foremost to their social groups and are not universalized.

Israel

According to the Central Bureau of Statistics (2012), Israel has a population of 7 million people. The age group formed by people between 20 and 24 years old is constituted by 578,000 emerging adults, which accounts for 7 percent of the total population.

Research on this Middle-Eastern country has shown that Jewish Israeli participants tend to emphasize affective autonomy (e.g., exciting life, varied life) and mastery (e.g., social recognition, independence), landing relatively close to English-speaking countries in terms of cultural values (Schwartz, 2004). According to Schwartz (2007), Israel presents a broad moral universe (scoring 3.5 in moral inclusiveness), suggesting that citizens consider that the moral values and rules they endorse apply to all humans. Despite its level of emphasis on individualistic cultural values, Israel is still considered a moderately collectivistic culture (Hofstede, 2001), "a unique blend of community oriented practices, and those inherited from the past British presence" (Kulkarni, Hudson, Ramamoorthy, *et al.*, 2010, p. 95).

Japan

According to the Statistics Bureau, from the Ministry of International Affairs and Communications – MIC (2010), Japan has a population of 127 million people. Approximately 45 percent of the total population lives in the three major metropolitan areas, that is, Tokyo, Osaka, and Nagoya. The age group formed by people between 20 and 24 years old accounts for 6 percent of the total population, with 7 million Japanese emerging adults.

This Asian country places a strong emphasis on family ties and individual reputation (Guerra, Giner-Sorolla, & Vasiljevic, 2013; Jun'ichi, 2005). It is usually considered a collectivistic culture (Hofstede, 2001), presenting a balanced endorsement of cultural dimensions, strongly emphasizing mastery and intellectual autonomy, but presenting lower scores on hierarchy (Schwartz, 2004, 2006). According to Schwartz (2007), this cultural group presents a broad moral universe (scoring 3.3 in the index of moral inclusiveness), being considered similar to Israel in terms of the inclusiveness of their moral values.

English-speaking countries

The final two samples were taken from the United Kingdom and New Zealand. New Zealand's current population is formed by 4 million people, with 6 percent of this total (approximately 395,000 people) within the age group that ranges from 18 to 23 years (Statistics New Zealand, 2012). The total population in England and Wales, where our data were collected, is currently approximately 62 million people. From this total, nearly 7 percent is formed by emerging adults within the 20 to 24 years age group, which accounts for approximately 4 million people (Office of National Statistics, 2011).

These countries are usually considered individualist cultures (Hofstede, 2001). According to Schwartz (2004), English-speaking countries share an emphasis on affective (e.g., exciting life, pleasure) and intellectual autonomy (e.g., freedom, creativity). Both countries also present a broad moral universe (New Zealand scoring 3.0 and the United Kingdom scoring 4.0 in the index of moral inclusiveness), similarly to Israel and Japan.

The present sample and questionnaire

A total of 792 university students answered a questionnaire in their native language (Portuguese, Hebrew, Japanese, or English) on a voluntary basis.

Table 6.1 *Sample characteristics*

	Brazil	Israel	Japan	New Zealand	United Kingdom
Sample size	264	94	100	90	244
Female (%)	67%	57%	69%	82%	80%
Age range	18–23	19–23	18–23	18–23	18–23
Mean age (*SD*)	20.4 (1.50)	21.8 (1.28)	20 (0.98)	18.9 (1.30)	19 (1.05)
Sample religious majority	Catholic (52%)	Jewish (73%)	No beliefs (35%)/ Buddhist (20%)	No beliefs (34%)/ Catholic (9%)	No beliefs (26%)/ CoE (16%)
Mean level of religiosity (*SD*)	3.49 (1.13)	2.86 (1.27)	2.23 (1.05)	2.19 (1.06)	2.61 (1.26)

Note. Level of religiosity was measured on a scale ranging from 1 = not at all religious to 5 = extremely religious. CoE = Church of England.

The number of participants in each sample was determined based on response numbers over a specific period of 3 months for each sample and was not increased in response to preliminary data analysis. Paper-based questionnaires were used in Brazil and Japan, and an online data collection was used in Israel, New Zealand, and the United Kingdom. Table 6.1 provides an overview of demographic characteristics of the samples from each country. The national samples were divided in two age groups: participants entering emerging adulthood (from 18 to 20 years of age; $M = 19$, $SD = 0.78$) and participants in early emerging adulthood (21–23 years; $M = 21.88$, $SD = 0.83$).

Morality scale

Degree of use of the three ethics was measured with the Community, Autonomy, and Divinity Scale (CADS; Guerra & Giner-Sorolla, 2010). See Appendix B in this volume for the complete scale. CADS consists of forty-four items. Participants are requested to read each item and indicate with what frequency (from 1 = *never* to 7 = *always*) the items justify someone's action as right or wrong by completing the question "An action or behavior is morally right/wrong if . . . " Validation of the complete version of the CADS was originally conducted on Brazilian and British samples, including tests of exploratory and confirmatory factor analyses as well as cross-sample measurement invariance (Guerra & Giner-Sorolla, 2010). Further validation analyses have also been performed in samples from Israel, Japan, Macedonia, New Zealand, and the United States (Guerra, 2009).

Here, we used a shorter version of the scale (Guerra, in press), composed of thirty items, which are also divided into the three dimensions: Community, which emphasizes moral norms and values based on social (e.g., *It is socially accepted*) and family rules (e.g., *The family considers it unacceptable*); Auton-omy, which suggests that people should do as they please, expressing their positive rights (e.g., *It expresses someone's autonomy*), but only if their actions do not harm anyone, expressing negative rights (e.g., *It restricts individual's rights*); and Divinity, which emphasizes moral norms and values based on reli-gious rules (e.g., *It is God's will*) and on natural law (e.g., *It is unnatural*).[1] The shorter version of the CADS uses the same instructions presented in the complete version.

Main hypotheses

On the basis of the cultural-developmental template (Jensen, 2011b) and the previous cross-cultural research reviewed above, we had four hypotheses:

H1: Autonomy would receive the highest endorsement for the sample as a whole (Guerra & Giner-Sorolla, 2010).
H2: Use of Autonomy would be higher in English-speaking countries than in the other three countries. Brazil, Israel, and Japan would have higher levels of Divinity and Community Ethics use than the UK and New Zealand would.
H3: Overall, because of the possibility that greater conformity to social roles and norms is seen in general as a sign of adulthood, we advanced the exploratory hypothesis that Community and Divinity, but not Autonomy, endorsement would increase with emerging adulthood; that is, an Age × Ethic interaction.
H4: Endorsement of Divinity, and possibly Community, would be more pronounced with age in countries showing stronger endorsement of this moral code to begin with (such as Brazil), because accepting this ethic would be considered a more stable part of moral development into adulthood. H4 would be testable through the Age × Country × Ethic interaction.

Findings

Analysis plan

We tested our hypotheses by means of a full design – Country (between-subjects, 5 levels) × Age group (between-subjects, 2 levels) × Ethic (within-subjects, 3 levels), with different hypotheses being addressed by different main and interaction effects. We used this analytic approach because it was desirable to control for nonindependence of factors using Type III sums of squares with a general linear model (GLM). As the three ethics are entered as within-subject

---

[1] Cronbach's alpha ranges for each country were as follows: Brazil, between 0.80 (Autonomy) and 0.88 (Divinity); Israel, between 0.64 (Autonomy) and 0.77 (Divinity); Japan, between 0.78 (Divinity) and 0.84 (Community); New Zealand, between 0.84 (Autonomy) and 0.89 (Community); and United Kingdom, between 0.88 (Autonomy) and 0.91 (Divinity).

variables, our main dependent variable is the overall score on the CAD Scale. Hypothesis 1 focused on the main effect of Ethic, suggesting the overall importance of Autonomy across all age groups and countries. Hypothesis 2 focused on the Country × Ethic interaction, comparing the countries on the relative endorsement of each of the three ethics. Hypothesis 3 tested the Age group (between) × Ethic (within) interaction, again looking at the relative endorsement of each ethic by the two age groups. And, finally, hypothesis 4 focused on the three-way interaction to see whether any interactions between age and ethics were moderated by country.

Main effects

As predicted (H1), we observed a main effect of Ethic, $F(2, 1564) = 171.49$, $p < 0.001$, partial $\eta^2 = 0.180$, with Autonomy ($M = 4.81$) presenting a stronger endorsement across all countries when compared to other types of moral codes (Community $M = 4.39$; Divinity $M = 3.79$).

A main effect of Country was also observed, $F(4, 782) = 27.177, p < 0.001$, partial $\eta^2 = 0.122$, with Brazil ($M = 4.72$) and Israel ($M = 4.67$) presenting the highest overall endorsement across ethics; New Zealand ($M = 4.16$) and the United Kingdom ($M = 4.25$) presented similar estimated means; and Japan ($M = 3.85$) presented the lowest endorsement across ethics. Post hoc analysis (Bonferroni test) showed significant differences, with participants from Brazil and Israel not differing from each other but significantly differing from all other countries. New Zealand and the UK also do not differ from each other, and all countries differ significantly from Japan. No significant main effect of Age group was observed, $F(1, 782) = 1.312, p = 0.252$.

Country × Ethics interaction (H2)

We observed a significant Country × Ethics interaction, $F(8, 1564) = 31.662$, $p < 0.001$, partial $\eta^2 = 0.139$. In order to clarify the interaction observed, we present graphs for each country's mean moral codes endorsement for all participants, separately for each of the code types, with *SE* error bars. Figure 6.2 presents these data.

Participants from most countries, except the UK, presented similar high endorsement of the Ethic of Community (Brazil $M = 4.44$; Israel $M = 4.46$; Japan $M = 4.40$; New Zealand $M = 4.33$; and the United Kingdom $M = 4.19$). Analysis of variance conducted afterward within Community (Bonferroni test) showed significant differences, with participants from the United Kingdom presenting significantly lower scores when compared to the scores of participants from Brazil and Israel, $F(4, 787) = 4.043, p = 0.003$.

Regarding the Ethic of Autonomy, Japan presented lower endorsement of this code type ($M = 4.32$) when compared to the other countries (Brazil

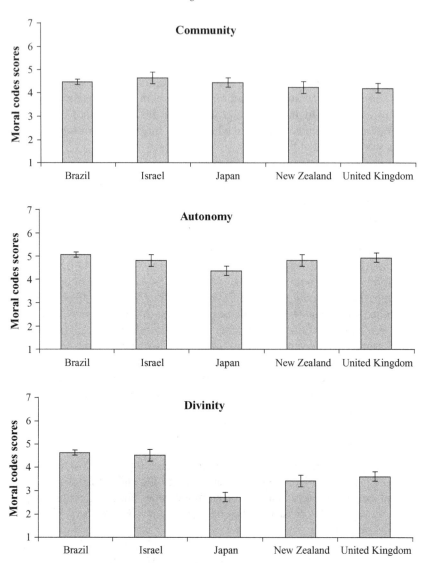

Figure 6.2 Profiles of moral codes in Brazil, Israel, Japan, New Zealand, and the United Kingdom

$M = 5.00$; Israel $M = 4.86$; New Zealand $M = 4.94$; and the United Kingdom $M = 4.88$). Post hoc analysis within Autonomy (Bonferroni test) confirmed the lower endorsement of the Japanese participants compared with endorsement from participants of the other nations, $F(4787) = 13.234$, $p < 0.001$.

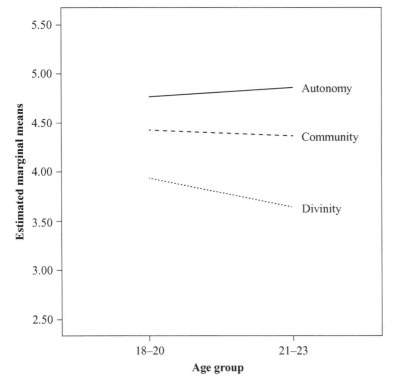

Figure 6.3 Moral codes marginal means according to age range

Finally, regarding the Ethic of Divinity, the pattern was grouped according to specific countries: in post hoc analysis (Bonferroni test), $F(4, 787) = 65.965, p < 0.001$. Brazil ($M = 4.58$) and Israel ($M = 4.17$) presented similarly higher endorsement of this moral code when compared to all other countries. New Zealand ($M = 3.64$) and the United Kingdom ($M = 3.71$) did not differ between themselves; Japan presented the lowest level of endorsement ($M = 2.73$) compared to all other countries. These findings in large part corroborate hypothesis 2, with a few exceptions; for example, Japan showed an unexpectedly low endorsement of Divinity, while New Zealand was as high in Community endorsement as were the non-English-speaking countries.

Age group × Ethics (H3)

We also aimed at identifying possible differences in endorsement of the three moral codes between the age groups. A significant Age group × Ethic interaction was observed, $F(2, 1564) = 6.166, p = 0.002$, partial $\eta^2 = 0.008$. Figure 6.3

presents these results, suggesting that the Ethics of Autonomy and Community are similar across age groups.

However, unexpectedly, the figure suggests that the Ethic of Divinity is lower for the oldest of the emerging adulthood groups (i.e., 21- to 23-year-olds). Therefore, hypothesis 3 was not corroborated, and in fact it was seemingly contradicted in the realm of divinity ethics. In general accord with the idea that culture moderates development, this variance could be explained by country differences. Therefore, in order to test hypothesis 4 (H4), it was necessary to observe results regarding the three-way interaction.

Age group × Ethics × Country (H4)

Figure 6.4 presents the estimated marginal means for the three ethics according to the age group by country in a cultural-developmental analysis. Although each country presents its own pattern of endorsement of the three ethics by age group, the three-way interaction was not significant, $F(8, 1564) = 0.442$, $p = 0.896$.

In Brazil, both age groups presented high and relatively stable endorsement of the three ethics. In Israel, participants who were entering the emerging adulthood phase endorsed the three ethics to an equal extent, with Community and Divinity being lower than Autonomy in the older group. In Japan, all three ethics were endorsed in a similar way by both age groups. New Zealand and the United Kingdom presented a similar pattern between age groups for endorsement of Autonomy and Community. Divinity, however, appeared slightly lower for the oldest group. Consequently, H4 is only partially corroborated.

Discussion

Our main objective was to investigate the application of the cultural-developmental template across five national samples of emerging adults. Results of this study support the use of this theoretical model, linking the endorsement of the three ethics to cultural and developmental differences.

First, it is important to emphasize that all three ethics were used in the five countries. This supports Shweder, Much, Mahapatra, and Park's (1997) proposal that the three ethics are widespread. Also, level of endorsement of the ethics varied by country. This also fits with Shweder's proposal and with previous findings by other researchers (Haidt, Koller, & Dias, 1993; Jensen, 1998; Rozin, Lowery, Imada, *et al.*, 1999; Shweder, Much, Mahapatra, *et al.*, 1997; Vasquez, Keltner, Ebenbach, *et al.*, 2001).

With respect to age, the use of the Ethics of Autonomy and Community was constant when comparing the group entering emerging adulthood (18–20

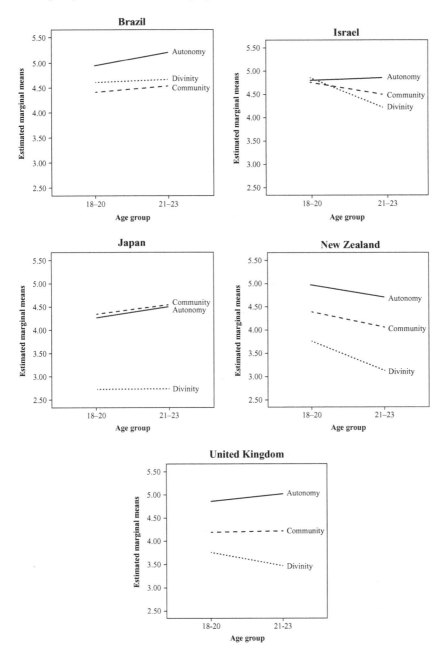

Figure 6.4   Moral codes marginal means according to age range studied in five countries

years) to those who were in the early phase of this developmental stage (21–23 years). Divinity, however, was lower for the older group. These results regarding stability of moral codes' endorsement for emerging adults are noteworthy. This age period is marked by many changes in terms of identities, relationships, education, and career-related choices. However, these findings suggest that there are not many changes in terms of values in the present five countries examined – at least not for the age range included here. Next, we turn to an elaboration of our findings for each of the three ethics.

Autonomy

The high overall endorsement of the Ethic of Autonomy moral code is consistent with literature on the three ethics (Arnett, Ramos, & Jensen, 2001; Guerra & Giner-Sorolla, 2010; Haidt, Koller, & Dias, 1993). This moral code emphasizes the importance of concepts such as fairness and justice, which research has shown to be endorsed across cultures (Vauclair & Fischer, 2011). Our results confirmed not only the centrality of this ethic to the moral life of all the cultural groups but also the stability of this ethic through developmental stages (Jensen, 2011a).

Japanese participants presented the lowest endorsement when compared with other countries; however, the use of this ethic was not below average in this country; that is, Japanese participants still presented high endorsement of the Autonomy moral code, which is in accordance with the literature on cultural values (Schwartz, 2006). Japan is a culture that emphasizes mastery (e.g., social recognition, independence) and intellectual autonomy (e.g., freedom, creativity) as cultural values, as well as self-expression in terms of personal values (Inglehart & Oyserman, 2004).

The emerging adulthood phase is characterized by a delay in life-changing decisions, such as long-term relationships and career choices (Arnett, 2007b), while individuals explore possible identities (Smetana, Campione-Barr, & Metzger, 2006). In this developmental period, the Ethic of Autonomy may provide a moral base for these choices. Certainly, the Ethic of Autonomy was prominent in the reasoning of both groups of emerging adults across the countries.

Community

In contrast to the Ethic of Autonomy, the Ethic of Community emphasizes the moral authority of one's social group and family. This moral code, which expresses the importance of conforming to norms and social rules, presented the second highest level of endorsement across samples, with the exception of Japan. The importance attributed by Japanese emerging adults to Community considerations such as family ties and social norms was as high as their autonomy considerations. This fits with recent work by Jun'ichi (2005), who observed that Japanese people tend to emphasize family ties and individual reputation, and the importance of one's honor is associated with "saving face," that is, one's concern for one's own image in the eyes of others (Guerra, Giner-Sorolla, & Vasiljevic, 2013; Oetzel & Ting-Toomey, 2003).

The UK presented the lowest endorsement of the Ethic of Community, significantly lower when compared to Brazil's and Israel's scores. However, British participants did not differ from Japanese and New Zealanders regarding this moral code, which is not as important as Autonomy in English-speaking countries. According to Schwartz (2004), the UK, New Zealand, and Japan and tend to present similar cultural values and are considered high in individualism (Hofstede, 2001). These results may reflect cultural differences similar to those found by Arnett (2003) in that, among less individualistic cultures or ethnic groups, upholding social roles may be more important, especially during transition to adulthood. We found that Community did not differ for the two age groups of emerging adults. This ethic, as proposed by Shweder (2003) and Miller (2001), emphasizes roles within families and how social groups define one's identity. The moral values emphasized would be related to one's relationships and interdependence with the group, such as loyalty, respect, obedience to authority, and self-control, all consistent with conformity to social norms. Emerging adults, however, are delaying adult decisions and responsibilities. We think it quite likely that this ethic would increase in use after these adult decisions are made and responsibilities are taken on. Thus, akin to the cultural-developmental model, we would propose additional research with participants at the end of emerging adulthood and the start of young adulthood to examine the degree and types of Ethic of Community reasoning used. We would expect that the formation of long-term relationships and the start of parenthood would make a difference.

Divinity

Finally, Divinity was the least endorsed moral code when compared with Autonomy and Community across almost all the cultures and age groups. This finding corroborates previous ones (Guerra, 2009) that showed a similarly low role overall for Divinity compared to the other ethics. It is important to note that Brazilian emerging adults presented a stable and relatively high use of the Ethic of Divinity across age groups, which is in line with previous findings (Guerra & Giner-Sorolla, 2010; Haidt, Koller, & Dias, 1993) and extends them to a sample of emerging adults.

We also think that it is important to reflect further on the results for the Japanese emerging adults. They had the lowest average scores on Divinity.

On one hand, this is consistent with previous research in the values literature that characterizes Japan as emphasizing secular-rational and self-expression values (Inglehart & Oyserman, 2004). On the other hand, we think that this low endorsement of the Divinity moral code among the Japanese sample could be explained by scale items – in our study and in the research by others on values – that mostly emphasize religious rules and religious institutions as moral authority (see also Guerra, 2009). When answering the CADS items regarding the importance of nature as a source of moral authority, Japanese participants presented a moderate endorsement of this subscale ($M = 4.20$) – akin, for example, to the Israeli groups of 21- to 23-year-olds). We think that this indicates that the content of the Divinity moral code matters for research on this culture and that there is a need for research focusing more specifically on what is natural and the laws of nature. Such precepts form an important part of Japanese folk and formal religion, transmitted through the belief systems of Shinto (Reader, 1991). According to Satoko (2005), Shinto rites and practices were associated with Buddhism, with most of the religious population presenting multiple religious affiliations. The association of Shinto and Buddhist philosophies is one of the bases of the Japanese cultural concern for ancestral memory and filial piety, the emphasis placed on the purity of the human soul and the importance of nature as sanctuary (Nitobé, 1908). Consequently, more research is needed to understand the moral conception of nature held by Japanese participants.

As expected, New Zealand and the United Kingdom were similar on Divinity endorsement, consistent with previous literature on the three ethics (Guerra, 2009; Guerra & Giner-Sorolla, 2010) and on cultural values (Inglehart & Oyserman, 2004). Arnett and Jensen (2002) observed a decrease in religious attendance in the United States for those in their late teens and early twenties associated with "becoming busy with other activities, doubting previously held beliefs, and simply losing interest in being involved in a religious institution" (p. 451). This also seems to be true in three of our national samples: Israel, New Zealand, and the UK. Likewise, research reviewed by Trommsdorff (2015) suggests that adolescence is a time of particular religious fervor in many cultures so that the decline in divinity concerns in early adulthood may represent the continuation of this trend. These findings generally represent the process of becoming an adult in individualistic cultures, as the decision regarding one's own beliefs and values is considered to be an important developmental task, which suggests search for independence from parents along with lessening of ties to family and religious institutions (Arnett & Jensen, 2002). However, Arnett and Jensen (2002) suggest that as emerging adults get married and start their own families in their mid- to late twenties, there may be an increase in their level of religiosity with a consequent increase in the use of the Divinity moral code. They suggest this for the United States, a Western country with a relatively high level of religiosity. However, for the UK and New Zealand, where religious belief is lower, such a developmental trend may not hold.

Limitations

It is necessary to discuss possible limitations that could have had an impact on the outcomes of this study. The use of only two age groups – spanning a fairly short period of 6 years – may not represent properly any possible changes in the use of each ethic.

Another important limitation of this study is the reliance on university students to represent emerging adults. Although members of these age groups might be expected to still undergo some of the life events characteristic of emerging adulthood in industrialized countries (Arnett, 2007b) – for example, forming more stable relationships, completing schooling, leaving the parental home (Buchmann & Kriesi, 2011) – the fact that they are in a university setting has several implications that are not characteristic of the general population. The university environment encourages learning and questioning. Also, persons pursuing university degrees are usually looking to change and improve their station in life rather than to settle down into an established role. Both these factors might tend to suppress the crystallization of belief in authority measured by endorsement of Community and Divinity ethics. On the other hand, by sampling university students exclusively, we have removed many confounding variables that would arise from comparing people in different life circumstances. Thus, the differences we have observed can genuinely be said to represent effects of culture and age groups or of other life experiences besides current socioeconomic and occupational status. These considerations remind us that a general population sample of emerging adults in different walks of life would be a useful complement to the present data.

Conclusion

This study focused on the use of the three ethics (Shweder, Much, Mahapatra, *et al.*, 1997) in different cultures and different age groups of emerging adults. Many future research possibilities could be derived from the present findings along with the cultural-developmental model of moral reasoning (Jensen, 2011a, 2011b). We used a cross-sectional design to facilitate cross-cultural data collection, consequently emphasizing the cultural aspects of the model. However, longitudinal studies on the endorsement of moral codes would provide a better test of the developmental aspects of this model. Both methods of investigation are needed in future research.

Further cross-cultural research should also be conducted to directly associate the three ethics (Shweder, 2003; Shweder, Much, Mahapatra, *et al.*, 1997) with cultural dimensions (Schwartz, 2004, 2006; Schwartz & Ros, 1995) and personal values (Gouveia, 2013) using the cultural-developmental template. Level of moral inclusiveness, as proposed by Schwartz (2007), could also be included. This variable could provide valuable information regarding the breadth or narrowness of the application of each of the three ethics that characterizes people from different cultures and of different ages.

Future research should also look into the association between development of moral codes and values change (Bardi & Goodwin, 2011; Bardi, Lee, Hofmann-Towfigh, *et al.*, 2009). In a manner that is consistent with the proposed model and data, literature on values suggests a decrease in the importance of religiosity during the late teens and early twenties followed by an increase in the importance of this value in the late twenties. Values may change based on psychosocial and developmental changes, such as new life situations: for example, emerging adults may place a stronger emphasis on promotion values (e.g., success, prestige) when beginning their careers (Vione, 2012).

A national study conducted in Brazil by Vione (2012) with 16,000 emerging adults (from 19 to 34 years old) indicated that women show an increase in the importance of *excitement* (e.g., pleasure, sexuality), *existence* (e.g., survival, health), and *suprapersonal* values (e.g., knowledge, maturity) during this period when compared with the importance of these values in adolescence; men, similarly, show an increase in the endorsement of *existence* and *suprapersonal* values but also of *normative* values (e.g., religiosity, tradition) and a decrease in *excitement* values during this period when compared with endorsement during adolescence. These results could indicate that development in the endorsement of specific ethics could reflect changes in the values hierarchy.

According to Arnett (2011), demographic and economic changes are responsible for the rise of emerging adulthood in developed and developing countries. Following these changes are also many changes in cultural beliefs and social norms that help shape this life period. As a cultural and developmental theory, emerging adulthood is directly related to the use of moral values and the beliefs these values are based on in each specific culture.

The cultural-developmental template (Jensen, 2011b) can be considered a fruitful theoretical and empirical way of studying the emerging adulthood life stage (Arnett, 2011) in relation to morality. More specifically, this model and the results of this specific study clarify and confirm the roles that culture and development play in morality, not disconnected from each other but intertwined.

REFERENCES
Allen, M. W., Ng, S. H., Ikeda, K., Jawan, J. A., Sufi, A. H., Wilson, M., & Yang, K-S. (2007). Two decades of change in cultural values and economic development in

eight East Asian and Pacific Island nations. *Journal of Cross-Cultural Psychology*, 38(3), 247–269. doi:10.1177/0022022107300273

Arnett, J. J. (2000). Emerging adulthood: A theory of development from the late teens through the twenties. *American Psychologist*, 55(5), 469–480. doi:10.1037/0003-066X.55.5.469

(2003). Conceptions of the transition to adulthood among emerging adults in American ethnic groups. *New Directions for Child and Adolescent Development*, 100, 63–75. doi:10.1002/cd.75

(2007a). Emerging adulthood: What is it, and what is it good for? *Child Development Perspectives*, 1(2), 68–73. doi:10.1111/j.1750-8606.2007.00016.x

(2007b). The long and leisurely route: Coming of age in Europe today. *Current History*, 106, 130–136. Retrieved from www.jeffreyarnett.com/articles/Arnett_2007_CurrHist.pdf

(2007c). Suffering, selfish, slackers? Myths and reality about emerging adults. *Journal of Youth and Adolescence*, 36, 23–29. doi:10.1007/s10964-006-9157-z

(2011). Emerging adulthood(s): The cultural psychology of a new life stage. In L. A. Jensen (Ed.), *Bridging cultural and developmental approaches to psychology: New syntheses in theory, research, and policy* (pp. 255–275), New York, NY: Oxford University Press.

Arnett, J. J., & Jensen, L. A. (2002). A congregation of one: Individualized religious beliefs among emerging adults. *Journal of Adolescent Research*, 17(5), 451–467. doi:10.1177/0743558402175002

Arnett, J. J., Ramos, K. D., & Jensen, L. A. (2001). Ideological views in emerging adulthood: Balancing autonomy and community. *Journal of Adult Development*, 8, 69–79. doi:10.1023/A:1026460917338

Bardi, A., & Goodwin, R. (2011). The dual route to value change: Individual processes and cultural moderators. *Journal of Cross-Cultural Psychology*, 42, 271–287. doi:10.1177/0022022110396916

Bardi, A., Lee, J. A., Hofmann-Towfigh, N., & Soutar, G. (2009). The structure of intraindividual value change. *Journal of Personality and Social Psychology*, 97, 913–929. doi:10.1037/a0016617

Buchmann, M. C., & Kriesi, I. (2011). Transition to adulthood in Europe. *Annual Review of Sociology*, 37, 481–503. doi:10.1146/annurev-soc-081309-150212

Calligaris, C. (2000). *Adolescência [Adolescence]*. São Paulo, Brazil: Publifolha.

Carrano, P. C. (2000). Juventudes: As identidades são múltiplas. [Youth: Multiple identities]. *Movimento. Revista da Faculdade de Educação da Universidade Federal Fluminense*, 1, 11–27. Retrieved from http://portalmultirio.rio.rj.gov.br/sec21/chave_artigo.asp?cod_artigo=1086

Central Bureau of Statistics. (2012). Population aged 15 and over, by religion, marital status, sex and age. *Statistica Abstract of Israel*, 63. Retrieved from www.cbs.gov.il/reader/shnaton/templ_shnaton_e.html?num_tab=st02_20x&CYear=2012

Fischer, R. (2006). Congruence and functions of personal and cultural values: Do my values reflect my culture's values? *Personality and Social Psychology Bulletin*, 32, 1419–1431. doi:10.1177/0146167206291425

Fischer, R., Smith, P., Richey, B., Ferreira, M., Assmar, E., Maes, J., & Stumpf, S. (2007). How do organizations allocate rewards? The predictive validity of national values, economic and organizational factors across six nations. *Journal of Cross-Cultural Psychology*, 38, 3–18. doi:10.1177/0022022106295437

Gouveia, V. V. (2013). *Teoria funcionalista dos valores humanos: Fundamentos, aplicações e perspectivas* [Functionalist theory of human values: Foundations, applications, and recent perspectives]. São Paulo, Brazil: Casa do Psicólogo.

Greenfield, P. M., Keller, H., Fuligni, A., & Maynard, A. (2003). Cultural pathways through universal development. *Annual Review of Psychology*, 54, 461–490. doi:10.1146/annurev.psych.54.101601.145221

Groppo, L. A. (2000). *Juventude: Ensaios sobre sociologia e histórias das juventudes modernas.* [Youth: Essays on the sociology and history of modern youth]. Rio de Janeiro, Brazil: DIFEL.

Guerra, V. M. (2009). Community, Autonomy, and Divinity: Studying morality across cultures. (Unpublished doctoral thesis). University of Kent, Kent, United Kingdom.

(in press). Community, Autonomy, and Divinity Scale: Identifying facets of moral codes. In A. Roazzi, B. Campello, & W. Bilsky (Eds.), *Proceedings for the 14th Facet Theory Association Conference* (pp. 347–360). Retrieved from http://dspace.uevora.pt/rdpc/bitstream/10174/10933/1/Facet%20Theory%20-%20 Proceedings%2014FTC.pdf

Guerra, V. M., & Giner-Sorolla, R. (2010). Community, Autonomy, and Divinity Scale: A new tool for the cross-cultural study of morality. *Journal of Cross-Cultural Psychology*, 41, 35–50. doi:10.1177/0022022109348919

Guerra, V. M., Giner-Sorolla, R., & Vasiljevic, M. (2013). The importance of honor concerns across eight countries. *Group Processes & Intergroup Relations*, 16(3), 298–318. doi:10.1177/1368430212463451

Haidt, J., Koller, S., & Dias, M. (1993). Affect, culture, and morality, or is it wrong to eat your dog? *Journal of Personality and Social Psychology*, 65, 613–628. doi:10.1037//0022-3514.65.4.613

Hofstede, G. (2001). *Culture's consequences: Comparing values, behaviors, institutions, and organizations across nations* (2nd ed.). Beverly Hills, CA: Sage.

Inglehart, R., & Oyserman, D. (2004). Individualism, autonomy, self-expression and human development. In H. Vinken, J. Soeters, & P. Ester (Eds.), *Comparing cultures: Dimensions of culture in a comparative perspective* (pp. 74–96). Leiden, The Netherlands: Brill.

Instituto Brasileir ode Geografiae Estatística – IBGE. (2010). *Censo Demográfico* [Demographic census]. Retrieved from www.ibge.gov.br/home/estatistica/ populacao/censo2010/

Jensen, L. A. (1998). Moral divisions within countries between orthodoxy and progressivism: India and the United States. *Journal for the Scientific Study of Religion*, 37, 90–107.

(2008). Through two lenses: A cultural-developmental approach to moral psychology. *Developmental Review*, 28, 289–315.

(2009). Moral development. In R. A. Shweder, T. R. Bidell, A. C. Dailey, S. D. Dixon, P. J. Miller, & J. Modell (Eds.), *The child: An encyclopedic companion* (pp. 624–629). Chicago, IL: University of Chicago Press.

(2011a). The cultural development of three fundamental moral ethics: Autonomy, Community, and Divinity. *Zygon*, 46(1), 150–167. doi:10.1111/j.1467-9744.2010.01163.x

(2011b). The cultural-developmental theory of moral psychology: A new synthesis. In L. A. Jensen (Ed.), *Bridging cultural and developmental psychology: New syntheses in theory, research, and policy* (pp. 3–25). New York, NY: Oxford University Press.

Jun'ichi, I. (2005). Deconstructing "Japanese religion": A historical survey. *Japanese Journal of Religious Studies*, 32, 235–248.

Kulkarni, S. P., Hudson, T., Ramamoorthy, N., Marchev, A., Georgieva-Kindakova, P., & Gorskov, V. (2010). Dimensions of individualism-collectivism: A comparative study of five cultures. *Current Issues of Business and Law*, 5, 93–109. doi:10.5200/1822-9530.2010.03

Leong, C., & Ward, C. (2006). Cultural values and attitudes towards immigrants and multiculturalism: The case of the Eurobarometer survey on racism and xenophobia. *International Journal of Intercultural Relations*, 30(6), 799–810. doi:10.1016/j.ijintrel.2006.07.001

Miller, J. (2001). Culture and moral development. In D. Matsumoto (Ed.), *The handbook of culture and psychology* (pp. 151–170). New York, NY: Oxford University Press.

Nitobé, I. (1908). *Bushido: The soul of Japan*. Retrieved from www.gutenberg.org/files/12096/12096-h/12096-h.htm

Oetzel, J. G., & Ting-Toomey, S. (2003). Face concerns in interpersonal conflict: A cross-cultural empirical test of the face negotiation theory. *Communication Research*, 30(6), 599–624. doi:10.1177/0093650203257841

Office of National Statistics. (2011). *Census: Population estimates for the United Kingdom – female and male usual resident population by five-year age group*. Retrieved from www.ons.gov.uk/ons/taxonomy/index.html?nscl=Ageing

Rabinovich, E. (2008). Commentary: How far is Brazil from Africa? *Culture & Psychology*, 14, 145–152. doi:10.1177/1354067×07082801

Reader, I. (1991). *Religion in contemporary Japan*. Basingstoke, United Kingdom: Macmillan.

Rozin, P., Lowery, L., Imada, S., & Haidt, J. (1999). The CAD triad hypothesis: A mapping between three moral emotions (contempt, anger, disgust) and three moral codes (Community, Autonomy, Divinity). *Journal of Personality and Social Psychology*, 76, 574–586. doi:10.1037/0022-3514.76.4.574

Satoko, F. (2005). Survey on religion and higher education in Japan. *Japanese Journal of Religious Studies*, 32(2), 353–370.

Schwartz, S. H. (2004). Mapping and interpreting cultural differences around the world. In H. Vinken, J. Soeters, & P Ester (Eds.), *Comparing cultures: Dimensions of culture in a comparative perspective* (pp. 43–73). Leiden, the Netherlands: Brill.

(2006). A theory of cultural value orientations: Explication and applications. *Comparative Sociology*, 5(2–3), 137–182.

(2007). Universalism values and the inclusiveness of our moral universe. *Journal of Cross-Cultural Psychology*, 38, 711–728. doi: 10.1177/0022022107308992

Schwartz, S. H., & Ros, M. (1995). Values in the West: A theoretical and empirical challenge to the individualism-collectivism cultural dimension. *World Psychology*, 1(2), 91–122.

Shweder, R. (2003). *Why do men barbecue? Recipes for cultural psychology*. Cambridge, MA: Harvard University Press.

Shweder, R., Much, N., Mahapatra, M., & Park, L. (1997). The "Big Three" of morality (Autonomy, Community, Divinity) and the "big three" explanations of suffering.

In A. Brandt & P. Rozin (Eds.), *Morality and health* (pp. 119–169). London, United Kingdom: Routledge.

Smetana, J. G., Campione-Barr, N., & Metzger, A. (2006). Adolescent development in interpersonal and societal contexts. *Annual Review of Psychology*, 57, 255–284. doi:10.1146/annurev.psych.57.102904.190124

Statistics Bureau. (2010). *Japan population census: Population by age.* Ministry of Internal Affairs and Communications. Retrieved from www.stat.go.jp/english/data/nenkan/1431-02.htm

Statistics New Zealand. (2012). Estimated resident population by age and sex. Retrieved from www.stats.govt.nz/infoshare/ViewTable.aspx?pxID=7a0ca8a8-aab7-4a24-91cb-d8609622f3ae

Trommsdorff, G. (2015). Cultural roots of values, and moral and religious purposes in adolescent development. In L. A. Jensen (Ed.), *The Oxford handbook of human development and culture: An interdisciplinary perspective.* New York, NY: Oxford University Press.

United Nations. (2011). World population prospects, the 2010 revision. Retrieved from http://esa.un.org/unpd/wpp/Excel-Data/population.htm

Vasquez, K., Keltner, D., Ebenbach, D., & Banaszynski, T. (2001). Cultural variation and similarity in moral rhetorics: Voices from the Philippines and the United States. *Journal of Cross-Cultural Psychology*, 32, 93–120. doi:10.1177/0022022101032001010

Vauclair, C-M., & Fischer, R. (2011). Do cultural values predict individuals' moral attitudes? A cross-cultural multi-level approach. *European Journal of Social Psychology*, 41, 468–481. doi:10.1002/ejsp.794

Vione, K. C. (2012). *As prioridades valorativas mudam com a idade? Testando as hipóteses de rigidez e plasticidade* [Do values priorities change with age? Testing the rigidity and plasticity hypotheses] (Dissertação de mestrado). Programa de Pós-Graduação em Psicologia Social, Universidade Federal da Paraíba.

Wan, C., Chiu, C., Peng, S., & Tam, K. (2007). Measuring cultures through intersubjective cultural norms: Implications for predicting relative identification with two or more cultures. *Journal of Cross-Cultural Psychology*, 38, 213–226. doi:10.1177/0022022106297300

Wong, S., Bond, M., & Rodriguez-Mosquera, P. (2008). The influence of cultural value orientations on self-reported emotional expression across cultures. *Journal of Cross-Cultural Psychology*, 39, 224–229. doi:10.1177/06022022107313866

7 The dynamics of ethical co-occurrence in Hmong and American evangelical families: new directions for Three Ethics research

Jacob R. Hickman and Allison DiBianca Fasoli

If there is one central critique coming from cultural psychology about moral development, it is that the process of moral development – and even the moral domain itself – is not as uniform as traditional psychological theories have put forth. The Three Ethics framework (Autonomy, Community, Divinity) emerged out of just such a critique, providing critical perspectives on cultural variation to the ways that we theorize and imagine moral development (i.e., Jensen, 2008; Shweder, Mahapatra, & Miller, 1987; Shweder, Much, Mahapatra, *et al.*, 1997). Many of the chapters in this volume build on this framework and this cultural critique of moral development. In this chapter we offer critical nuance to this line of inquiry. We suggest some new directions for Three Ethics research that would move toward analyses of the dynamic relations of the three ethics as they co-occur within individuals' moral discourse. Doing so reveals important culturally specific trends, such as the mutual imbrication and ontogenetic inter-dependence of Autonomy, Community, and Divinity. These trends represent significant developmental patterns that would otherwise be overlooked and, we argue, would be hard to detect without such an explicit focus on ethical co-occurrence.

We suggest that this kind of relational analysis of ethical co-occurrence is fruitful for cultural-developmental research for three reasons. First, we find that the co-occurrence of ethics within one line of thinking is common and may take several different forms. Taken together with other research findings (e.g., Pandya & Bhangaokar, Chapter 2, this volume; Vainio, Chapter 3, this volume; Padilla-Walker & Nelson, Chapter 5, this volume), we argue that there is mounting empirical evidence to suggest that ethical co-occurrence is an important aspect of individuals' moral reasoning that researchers should attend to in their analyses of moral thinking across the life course. However, we also find evidence of deeper forms of relation between the three ethics, which we call ethical imbrication – the inextricable integration of seemingly disparate (from a theoretical perspective) moral discourses into a single line of moral reasoning. In these imbricated forms of co-occurrence, the delineation of reasoning into separate ethics is arbitrary from an emic point of view. Following from this point, our second argument for using the Three Ethics framework to analyze the relations between justifications is that it can reveal whether these distinctions are meaningful to participants. By uncovering aspects of moral thinking in which the analytic categories of Autonomy, Community, and Divinity are "imbricated" (from the point of view of the analyst), we can reconstruct cultural logics that underlie particular ethical constellations. Third, such relational analyses of ethical co-occurrence can also reveal imbricated processes of moral development. In other words, we argue that imbrication occurs within an individual's moral reasoning not only at a single point in time but also developmentally, where one ethic may provide a developmental foundation for the emergence of another ethic.

These insights rest on innovative methodological uses of the Three Ethics framework. Specifically, examining the relation between justifications in individuals' moral discourse requires various forms of discursive analysis, such as cultural discourse analysis and language-interaction analysis. Such analyses, we argue, can uncover culturally distinct visions of the moral realm and culturally distinct developmental processes through which individuals come to adopt those visions in ways that comparative analyses of the distributions of the three ethics cannot. Moving Three Ethics research in this direction provides a critical nuance to the approach that can help analysts stay closer to the construction of the moral domain as research participants themselves experience it – the original intent behind developing this framework.

We build these arguments through our analysis of moral reasoning in two different empirical projects. DiBianca Fasoli's data are derived from research that aims to understand the socialization of a divine moral code in American evangelical Christian families in Boston, whereas Hickman's data come from a comparative ethnography of the transnational and intergenerational patterns of moral thinking of Hmong families in both Thailand and the United States. Despite the distinctness of these two projects, they converge by revealing aspects of ethical co-occurrence that were not sufficiently accounted for in existing Three Ethics scholarship. Crucially, it was by combining the Three Ethics framework with various cultural discourse approaches that enabled us to recognize the implications of these aspects of ethical co-occurrence, and each distinct data set provided evidence toward this end.[1] Specifically, the ethnographic approach of Hickman's transnational data on moral reasoning

---

[1]   In our separate analyses, we were finding similar trends of ethical co-occurrence that led us to simultaneously draw the conclusions that we lay out in this chapter. The distinct character of our different populations suggests that ethical co-occurrence is a broader phenomenon that deserves greater consideration.

enabled him to interpret the co-occurrence of ethics as ethical imbrication. The parent-child conversation approach of DiBianca Fasoli's data on moral reasoning enabled her to interpret the co-occurrence of ethics in terms of their developmental implications for ethical imbrication. We believe this convergence on ethical imbrication demonstrates the utility of these new directions for employing the Three Ethics framework across a diverse range of empirical projects.

We first review the Three Ethics research that has examined the relation of the ethics in moral thinking, outlining the ways in which this research has examined ethical co-occurrence and explaining, by contrast, what we mean by ethical imbrication. We build on this research by presenting three forms of co-occurrence that we recognized through discourse analysis of Hmong moral discourse and specify when co-occurrence can signal parallel justifications, divergent justifications, and ethical imbrication. We then address the ontogenetic implications of ethical co-occurrence by drawing on American evangelical moral discourse in parent-child conversations. We conclude by discussing future directions of Three Ethics research, with a particular focus on methodological approaches that can help us to better understand the nature and development of particular cultural moral codes.

Three Ethics

The Three Ethics approach to moral thinking and moral development emerged from work pioneered by Shweder and his colleagues in an effort to critique ethnocentric assumptions about moral reasoning embedded in much of the cross-cultural psychology research (Shweder, 1990; Shweder, Mahapatra, & Miller, 1987; Shweder & Much, 1991; Shweder, Much, Mahapatra, et al., 1997). Shweder and colleagues conducted ethnographic research on moral thinking and collected moral discourse in India and the United States. On the basis of this research and in conjunction with a review of the developmental and cultural literature, Shweder and colleagues ultimately derived three central ethics, labeled Autonomy, Community, and Divinity. Conceptually, each ethic is grounded in a distinct conception of the self, as an "individualized preference structure" (Autonomy), as an "office-holder" (Community), or as a "divine soul" (Divinity).

The three ethics provide a minimalistic framework for understanding culturally varying deontological moral discourses (Jensen, 1993, 1995, 2004; Shweder, 1990; Shweder, Much, Mahapatra, et al., 1997). The central aim of this framework is to capture cultural variations in moral rationalization in a way that does not favor any particular view of the good. More specifically, Community and Divinity can be rationalized and considered ultimate moral goods in the same way as liberal individualism (or Autonomy), which psychological theories of moral development had typically framed as the sole ultimate moral good. Through a sophisticated discourse analysis of a Brahmin priest, for example, Shweder and Much (1991) demonstrate that communal ethics reach beyond mere conventionalism and can be grounded in a transcendent Ethic of Community, providing an "alternative version of an objective postconventional moral world" (p. 229). Thus, by proposing three distinct moral ethics and outlining how they develop in different cultural contexts, the Three Ethics approach has provided an important corrective to traditional theories of moral development that emphasized the uniformity of the moral realm. As such, this approach is appealing because it provides a means of identifying similarities in the rational processes underpinning culturally distinct moral systems while also allowing for a great degree of complexity and cultural specificity in various conceptions of the moral domain. Various cultural visions of the good provide unique configurations of Autonomy, Community, and Divinity and fill these ethics out in culturally distinct ways.

Much research has used the three ethics to trace similarities and differences in moral reasoning in different cultural contexts and developmental periods (e.g., Arnett, Ramos, & Jensen, 2001; Guerra & Giner-Sorolla, 2010; Haidt, Koller, & Dias, 1993; Jensen, 1998; Vasquez, Keltner, Ebenbach, *et al.*, 2001). For example, in Shweder and colleagues' original research, they suggested that liberal individualists were more likely to prioritize the principles reflecting Ethics of Autonomy and Community in their moral rationalization than the Ethic of Divinity, whereas Brahmin priests might draw more heavily from Ethics of Divinity and Community than from Autonomy.

A common finding generated by these research endeavors is that, although the three ethics are differentially patterned across individuals from diverse cultural groups, nonetheless, all three ethics can be recognized in all societies and even within the responses of many individuals (e.g., Haidt, Koller, & Dias, 1993; Jensen, 1995, 1997a, 1997b, 2008; Rozin, Lowery, Imada, *et al.*, 1999). Consequently, one implication of these largely quantitative analyses is that the co-occurrence of multiple ethics in moral responses is a common psychological experience. How multiple ethics are psychologically related for individuals as well as how multiple ethics are related developmentally are central questions for the cultural psychology of morality and for the present volume. Our goal in this chapter is to push our understandings of this co-occurrence in new directions and emphasize its importance for a cultural-developmental approach to morality.

Relation of three ethics in moral thinking

The co-occurrence of Autonomy, Community, and Divinity has been empirically examined at various levels of analysis. Most broadly, research has demonstrated ethical co-occurrence at the group level, finding that certain groups may show equally high preference for more than one ethic (Haidt, Koller, & Dias, 1993; Jensen, 1995; Shweder, Much, Mahapatra, *et al.*, 1997). Other research has demonstrated ethical co-occurrence at the level of the individual or even the response. Vasquez, Keltner, Ebenbach, and Banaszynksi's (2001) analysis of moral examples generated by Filipino and American participants demonstrated not only that all three ethics can be given "equal emphasis" within a cultural group, as evidenced in their sample of Filipino responses, but also that ethics can be "infused" within a single response (p. 107). Such ethical infusion was recognized when participants generated examples of one ethic that contained themes from another ethic (e.g., when an example of an auto-nomy breach included references to community themes such as duty, hierarchy, interdependence, or social status).

Guerra and Giner-Sorolla (2010) examined ethical co-occurrence at the individual level by measuring British and Brazilian individuals' degree of endorsement of a series of statements representing each ethic. In both sam-ples, researchers demonstrated positive correlations between various ethics. At minimum, these findings indicate that multiple ethics can be embraced simultaneously by an individual. They also indicate that in certain cultural con-texts, ethics can become linked to each other in an individual's reasoning. For example, Guerra and Giner-Sorolla found that both Brazilian and British partic-ipants' moral endorsements of certain community statements were associated with their endorsements of certain Divinity statements. Additionally, Brazilian participants' moral endorsements of autonomy statements were associated with their endorsements of Divinity statements. In turn, by associating these ethical correlations with cultural orientations, such as vertical and horizontal dimen-sions of individualism and collectivism, these researchers can point toward the particular cultural underpinnings of co-occurring ethics.

These quantitative analyses of ethical co-occurrence can reveal which ethics are likely to co-occur in certain cultural contexts.[2] However, these analyses have limited utility in revealing the dynamic of ethical co-occurrence itself – that is, how co-occurring ethics are related to one another. To our knowledge, there are only a few studies that have examined the relation between co-occurring ethics within individuals' moral reasoning. Arnett, Ramos, and Jensen (2001), in their study of ideologies among emerging adults in the United States, recognized multiple ethics in response to one question among a sizable minority of partic-ipants. Analysis of these qualitative statements indicated two ways that ethics were related in individuals' discourse. For some individuals, ethics appeared in a "mutually reinforcing" relationship (p. 78). In these cases, one ethic was framed as a logical prerequisite for another ethic, such that fulfilling one ethical

---

[2] It is worth noting that these quantitative analyses of ethical distributions largely include group-level comparisons, whereas the methodological approach that we push in this chapter can be much more sensitive to both group-level and individual-level differences in moral thinking.

goal enabled the fulfillment of another. For other individuals, ethics appeared in an "oppositional" relationship, such that justifications coded as one ethic were "explicitly embraced" and used to deny the legitimacy of a justification coded as another ethic. In other words, within the framework of one ethic, another ethic is "disparaged" as a "destructive force" (p. 78). Jensen (1995) also examined qualitative statements involving ethical co-occurrence in her analysis of moral reasoning across the life course among US individuals. Among midlife and older adults, she illustrated how different ethics compounded on one another as participants offered multiple, distinct lines of reasoning. In this way, ethics appeared side by side as parallel justifications to support a moral stance.

As these research examples illustrate, an examination of the relation between ethics requires situating coded justifications in their discursive contexts. This is because it is through various communicative and discursive moves that speakers position ethical justifications in relation to one another. Through using discursive methods to analyze these moments of ethical co-occurrence, this chapter builds on previous research to uncover various relations of ethical co-occurrence in a systematic fashion. Additionally, a more critical goal of this chapter is to propose a more serious consideration of the nature of one of these types of ethical co-occurrence that we call "ethical imbrication." By *imbrication* we are referring to the extent to which these seemingly distinct ethics (in this case Autonomy, Community, and Divinity) come into play in the same place and time in the production of moral discourse. In this way, our use of the term *imbrication* is meant to denote overlap, similarly to the way tiles on a roof overlap and coconstitute one another to make up the entirety of the roof structure. By making ethical imbrication itself an object of analysis in a way that has not been the case thus far, our analyses challenge some of our theoretical and methodological considerations as we engage in cross-cultural and developmental Three Ethics research.

Specifically, our analysis of ethical imbrication challenges firm conceptual distinctions between the three ethics. This kind of "conceptual essentialism" can be implied when cultures (or individuals) are characterized by their distributions of each ethic. Such analytic approaches treat the three Ethics of Autonomy, Community, and Divinity as distinct entities. These approaches ask what we can say about group differences given an assumed moral domain. Our focus, by contrast, is about the moral domain itself within these group discourses. Thus, while we find these distinctions to be analytically useful as Weberian ideal types, when it comes to analyzing moral discourse, our analysis of ethical imbrication suggests ways in which these ideas so deeply interpenetrate one another that it calls into question the empirical utility of these distinctions in characterizing a cultural moral code on its own terms. In this way, our purpose is to argue for a space in which the mutual distinctiveness of the three ethics can be called into question in the analysis of moral discourse. What our approach offers is a close phenomenological account of a moral system under analysis that seeks to avoid conceptual essentialism, such as imposing an a priori structure of the moral domain that may not provide a good fit to the moral domains revealed in the discourse of our ethnographic interlocutors.

This conceptual essentialism can occur on at least two levels. On the one hand, the analyst may conceptualize certain moral categories as philosophically or empirically distinct. This kind of essentialism can be implied when cultures (or individuals) are characterized by their distributions of each ethic. On the other hand, the individuals producing the moral discourse may essentialize certain moral ideals or concepts in the ways that they conceptually carve up the moral domain according to various ethnotheoretical perspectives on morality and ethics. This chapter deals more substantively with the former type of conceptual essentialism (that imbued by the analyst), while also suggesting some ways to more effectively document ethnotheoretical conceptual essentialism. The Three Ethics framework has already built into it a cultural flexibility by allowing for different configurations (both in kind and quantity) of the three ethics in culturally distinct visions of the good. We advocate furthering this flexibility by suggesting that close discursive analysis of ethical co-occurrence opens up new avenues for understanding the ways that convergent and divergent ethical concepts are discursively wielded in the production of particular moral discourses in distinct social contexts.

Method: discourse analysis of moral vignettes

As mentioned above, the examples of moral reasoning that we present here were derived from interviews with Hmong families in the United States and Thailand (Hickman, 2011) and American evangelical families in Boston (DiBianca Fasoli, 2013). Each of us developed a series of culturally relevant moral vignettes based on our prior ethnographic work with each community. These vignettes were designed to portray realistic instances of moral breaches relevant to each community, and in some cases the moral breaches came directly from ethnographic observations in these communities.[3] In each project, vignettes were followed by a series of prompts (asked verbally by Hickman, presented in written form by DiBianca Fasoli) designed to assess various dimensions of participants' moral reasoning. These included the participant's moral evaluation of the breach, the relative degree of the breach, justification for the moral stance taken, and whether the participant would condone or suggest interference in the breach.[4] These questions were built on prior research

---

[3] Some vignettes were adapted from Shweder, Mahapatra, & Miller (1987) but only when the situations represented in the vignettes were deemed ethnographically relevant.

[4] Examples of these included "Would it be OK for someone to try and make Sarah help, or is it up to Sarah whether she helps or not?" as well as "What if no one knew this had been done. It was done in private or secretly. Would it be wrong then?" The complete protocols can be provided by the authors on request.

utilizing this vignette approach (Haidt, Koller, & Dias, 1993; Jensen, 1995, 1998; Miller & Bersoff, 1998; Miller, Bersoff, & Harwood, 1990; Shweder, Mahapatra, & Miller, 1987).

Vignettes were presented to Hmong parent-child dyads separately in two subsamples: a set of nine transnational kinship groups with members in both Thailand and the United States[5] and a set of ten Hmong families living in the midwestern United States.[6] In order to harness naturally occurring speech genres in the production of moral discourse, the vignettes and discussion were framed according to ethnographic research on communicative practices and moral discourse in each community (compare to Briggs, 1986; see Hickman, 2011, and DiBianca Fasoli, 2013, for a more comprehensive account of these methods). In the Hmong sample, a speech genre wherein Hmong members of a community narrate and comment on moral tales was mimicked in order to collect quasi-naturalistic discourse surrounding the predetermined vignettes. Among the American evangelical sample, vignettes were presented to sixteen parent-child dyads (children's ages ranged from 6 to 9 years), who responded to vignettes together, without an interviewer present. Specifically, dyads were asked to read and respond to each prompt aloud. They were told that the goal of these prompts was to generate conversation and thus to move to subsequent prompts when they felt their conversation was exhausted. This procedure was designed to elicit moral reasoning in the context of parent-child verbal interactions, taken as a window onto socialization processes of moral reasoning.

Analysis of each data set began by using the Three Ethics framework to analyze the distribution of the three ethics by different subgroups and, subsequently, to identify and extract instances of moral discourse reflecting multiple ethics. Hickman utilized cultural discourse analysis (Quinn, 2005a, 2005b; Strauss, 2005) – based on cultural model and cultural schema theory (e.g., Shore, 1996; Strauss & Quinn, 1999) – to analyze the nature of co-occurring ethics and to point out when such instances signaled imbrication. DiBianca Fasoli utilized a form of language interaction analysis, which draws on the methods of talk-in-interaction and conversation analysis and has been fruitfully used by researchers to analyze the making of morality in social interaction (Fasulo, Loyd, & Padiglione, 2007; Fung & Chen, 2001; Sterponi, 2003). She employed these analytic methods to examine the sequential organization of coded justifications in parent-child verbal interaction.

---

[5] Parents' ages ranged from 39 to 85 years, with a mean of 55 years, and children's ages ranged from 18 to 37 years, with a mean of 24 years. Hickman separately interviewed a parent and one of that parent's children in each kinship group in each location. The data in Table 7.1 come from this first subsample, but both are used for Hickman's (2011) analysis of intergenerational patterns of Hmong moral discourse.

[6] Parents' ages ranged from 37 to 65 years with a mean of 52 years, and children's ages ranged from 18 to 23 years, with a mean of 20 years.

Table 7.1 *Frequency of ethical co-occurrence in Hmong and American Evangelical moral discourse*

	Hmong sample		American Evangelical sample	
	# Vignettes	% of total	# Prompts	% of total
Autonomy alone	13	6.6	–	–
Community alone	39	19.7	–	–
Divinity alone	21	10.6	27	43.5
Subtotal no co-occurrence	73	36.9	27	43.5
Autonomy + Community (co-occurring)	82	41.4	–	–
Autonomy + Divinity (co-occurring)	7	3.5	25	71.4
Community + Divinity (co-occurring)	18	9.1	5	14.3
Autonomy + Community + Divinity (co-occurring)	18	9.1	5	14.3
Subtotal co-occurrence	125	63.1	35	56.5
Total	198		62	

How prevalent is ethical co-occurrence?

In both analyses of the present data sets, instances in which ethics co-occurred in participants' moral reasoning were common. Hickman (2011) examined co-occurrence at the level of the vignette, using the whole of moral discourse produced in response to each vignette as a unit of analysis. When employing the Jensen (2004) coding manual for the three ethics, analysis suggests that in the majority of vignettes (63.1 percent) respondents employed justifications from more than one ethic. In other words, there were only 73 out of 198 vignettes presented to participants for which a single ethic was coded in the participant's resulting moral discourse.[7] Table 7.1 parses out the patterns for each ethic, giving the raw number of vignette responses where each ethic was coded alone versus when it was coded along with another ethic. In the majority of moral discourse prompted by each vignette, participants utilized these ethics in concert with others.

DiBianca Fasoli's analysis focused on the Ethic of Divinity, as the original research question was to understand the socialization of spiritual concepts in moral thinking among evangelical Christian families. Using the Jensen (2004) manual to code justifications at the level of the prompt, 62 prompt responses that included Divinity were identified (from a possible 240 prompt responses),

---

[7] There were 6 vignettes in addition to the 198 for which no discernible ethic was coded using the Jensen manual. Interrater reliability indices and analysis indicated decent reliability and are fully described in Hickman (2011).

and all other justifications that occurred in these prompt responses were coded (see also Appendix A, this volume). The results reported in Table 7.1 suggest that in parent-child verbal interactions, children are just as likely to encounter Divinity principles in relation to other ethics (56.5 percent) as they are to encounter them independently (43.5 percent), even at the level of the prompt.

Together, these analyses suggest that ethical co-occurrence appears frequently in the moral reasoning of our American evangelical and Hmong participants. Although the frequency of such co-occurrence may vary from community to community, its prevalence in these two distinct samples suggests that the phenomenon is worth examining in greater detail.

Forms of ethical co-occurrence

Given that individuals use multiple ethics in their moral reasoning, the next question is to determine how individuals are relating those ethics in their moral reasoning. We suggest three distinct forms of ethical co-occurrence that we identified using the analytic categories of Autonomy, Community, and Divinity. Below we provide a brief overview of each of these three forms and then present cultural discourse analysis of examples of moral reasoning of Hmong participants. In particular, we use ethnographic findings to demonstrate how instances of ethical co-occurrence may signal ethical imbrication.

We label the three forms of ethical co-occurrence that we recognized "parallel justifications," "divergent justifications," and "imbricated justifications." (1) Co-occurrence as *parallel justifications* entails the use of multiple lines of moral discourse that can be demonstrably represented as distinct rationales (e.g., Autonomy and Community), yet they converge on the same moral judgment. In other words, they compound on one another in order to provide a more expanded rationale for a singular moral assessment. Distinct from this type of co-occurrence, (2) *divergent justifications* refers to instances that we interpret as a kind of moral-cognitive dissonance. In these cases, our interlocutors employed moral discourse representing discrete ethics (e.g., Autonomy and Community), but each toward distinct and often incompatible moral ends. In other words, our interlocutors felt conflicted about their moral judgment and utilized different lines of reasoning that pushed them in different directions with regard to their moral assessment. (3) Co-occurrence as *imbricated justifications* denotes instances in which interlocutors could be recognized as employing elements of multiple lines of moral discourse (e.g., Autonomy and Community), woven into a single rationale, such that it becomes impossible to extract the autonomy dimensions or the community dimensions from the discourse that was produced without the original rationale falling apart. This last set of cases points toward a kind of integration of analytic categories that is so deep that it suggests that the analytic distinction between ethics is not one that is necessarily meaningful in participants' moral outlooks.

    Parallel justifications. As an example of a parallel justification, one participant in the United States responded in the following way when presented with the following vignette:

A poor man went to the hospital after being seriously hurt in an accident. At the hospital they refused to treat him because he could not afford to pay.

While describing why he thinks the doctors and medical staff in this situation were morally wrong in not providing treatment to the individual in the vignette, a 64-year-old Hmong man responded (in Hmong):[8]

P: . . . the right thing to do is that they [the doctors] must help the person as much as   1

they can, because it is their *responsibility. It's their job.*[9] And they need to know what   2

the sickness is, and how to fix it so they must help fix it. Even if there isn't enough   3

money for the doctors or medical staff, they must still help! If they don't help, then   4

it's like – if they are able to help but they – he doesn't have money to pay them and   5

now they won't fix him, then it's like – it's like they're killing that person and   6

disposing of them, because they [the doctors] are the ones who save people. This is   7

what I think. But who knows if I am correct! (smiles and laughs)[10]   8

I: (Laughs) So you think that perhaps they are wrong?   9

P: I think they are wrong.   10

I: This wrong, how heavy is the violation? Would you say it is not wrong, just a   11

little wrong, quite wrong, or extremely wrong?   12

P: I think it must be extremely wrong.   13

I: Why is that?   14

P: Because this is a poor person. If one compares it now to the law of heaven, one   15

can show grace, let's say this poor person didn't do anything wrong to you, but just   16

comes to you sick but doesn't have money to pay you, and doesn't have relatives to   17

help, and you don't heal him, then – if you do this then you did not show grace to   18

him [the poor person], and perhaps heaven *will not show grace to you either.*   19

---

[8] Transcripts of the vignettes and the responses in the original language are available from Hickman upon request. P = Participant, I = Interviewer (Hickman), and a dash (–) indicates a slight pause in all of these transcripts that follow, which in many cases represents a hesitation or discursive change of direction.

[9] The term used for both "responsibility" and "job" here is *txoj hauj lwm*, which he repeated twice with emphasis. This term denotes both a line of work and the responsibilities of a certain social position, and the translation here reflects both of these senses.

[10] This is a culturally typical qualification that discursively marks the humility of his position.

Utilizing the Jensen (2004) coding scheme, the emphasis this person placed on the place in society of doctors and their role and responsibility to heal the sick was coded as Community. In line 2 he emphatically repeated that it is the doctors' responsibility in society, and again in line 7. However, this respondent went on to provide a further justification that invokes "the law of heaven" (*kev cai ntuj*) and the karmic principle of just desert (lines 15–19). While this participant invoked both a community-based responsibility (i.e., the essential role of doctors in society) as well as a divinity-based response, these multiple ethics are appealed toward the same moral end – the doctors must treat the man regardless of his ability to pay. In this sense, these parallel justifications converge on the same moral assessment, while providing distinct rationales that can clearly be coded under different ethics in the Three Ethics framework.

Compared to the other forms of ethical co-occurrence we discuss below, parallel justifications can be accounted for by current methodologies most easily. For example, the common practice of computing the total frequencies of each ethic in the moral profile of a given individual or group does not require only a single ethic to be at play in response to a single item (e.g., vignette or question). This form of co-occurrence is perhaps the most commonly noted in the literature and has been observed and documented by Jensen (1995) and Arnett, Ramos, and Jensen (2001) in American samples. Jensen (1995) argues that with age, midlife and older Americans "become more concerned with the goals of the community and with integrating the self into a natural and sacred order" (p. 85). In other words, later in life they begin to compound the Ethic of Autonomy with Community or Divinity in their moral reasoning. Arnett, Ramos, and Jensen (2001) also described examples of ethical co-occurrence, including how some emerging adults regarded autonomy as a foundation for the development of healthy communal relationships. Our analyses build on these findings to demonstrate the work that is being done by individuals when parallel justifications factor into a person's moral discourse. Among other things, parents can use parallel justifications to socialize their children into particular modes of moral thinking, thus providing important developmental pathways to intended moral outlooks in culturally particular visions of the good. We address this point in greater detail below.

Divergent justifications. Divergent moral justifications occur when an individual seems to be conflicted about the ultimate moral judgment at hand, with different ethics pulling the individual's rationales in different directions. We argue that this can be characterized as a kind of moral-cognitive dissonance. As an example, consider responses to the following vignette, both by young Hmong males living in the United States:

A letter arrived addressed to a 14-year-old son. Before the boy returned home, his father opened the letter and read it.

One 23-year-old Hmong man responded (in English):

P: The father still has the right to know what is it, who is it that – the son is still   1
    fifteen years old so he's still a minor, so he can't be independent yet. So if the
    father   2
    reads it, if there's a problem, then he can solve it, then they can solve it.   3

. . .

I: So what if the son was eighteen years old?   4
P: Eighteen years old? Then really, then it's too the point, I feel it gets to the
    point   5
    where the father has to slowly step back, slowly step back. If it's a letter that
    says   6
    maybe an – it's from the college or university, then maybe the father can just
    let that   7
    one slide and give it to him, the son, to look at. Then that's okay, I feel that
    that's –   8
I: What if it was a personal letter?   9
P: If it's a personal letter, let's say, um, maybe, his girlfriend maybe? Hypothet-
    ically   10
    if it's his girlfriend, I think he should also let it slide, too. Let it slide just a
    little bit.   11
    But, for the first few times he see that, he should at least take a look at it to
    see if   12
    there is anything serious such as –   13
I: Even if he is eighteen years old?   14
P: Even if he's eighteen years old. Because what if the letter says that, you got
    me   15
    pregnant, you've got to take care of me, then the father, if the son keeps that
    a secret,   16
    then that's going to be a situation.   17

. . .

I: Is it a sin? [*Nws puas muaj txim?*][11]   18
P: Uh, in this – in this context here, uh, no. Because the father really take – the
    goal   19
    of the father is really to keep watch of the son, so that – to keep him safe, to
    keep   20
    him on track so that he can become a good person. I think that's what he –
    That's   21
    what it does.   22

In response to the same vignette, another 18-year-old Hmong man explained (in English):

---

[11] When interviewing bilingual Hmong youth in the United States, Hickman would give this question in both Hmong and English in order to maintain the same sense as his interviews conducted solely in Hmong.

P: because it's, well, his father should have permission to like – *I know it's a
   privacy*   1
   thing, but if it's important to his parents, his father should be able to check
   his   2
   personal things. He is the household leader anyway.   3

   . . .

P: Well, if it's personal letter, I think he could uh – uh – he'll probably – I
   don't –   4
   I don't really think it's – I think it's okay, because it's – the father probably
   will   5
   understand if it's a personal letter and go back and give it to him.   6
I: And what if the father reads it before the son reads it, is that wrong?   7
P: I think it's – as far if he'd read like a personal letter, because he should
   understand   8
   we have our personal rights, besides just a family thing, you know? So, also
   that's   9
   like the other side of that.   10
I: So if the father's reading a letter to the son, and it's a personal letter, then it is 11
   wrong?   12
P: Yeah, it is wrong. That's a privacy thing. We all have, you know, an outside
   life of   13
   the house. It's okay if we get [them at] this point, but I mean sometimes you
   don't   14
   want to get families involved in [some of these things].   15

In both of these responses there are two distinct and competing ethics at play.
On the one hand, the father is seen as having a particularly important role of
watching over and guiding his son toward being "a good person" (line 21 in the
first transcript). Other participants phrased this in terms of protecting the son
against his own ignorance and making sure the father is able to help the son
resolve any troubles in his life. The key here is that the role of the father as a
father vis-à-vis his son is foregrounded, and this hierarchical role relationship
is the ethical principle that grounds this argument (i.e., "he is the household
leader anyway," line 3 of the second transcript, or the argument in lines 5–6 of
the first transcript that as the son ages his father needs to "step back" and grant
the son his independence). Such reasoning can be recognized as an Ethic of
Community. On the other hand, the rights to privacy of the son – such as the
privacy of a letter addressed to him – is painted as a competing ethic (i.e., "We
all have, you know, an outside life of the house," lines 13–14 in the second
transcript). This notion of privacy clearly falls under the rubric of Autonomy.

One can see the back-and-forth in these responses. In the first transcript the
speaker is working out a compromise between the responsibilities of the father
and the autonomy of the son throughout his response. The second transcript
makes this ambivalence particularly clear. The phrase "also that's like the other

side of that" (lines 9–10) and the hesitations and discursive course corrections are all telling. In lines 4–5 the dashes represent the constant changing of direction in his discourse. He also starts his statement with the qualification "well." Both of these discursive characteristics are representative of the ambivalence that this young Hmong man is experiencing as he weighs the competing ethics in this situation.

Hickman discusses the developmental significance of this moral-cognitive dissonance elsewhere (see Hickman, 2011, for an ethnographic description of the lives of these youth and an intergenerational-transnational comparison of patterns in moral discourse), but for present it is sufficient to note that these youth did manifest higher levels of this type of moral-cognitive dissonance than their parents did. Critically, these young Hmong were born right about the time that their parents resettled to the United States as refugees from Laos. One explanation of this increased moral ambivalence for the younger generation, then, may be that they are struggling with competing moral goods offered by their parents and peers. In other words, they are dealing with the competing demands of Hmong moral models handed to them by their parents and relatives versus those that are more prevalent in American society (such as their non-Hmong peers) and more typical of American emerging adults in particular (see Jensen, 1995). This is an important dynamic for understanding the moral worlds of these migrant youth, and it suggests a more complicated picture of the development of moral identity (see Hardy, Walker, Olsen, *et al.*, 2013). Critically, this trend would be overlooked by an approach that stops at coding the mere presence of the three ethics rather than analyzing the particular dynamic of competing moral goods in the discourse. The key methodological point here is that employing the Three Ethics framework within a cultural discourse analysis reveals psychocultural underpinnings of moral motives – in this case a manifest moral ambivalence that would otherwise be missed.

Ethical imbrication, or coconstitution of "distinct" ethics. Beyond parallel and divergent justifications, we also found many instances across our data sets where the analytical categories of Autonomy, Community, and Divinity co-occurred but could not be extricated from one another in the participants' moral discourse in a culturally meaningful way. In the following example, the vignette which was used to elicit moral speech went as follows:

A father and son lived together in their village. One day, the father committed a serious moral transgression that made him lose face, and made the son very embarrassed. The son decided to move to another village, and he changed both his given name and his clan name, so no one would know whose son he is. Is a son that does this morally wrong?

In an interview in Thailand, a 48-year-old Hmong father, whom we will call Txawj Pheej, responded to this vignette in the following way after indicating that the son in this situation was wrong and should be corrected (the interview was in Hmong):

I: What would you say to him?   1
P: I would say to him that those people are your mother and father that gave birth
      to   2
    you! (emphatic intonation) You have to just take responsibility for
      admitting /   3
    confessing (*lees*) them to be your parents. One must tell him [the son] this.
      And, he is   4
    just a little mad (*chim*), right, just a little mad, then say to him – he still has to
      accept   5
    his mother and father also, as he is only a little ashamed (*txaj muag me me
      xwb*).   6
I: But what if he says that "I can't accept them because I am too embarrassed.
      My   7
    father has lost face, I have also lost face." If he says this and that he just wants
      to run   8
    away, what would you say to him?   9
P: Um, even if he says that, he can't do it. Because they are his parents and they 10
    raised him, so he can't do that. One must tell him that he must absolutely own
      up to   11
    them.   12
I: Oh.   13
P: Being ashamed, losing face, is not as important as the fact that one's parents   14
    provide one's fate and fortune (*txoj hmoov*) – which is more important.   15
I: Is that right?   16
P: Yes, [this is] much more important.   17

    . . .

I: Is this a violation of social convention or a violation of heaven's law [i.e.,
      natural   18
    law]?[12]   19
P: [It's] a sin against – heaven's law.   20
I: This is a transgression of heaven's law – of heaven's law just a bit, is that
      right?   21
P: Yes. It's a minor violation of heavenly law.   22
I: Why is it a violation of heavenly law, but not just a matter of social convention?
                                                                              23
P: Because he is not thinking sufficiently – not thinking about everything –
      about   24
    his parents that raised him, which is the most important thing for fate and
      fortune   25
    (txoj hmoov).   26

---

[12] The phrasing of these terms (heaven's law and social convention, respectively) that was used
    in the interview in Hmong can most literally be translated as "the way/law of heaven" (*kev cai
    ntuj*) or "the way/law/customs of people" (*kev cai tib neeg*).

I: Oh.   27
P: So if you don't accept the wrong that your parents did – Doing something
        wrong,   28
    whoever did it, will only hurt that person.   29
I: Uh-huh.   30
P: So if your parents do something wrong and you are not going to accept them,
        that   31
    is not right. Wherever you run to, you shouldn't change your last name. You
        should   32
    remember who your parents are – They are these people.   33
I: Uh.   34
P: Doing this, you won't wrong the heavens.   35

On the one hand, the behavioral prescription here is that the son should respect and honor his parents because of their relationship to him and his filial obligation to them (lines 2–3). This seems to fit squarely under an Ethic of Community. On the other hand, what Txawj Pheej is marking here is the importance of the son's fate or fortune, as mediated by his parents (lines 14–15) and the potential impact that their influence will have on his interests. The issue here is that one's selfish interest and ultimate welfare is tied up in one's communal and kinship obligations and, further, that these moral obligations are based on an ontology that fits squarely under the Ethic of Divinity. That is, the welfare of the soul (both the parents' and the son's) here is indistinguishable from one's "secular" interests that might be stressed under an Ethic of Autonomy. Third, all of this is based on a divine ontology, namely, the conception of ancestors and their ability to mediate the fate or fortune of the self, as well as the conceptions of the eternal life course and life and death more broadly.

The most fundamental point to be made here is that what Txawj Pheej is doing is not simply negotiating between competing ethics in his moral assessment of the son's actions here. Rather, at least in this instance, he is expressing a deontological stance that contains essential elements from all three ethics. If the assumptions of any one of these ethics were minimized or extracted from Txawj Pheej's rationale, his moral argument would disintegrate. Without the Ethic of Autonomy operating here, the son would not have as significant of a motivation to follow through with his filial obligation. In fact, Txawj Pheej implicitly argues here that the benefits to the personal preferences of the son are a primary reason for why he should respect his parents (the phrasing in lines 14–15 and 24–26 is undergirded by this assumption), despite any personal issues of shame or suffering (lines 5–6). The Ethic of Community is even more obvious and apparent in this example, but without the Ethic of Divinity and a metaphysical understanding of how elders and ancestors mediate one's own well-being, the basis for the personal incentive to be pious would also fall apart. In sum, Ethics of Autonomy, Community, and Divinity work in concert to fill out this particular moral rationale. Although they may seem like principles that work in opposite directions, at least in some instances, this example of Hmong moral discourse depends explicitly on two or more of these ideal types.

Other aspects of Hmong metaphysics and ancestral beliefs make this point even more apparent. As described in detail elsewhere (Hickman, 2011, in press), a Hmong view of the life course extends one's existence and filial obligation far beyond the supposed barrier of death. Ancestral rituals involve intimate interactions with deceased ancestors that mirror living relationships, and these ancestral rites are even anticipated in informal rites while elders are still alive. In this context of a Hmong ethnotheory of the life course, it does not make much sense to make a strong distinction between the kinship dimensions of an Ethic of Community, on the one hand, and an Ethic of Divinity that concerns the transmigration of souls to ancestral villages, on the other. Consequently, in coding systems that make such sharp distinctions, it would seem that once an ancestor dies, one's filial obligation to that ancestor turns from communal to divine. We argue that from the standpoint of a Hmong ethnotheory of the life course, this is a fairly arbitrary distinction.

In this section we have sought to illustrate various forms of ethical co-occurrence by presenting cultural discourse analysis of examples of moral reasoning from Hickman's (2011, in press) larger ethnographic study. We argue that trends in ethical co-occurrence itself can tell an important story about the moral outlooks of people from varying cultural backgrounds that analyses of the mere distribution of ethics cannot. We further argue that analyses of ethical co-occurrence can help researchers see where these analytic categories do not represent meaningful categorical distinctions in the moral outlook of research participants. At the same time, however, what we hope our analysis has illustrated is how one can reconstruct the moral outlook of participants in culturally meaningful terms through employing these categories within a cultural discourse analysis, in conjunction with rich ethnographic data. In other words, the Three Ethics framework provides a critical epistemological means of discovering ethical imbrication and other forms of ethical co-occurrence. That is, even if the theoretical separation of the three ethics does not map exactly onto the emic worldviews of participants, this framework provides a good heuristic and starting point for detecting differences and filling out those worldviews in their cultural specificity. Researchers should take advantage of the utility of this framework for investigating cross-cultural patterns in moral thought but ought not to overdetermine the extent to which these theoretical distinctions inhere in the actual moral discourse that researchers collect and analyze. In sum, the interactions *between* the three ethics provide critical insights into both cultural and developmental moral dynamics. It is to the latter that we now turn.

Ontogenetic implications of ethical co-occurrence (or the developmental story)

DiBianca Fasoli's data on Divinity reasoning illustrates how a close language-interaction analysis of parent-child interaction can be used to examine the socializing potential of ethical co-occurrence. In this section, we highlight what such an analysis can tell us about the processes through which moral thinking may develop in particular cultural contexts.

In the parent-child interaction data, instances in which Divinity co-occurred with other ethics typically followed a common format, such that parents introduced the justification coded as Divinity and children contributed justifications coded as Autonomy. Analysis of these instances suggests three ways Autonomy and Divinity were typically related in these interactions. Together, these relations suggest a process whereby parents socialized their children into an Ethic of Divinity by reframing children's self-generated Autonomy reasoning.

The first way that Divinity-coded and Autonomy-coded justifications were related to one another was in opposition. Parent-child conversations created such an oppositional relationship when parents used Divinity principles to counter their child's Autonomy principles, which were typically Autonomy principles of exchange relations based on reciprocity or social contracts. This type of co-occurrence was recognized in the interactions of 31 percent of the dyads. In these instances, parents did not disagree with their child's judgment of the action as right or wrong but rather with the child's justification for that judgment. For example, one father-son dyad negotiated why they thought it was wrong for the protagonist of the vignette, Jack, to refuse to give some money to Sam, a classmate who had lost his lunch money:

CHILD: Because it [giving some money] would be fair,	1
even and fair if, um, Jack had given him some of his money for lunch.	2
DAD: Well, sometimes you do things and you don't get anything back, right?	3
Sometimes you do things, ah, just to be helpful,	4
just because God is leading you to help.	5

The child justified his position by appealing to equality and fairness – concerns both classified under the Ethic of Autonomy. However, the father voiced doubt about these appeals when he said "well" to introduce his own position. He continued by providing a different line of reasoning, one that evaluated the moral status of the act in terms of God. By appealing to spiritual concerns to discourage concerns relating to equality and fairness, the parent can be recognized as conveying that Divinity-based reasoning is a more appropriate ground for moral judgment than certain Autonomy principles are in this case.

A very different relation between Autonomy and Divinity was available to children when parents legitimated their child's Autonomy reasoning through further appealing to Divinity principles. In these instances, which were apparent in the reasoning of 50 percent of dyads, parents reinforced children's Autonomy-coded evaluations through using Divinity-coded justifications as an additional layer of meaning in the situation.

To illustrate, consider the conversation between 7-year-old Rachel and her mother Laurel as they responded to the Lunch Story (described above). Laurel read the standardized prompt, asking her daughter whether she thought refusing to give money in this situation was a sin:

RACHEL: Yes	1
LAUREL: How come?	2
R: Because she was saying, "no I don't want you to have my money,	3
because it's my money	4
and I want to get all these extra things"	5
and she could've actually had food than having no food at all.	6
L: Mhm that's right, that's right	7
L: And, the, do you remember there's another thing,	8
that Jesus says about feeding the hungry.	9
R: Huh!?	10
L: He says something like, when you feed . . .	11
when you help the least of these,	12
when you give someone hungry something to eat,	13
it's like you're feeding me.	14
He asks us to take care of others.	15

In this exchange, we once again see the child appealing to principles recognized as Autonomy, namely, self-interest and the interest and welfare of another individual. First, in lines 3–5, Rachel cast self-interest on the part of the protagonist as selfish. She accomplished this by embedding the protagonist's words in her speech, thereby transforming those words into evidence to support her own stance. Within the reported speech, Rachel placed emphatic stress on "you" and "my," highlighting the contrast between potential giver and receiver. This contrast was amplified in line 5 when she placed stress on the word "extra" and paired it with the word "all."

Second, Rachel described the consequences of self-interest on another's welfare through an implicit counterfactual statement in line 6. Here, she evoked a world where the classmate "could've actually had food." She then explicitly contrasted the imagined world and the current world such that in the imagined world the classmate "had food" while in the current world she had "no food at all." Meanwhile, in the current world, the character Sarah had "all" these things, which Rachel saw as "extras."

In response, the parent appealed to concerns that were coded under the Ethic of Divinity: she first evoked Jesus as a speaker (line 9) and then directly reported his words (lines 11–14). Within this reported speech, she also evoked Jesus as a recipient of giving, such that giving food to another is like feeding Jesus. To justify this claim, Laurel appealed to the authority of Jesus by attributing the claim itself to Jesus. Importantly, Laurel did not position this line of reasoning in opposition to her daughter's Autonomy reasoning but rather as coexisting, suggested through her use of the conjunction "and," the label "another thing" (line 8), and her affirmation "that's right, that's right" (line 7).

In this exchange, both Rachel and Laurel mobilized the speech of others as evidence to support their stances. However, Laurel appealed to the words of Jesus, presumably a higher authority than the words of Sarah, the potential giver. Moreover, while Rachel imagined alternate possible worlds of literal givers and receivers through her counterfactual, Laurel moved to a symbolic world that evoked Jesus as a third actor in giving. Thus, rather than solely an act of material exchange between the giver and receiver – as her daughter suggested – the mother constituted helping as also a symbolic act of giving to Jesus. These were not necessarily in opposition but simply different layers of meaning – a kind of strategic deployment of parallel justifications toward the ends of the socialization goals of the parent.

Finally, a third and similar way in which justifications coded as Autonomy and Divinity were related in parent-child interactions was when parents scaffolded their child's Divinity reasoning through Autonomy reasoning. In these instances, parents first prompted children to interpret the protagonist's action in terms of self-interest versus other-interest (Autonomy) and then introduced God (Divinity) to judge the moral worth of the Autonomy-based interpretation. In other words, an Autonomy-based *interpretation* of an event was used to arrive at a Divinity-based *evaluation* of that event. In the following excerpt, the mother, Martha, invited her daughter, Lydia, to participate in this logic by first prompting her to interpret the situation in terms of self- and other-interest. The excerpt opens with Lydia reasoning why it was wrong to refuse to comfort a neighbor before surgery:

LYDIA: [It was wrong] because she could see that movie anytime.	1
Her friend only has one life, she, this is the only time, she can see her friend do that.	2
She can't just take a time machine and – go back.	3
That's the only, that's a one in life time. That movie she could see anytime.	4
MARTHA: But she had broken her leg and was going to the hospital	5
and that was happening then and there, right?	6
L: Yeah.	7
M: So you're saying she should right at that moment do what was right.	8

L: Yeah.   9
M: And put off the movie.   10
    Who is she, who is she thinking about if she goes with her friend to the
        hospital?   11
L: Her friend.   12
M: And who is she thinking about if she goes to the movie?   13
L: Herself.   14
M: Herself.   15
    And what does God ask us to do?   16
L: Do unto others as they would have you do unto you. As you would have them
        do unto   17
    you.   18
M: Mmm.   19
    Or to serve others, right?   20

In this excerpt, the daughter first appealed to the uniqueness and urgency of the opportunity to help (lines 1–4) to justify her stance. After some clarification in lines 5–10, the mother then introduced additional considerations, namely, principles of self-interest and other-interest (subcategories of Autonomy in Jensen's 2004 coding manual). She introduced these considerations as questions, inviting her daughter to interpret the situation in terms of self-interest and other-interest (lines 11–14). The mother then introduced God's interests (Divinity), again in the form of a question she posed to her daughter (line 16). In this way, the mother used her daughter's understanding of certain Autonomy and Divinity principles to scaffold her daughter's expression of those principles as moral justifications. In doing so, she suggested that the relative moral worth of two Autonomy principles (self-interest and other-interest) were to be decided in terms of Divinity principles (God's wants and desires).

Together, these data suggest that parents used spiritual concerns to selectively encourage and discourage a set of concerns recognized as Autonomy. Specifically, the Autonomy concerns of "reciprocity" and "self-interest" were devalued, but "other-interest" was elevated to divine status. Consistent with these findings, Jensen (Chapter 8, this volume) found that the use of reciprocity in evangelical Christians' moral reasoning declined across the life course, such that it was used frequently by children, minimally by adolescents, and not at all by adults. The current findings suggest the processes that produce this pattern – namely, that such concerns may be cast by socializing agents as "morally objectionable" within an Ethic of Divinity.

At the same time, however, such opposing relations between Autonomy and Divinity represent only a partial view of their potential relations. Other findings of this study demonstrated several other types of Divinity-Autonomy co-occurrence that were not opposing. Specifically, parents appealed to God and Jesus to legitimate their children's appeals to "other-interest," and parents also scaffolded their children's spiritual reasoning through "other-interest" and "self-interest." Such findings would explain the corresponding rise of Divinity and decline in Autonomy among highly religious individuals as due to increasing scope of Divinity over Autonomy rather than solely their opposition. These findings suggest that Autonomy may decline over the life course as it becomes increasingly superficial or proximal, that is, as it is encompassed by the increasing scope of Divinity as an ultimate moral end.

These patterns of Autonomy-Divinity relations have implications for understanding the ontogenetic origins of the three ethics in moral reasoning. For example, one way that parents may socialize their children into an Ethic of Divinity is by building on their Autonomy reasoning. From this perspective, children come to see Divinity principles as relevant for moral reasoning through their initial link with Autonomy principles. Thus, rather than envisioning Divinity as having its own, distinct trajectory of development, it may be that Divinity is ontogenetically rooted in Autonomy. Consequently, in this community, Divinity may already be tied to and encompass certain forms of Autonomy reasoning when it emerges in individuals' self-generated moral reasoning. In other words, Divinity may emerge in moral reasoning already "imbricated" with Autonomy in this community.

In sum, discursive analysis of ethical co-occurrence in parent-child interactions suggests specific dynamics between ethics, namely, Autonomy and Divinity. The specific ways in which Divinity and Autonomy co-occurred in these interactions was nuanced, but in all cases, a relationship between Autonomy principles and Divinity principles was made available for children. Attending to such moments of ethical co-occurrence provides a means of deessentializing these ethics in order to illuminate culturally grounded patterns of the development of moral thinking.

Conclusions: methodological and theoretical treatments of ethical imbrication

Let us conclude by briefly sketching some implications for analyzing moral discourse that extend from our argument against conceptual essentialism of the three ethics. We agree with philosophers Isaiah Berlin and David Wong that the negotiation between incommensurable goods constitutes an essential dimension that varies between cultural moral codes and that this incommensurability does not discount the ultimate rationality of any particular system (Gray, 1996; Wong, 2014). Rejecting the assumption of commensurability in the moral domain – that is, that all rationally defensible moral goods can be fulfilled simultaneously – allows for immense cultural variation in the moral domain without the conclusion that one system is more rationally coherent than another. It was in this spirit that the critiques that led to the Three Ethics approach first challenged our understanding of moral development in different cultural contexts (Shweder, 1990; Shweder, Mahapatra, & Miller, 1987). However, the conceptual essentialism implicated in some research on moral reasoning limits the types of cultural complexity that can be detected in the moral systems and developmental trajectories of our ethnographic interlocutors. This cuts against the grain of the spirit of the original critique that brought about the Three Ethics framework. Crucially, conceptual essentialism leads the analyst to give priority to abstract ethical categories that may preclude us from seeing the full vision of the good that members of a given society themselves may recognize or implicitly operate from. We therefore propose new directions of research that emphasize analyzing moral discourse for parallel justifications, divergent justifications, and ethical imbrication. Methods that accomplish such analyses will be more sensitive to culturally divergent views of the moral domain and the developmental trajectories that are engendered by them. These new directions offer ways of revealing the cultural logics that conceptually underlie particular constellations of ethics.

On the one hand, we need to be open to the possibility that these categories are often inextricably linked, can coconstitute one another, or even provide developmental precursors to one another in the cultural moral codes of our interlocutors – what we have termed "ethical imbrication." Thus, given the ways that our Hmong and American evangelical interlocutors frame their moral arguments, we are compelled to question contemporary trends of conceptual essentialism and consider the ways in which analytically distinct ethical goods can in fact be imbricated as part and parcel of the same threads of moral discourse (i.e., part of the same moral domain as experienced by our interlocutors). Such instances of ethical imbrication would not represent a simple trade-off, hierarchical ordering, or compartmentalization of discrete moral ideals. Rather, the mutual constitution of these concepts can run so deep that they require each other to exist as our interlocutors imagine them and as these principles inform the moral discourse that we collect. In such cases, justifications coded as separate ethics may be so imbricated that they cannot be meaningfully separated without dismantling the logic of the response.

On the other hand, our position is not to deny that people can hold moral ideals that are incommensurable in the same place and time. Rather, our descriptions of "parallel" and "divergent justifications" demonstrate how the production of moral discourse can have much to do with negotiations that people make *between* what they experience as competing moral goods.

This argument can be situated in a broader context of scholarship that has similarly suggested that paradoxically held beliefs can play important roles in driving a cultural system or socializing children into those systems. Nuckolls (1998) points to paradoxes of values as a critical source of cultural dynamism in his studies of American psychiatry, identity in Oklahoma, and emotional experience in Micronesia. Using these examples, Nuckolls (1998) argues that "culture is a problem that cannot be solved" (p. 32). In other words, cultural knowledge systems are often made up of a dialectic tension between ultimately incommensurable values. Nuckolls argues that it is the working out of these incommensurable values that drives cultural production of the ideas that we experience as natural. Applied to the Three Ethics framework, this argument suggests that the drive to resolve the (ultimately irresolvable) competing demands of incommensurable ethics such as Autonomy, Community, and Divinity constitutes the very knowledge systems of the people working out these differences, such as American evangelical parents socializing their children into a religious worldview or Hmong youth who simultaneously ascribe to competing cultural models of parent-child relationships.

Astuti (2011) makes a related developmental point in her description of the discrete sets of beliefs that provide ontogenetic precursors to one another among Vezo parents and children in Madagascar. Analyzing the developmental trajectories of ideas about the afterlife, Astuti (2011) points to developmental trajectories where children hold developmentally prior "ideas that are very different from – and not just immature versions of – those of their parents and elders" (p. 13). Whereas Vezo children eventually develop the "Vezo" eschatology as adults, Astuti demonstrates that children's views represent an altogether distinct eschatology. Rather than correcting these views, Vezo parents instead encourage or poke fun at them. Astuti argues that it is through ritual performance, rather than explicit teaching, that children eventually develop the adult set of beliefs about the afterlife and ancestors. Paired with our analysis of the various ways that American evangelical parents socialize Divinity thinking in their children, a developmental picture emerges here that is more complex than the increasing or decreasing prevalence of distinct ethics over the life course. Specifically, what we want to draw attention to with our concept of ethical imbrication is that the analytic categories of Autonomy, Community, and Divinity can be shown in some contexts to depend on one another for their very realization.

It is a major goal of this chapter to address this ethical imbrication directly, to argue for its potential salience, and to develop methodological and theoretical perspectives to productively use this ethical imbrication in research on moral thinking across the life course. It is critical to note here that the directions we propose are not necessarily inconsistent with current Three Ethics approaches. Ethical co-occurrence can readily be identified in current methodological implementations of the three ethics, as it is common practice to allow the coding of a single stretch of moral discourse under more than one ethic. Similarly, in our approach, employment of the Three Ethics framework was an essential first-step analytic to reveal moments of ethical co-occurrence. Such analyses involve tight distinctions between the three ethics (a requisite to claim co-occurrence). However, what we propose is that further analyses of ethical co-occurrence ought to be included as necessary post hoc analyses, designed to understand what is actually happening in the discourse when multiple ethics come into play. Indeed, in both empirical projects presented in this chapter, the discourse analyses performed began as post hoc analyses to a more conventional use of the Three Ethics approach. In this way, our critique encourages researchers to analyze the particular dynamics of ethical co-occurrence as a way to go beyond understanding moral codes as distributions of abstract ethical categories. When multiple ethics are coded in responses to particular moral situations, then researchers ought to investigate the implications here, with particular attention to the precise dynamics between and among the "different" ethics at play in the discourse. Doing so can reveal the cultural logics that make sense of the dynamic interplay of different ethical concepts as well as the socialization processes through which abstract ethical categories are acquired as ultimate moral goods.

Ethical imbrication has interesting implications for the development of moral thinking that build on cultural-developmental approaches (Jensen, 2008, 2011a). If two ethics are inextricably linked in a particular cultural logic, is this relationship reflected in moral development as well? Based on the present research, we suggest that it is. Specifically, by examining the relation *between* ethics in parent-child conversations, we can see how parents selectively cultivate and impede children's moral reasoning in ways consistent with their own moral vision. The findings of this particular investigation depict a socializing process whereby certain elements of Autonomy are selectively imbricated with – or absorbed within – Divinity. Thus, it was only by studying the relation between ethics that we were able to raise the hypothesis that Divinity, which emerges as self-generated reasoning during early adolescence (Jensen, 2011b; see also Trommsdorff, 2012), may be ontologically premised on children's expression of certain Autonomy concerns in this community. Similarly, an explicit emphasis on the dynamics of ethical co-occurrence – with the Three Ethics framework as an epistemological starting point – informed our analysis of the ways that Hmong youth navigate competing moral demands. Although these developmental processes are cut across by migration and are admittedly complex, the analytic moves we have argued for in this chapter are useful in starting to tease apart this complexity and derive a better understanding of the developmental pathways of migrant youth.

We have sought to delineate a mode of analysis that has important theoretical and methodological implications for how we think about Three Ethics theory and related frameworks. The developmental trends that we point to demonstrate that any cultural-developmental approach must take stock of ethical co-occurrence at various points in the life course. By employing discourse analysis methods to uncover the dynamics of parallel, divergent, and imbricated forms of ethical co-occurrence, researchers can develop more robust accounts of the nature and development of moral thinking across diverse cultural contexts.

REFERENCES

Arnett, J. J., Ramos, K. D., & Jensen, L. A. (2001). Ideological views in emerging adulthood: Balancing autonomy and community. *Journal of Adult Development,* 8(2), 69–79.

Astuti, R. (2011). Death, ancestors and the living dead: Learning without teaching in Madagascar. In V. Talwar, P. L. Harris, & M. Schleifer (Eds.), *Children's understanding of death: From biological to religious conceptions* (pp. 1–18). Cambridge, United Kingdom: Cambridge University Press.

Briggs, C. (1986). *Learning how to ask: A sociolinguistic appraisal of the role of the interview in social science research.* Cambridge, United Kingdom: Cambridge University Press.

DiBianca Fasoli, A. (2013). *Moral psychology and the socialization of helping among evangelical Christian families* (Doctoral dissertation). University of Chicago, Chicago, IL.

Fasulo, A., Loyd, H., & Padiglione, V. (2007). Children's socialization into cleaning practices: A cross-cultural perspective. *Discourse and Society,* 18(1), 11–33.

Fung, H., & Chen, E. C. H. (2001). Across time and beyond skin: Self and transgression in the everyday socialization of shame among Taiwanese preschool children. *Social Development,* 10(3), 419–437.

Gray, J. (1996). *Isaiah Berlin.* Princeton, NJ: Princeton University Press.

Guerra, V. M., & Giner-Sorolla, R. (2010). The Community, Autonomy, and Divinity Scale (CADS): A new tool for the cross-cultural study of morality. *Journal of Cross-Cultural Psychology,* 41(1), 35–50.

Haidt, J., Koller, S. H., & Dias, M. G. (1993). Affect, culture, and morality, or is it wrong to eat your dog? *Journal of Personality and Social Psychology,* 65(4), 613–628.

Hardy, S. A., Walker, L. J., Olsen, J. A., Woodbury, R. D., & Hickman, J. R. (2013). Moral identity as moral ideal self: Links to adolescent outcomes. *Developmental Psychology,* 50(1), 45–57.

Hickman, J. R. (2011). *Morality and personhood in the Hmong diaspora: A person-centered ethnography of migration and resettlement* (Doctoral dissertation). University of Chicago, Chicago, IL.

(in press). Ancestral personhood and moral justification. *Anthropological Theory.*

Jensen, L. A. (1993). *The ethics of Autonomy, Community, and Divinity: A theory and an exploratory study* (Unpublished manuscript). University of Chicago, Chicago, IL.

(1995). Habits of the heart revisited: Autonomy, Community, and Divinity in adults' moral language. *Qualitative Sociology,* 18(1), 71–86.

(1997a). Culture wars: American moral divisions across the adult lifespan. *Journal of Adult Development,* 4(2), 107–121.

(1997b). Different worldviews, different morals: American's culture war divide. *Human Development,* 40, 325–344.

(1998). Moral divisions within countries between orthodoxy and progressivism: India and the United States. *Journal for the Scientific Study of Religion*, 37(1), 90–107.

(2004). *Coding manual: Ethics of Autonomy, Community, and Divinity (Revised)*. Retrieved from www.lenearnettjensen.com

(2008). Through two lenses: A cultural-developmental approach to moral reasoning. *Developmental Review*, 28, 289–315.

(Ed.). (2011a). *Bridging cultural and developmental approaches to psychology: New syntheses in theory, research, and policy*. New York, NY: Oxford University Press.

(2011b). The cultural development of three fundamental ethics: Autonomy, Community and Divinity. *Zygon*, 46(1), 150–167.

Miller, J. G., & Bersoff, D. M. (1998). The role of liking in perceptions of the moral responsibility to help: A cultural perspective. *Journal of Experimental Social Psychology*, 34(5), 443–469.

Miller, J. G., Bersoff, D. M., & Harwood, R. L. (1990). Perceptions of social responsibilities in India and in the United States: Moral imperatives or personal decisions? *Journal of Personality and Social Psychology*, 58(1), 33–47.

Nuckolls, C. W. (1998). *Culture: A problem that cannot be solved*. Madison: University of Wisconsin Press.

Quinn, N. (Ed.). (2005a). *Finding culture in talk: A collection of methods*. New York, NY: Palgrave Macmillan.

(2005b). How to reconstruct schemas people share, from what they say. In N. Quinn (Ed.), *Finding culture in talk: A collection of methods* (pp. 35–82). New York, NY: Palgrave Macmillan.

Rozin, P., Lowery, L., Imada, S., & Haidt, J. (1999). The CAD triad hypothesis: A mapping between three moral emotions (contempt, anger, disgust) and three moral codes (Community, Autonomy, Divinity). *Journal of Personality and Social Psychology*, 76(4), 574–586.

Shore, B. (1996). *Culture in mind: Cognition, culture, and the problem of meaning*. New York, NY: Oxford University Press.

Shweder, R. A. (1990). In defense of moral realism: Reply to Gabennesch. *Child Development*, 61, 2060–2067.

Shweder, R. A., Mahapatra, M., & Miller, J. G. (1987). Culture and moral development. In J. Kagan & S. Lamb (Eds.), *The emergence of morality in young children* (pp. 1–83). Chicago, IL: University of Chicago Press.

Shweder, R. A., & Much, N. C. (1991). Determinations of meaning: Discourse and moral socialization. In R. A. Shweder (Ed.), *Thinking through cultures: Expeditions in cultural psychology* (pp. 186–240). Cambridge, MA: Harvard University Press.

Shweder, R. A., Much, N., Mahapatra, M., & Park, L. (1997). The "Big Three" of morality (Autonomy, Community, Divinity) and the "big three" explanations of suffering. In A. Brandt & P. Rozin (Eds.), *Morality and health* (pp. 119–169). London, United Kingdom: Routledge.

Sterponi, L. A. (2003). Account episodes in family discourse: The making of morality in everyday interaction. *Discourse Studies*, 5(1), 79–100.

Strauss, C. (2005). Analyzing discourse for cultural complexity. In N. Quinn (Ed.), *Finding culture in talk: A collection of methods* (pp. 203–242). New York, NY: Palgrave Macmillan.

Strauss, C., & Quinn, N. (1999). *A cognitive theory of cultural meaning*. Cambridge, United Kingdom: Cambridge University Press.

Trommsdorff, G. (2012). Cultural perspectives on values and religion in adolescent development: A conceptual overview and synthesis. In G. Trommsdorff & X. Chen (Eds.), *Values, religion, and culture in adolescent development* (pp. 3–45). Cambridge, United Kingdom: Cambridge University Press.

Vasquez, K., Keltner, D., Ebenbach, D. H., & Banaszynski, T. L. (2001). Cultural variation and similarity in moral rhetorics: Voices from the Philippines and the United States. *Journal of Cross-Cultural Psychology*, 32(1), 93–120.

Wong, D. (2014). Integrating philosophy with anthropology in an approach to morality. *Anthropological Theory*, 14.3, 336–355.

8 How liberals and conservatives are alike and apart: a research autobiography

Lene Arnett Jensen

I grew up in Denmark for most of my childhood. Unlike the United States, Denmark is not particularly diverse. This was even more true when I was a child, as there were fewer immigrants than now. The vast majority of Danes, then and now, value a society where all individuals have relatively equal access to education, health services, and work and civic opportunities. In turn, everyone is expected to contribute substantial time and taxes to make this vision a sustainable reality. It is a vision and a reality based on beliefs in individual autonomy coupled with collective responsibility (see also Vainio, Chapter 3, this volume). It is not, however, based on religious or spiritual beliefs (Arnett & Jensen, 2015; Zuckerman, 2008). Religion is largely absent from individual and collective consideration. For example, unlike in the United States, meetings in city hall do not start with a prayer. There is no pledge of allegiance invoking divinity. Nor does the monetary unit avow a "trust in God." The vast majority of Danes very rarely attend religious services. When they do it is typically to affirm family and communal ties and traditions, such as at weddings, rather than belief in God. On worldwide surveys assessing extent of religious and spiritual belief and behavior, Denmark repeatedly comes out rock bottom (Crabtree, 2010).

At 18, I immigrated with my family to the United States. Like many immigrants, we came with educational and occupational aspirations (Suárez-Orozco, 2015). We were hopeful and fascinated. We also felt apart and puzzled. Certainly, the religious side of the United States was mysterious. Living in Atlanta, we wondered on Sundays where all those cars with very well-dressed people were going during the morning hours. After a busy week, all we wanted to do was read the newspaper and drink strong Gevalia coffee. Where were those Americans going? It took us several Sundays to figure it out.

By the early 1990s, I had decided to delve more deeply and systematically into this American religious side. While a graduate student at the Committee

I thank Samantha Horsley, Carolyn Kraft, and Kristina Pecora for assistance with interviews and coding and Jessica McKenzie for assistance with analyses. I am profoundly grateful to the congregants, ministers, and church staff who saw value in scientific research on the present topic and contributed considerable time to make it a reality. I also thank The Pew Charitable Trusts and the Templeton Foundation for support.

on Human Development at the University of Chicago, I began to attend Baptist churches as part of a dissertation project on culture, religion, and morality that I was developing. Baptists engage in full-body immersion – from head to toe – to mark the moment in their lives when they "take Jesus into their hearts" and become "saved." For a couple of years, I attended five different Baptist churches, one large mainline church and four smaller ones that self-identify as fundamentalist. Certainly for me, attending church services a couple of times on Sundays and on Wednesday evenings (a common Baptist service time) and joining a wide variety of church community events on other days across the five churches was a kind of immersion, too. In a matter of a few weeks, I had spent more time in church than in all of my previous life put together.

This chapter describes key insights about the moral psychology of religiously liberal and conservative cultures that emerged from this ethnographic research and from interview and questionnaire research with adult church members. In turn, these insights, along with findings on moral development from other research traditions, led to my proposal of the cultural-developmental approach to moral psychology (Jensen, 2008, 2011b). The chapter also includes a review of recent research that tests and extends the cultural-developmental predictions through interviews with children, adolescents, and adults. These participants from religiously liberal and conservative communities discussed not only "public" moral issues, where judgments are applied to people in general, as in past research, but also "private" moral issues, where they made decisions for themselves. As we will see, it turns out that the two cultural groups share developmental features and moral reasoning, but with age they part company on what they think should be the "moral lingua franca" of society. This represents a new and nuanced way to understand what has commonly been termed the American "culture wars" (Hunter, 1991). As such, it also tells us something about moral reasoning and its fundamental and distinctive role in human societies and cultural socialization. This chapter, then, is a kind of research autobiography that brings together past and present insights with the hope of inspiring complex and creative new research.

Attending church: one program, different messages

The Baptist churches that I attended were all located in central Missouri, an area where smaller cities and towns, suburbs, and rural patches are puzzled together. After initially visiting some twenty churches of various denominations, I decided on the five Baptist churches that seemed good candidates for a comparison of religiously liberal and conservative congregations.[1] Sociologists

---

[1] I included one larger mainline church and four smaller fundamentalist ones in order to have enough of a pool of congregants for interviews and a questionnaire survey.

have noted that religious liberals and conservatives have come to form different kinds of cultures in the United States (e.g., Bellah, 1987; Wuthnow, 1989). Old lines among Catholics, Jews, and Protestants have in many ways been supplanted by splits within religious denominations and in American culture in general. As liberal and conservative political and nonprofit organizations work together across the old religious lines, the new split finds vociferous expression in public debates – to the point where Hunter (1991), in a careful analysis of this public realignment, termed it the "culture wars." The term, borrowed from the German *Kulturkampf* of the Bismarckian era, is striking. It is also rather muscular. There is, after all, not an armed conflict, and heated public debates have a way of obscuring more subtle and complex individual convictions and psychologies. Still, the new public ideological split is evident. In fact, some have proposed that the American division is one example of similar post–World War II divisions that are occurring worldwide between modernism and fundamentalism (Marty & Appleby, 1995).

Once I had decided on the five Baptist churches, I met with pastors to obtain their permissions to attend their churches as a researcher and to ask if they would author a letter to their congregants endorsing the interview and questionnaire components of my study. I had expected pastors to ask a series of questions about my research approach and even to show reluctance toward an outsider of indeterminate faith. Fundamentalist churches in particular have been characterized as closed off to researchers who are not kindred spirits (Ammerman, 1987). What I promised was to aim to capture the beliefs and behaviors of congregants in a way that they would clearly recognize, even if they might not share my terminology and research vantage point. I also promised to make my findings and writings readily available. To my surprise and delight, I was met with wide open doors. As time went on, I would come to realize that pastors and congregants were welcoming for a variety of reasons, all of which were positive, but not necessarily focused on the merits of scientific research.

When I entered through church doors to attend service, I sought to follow congregation norms. Typically, I arrived early and stayed late to converse with congregation members. I participated fully in worship greetings, singing, recital of prayers, and so on. I did not take part in communion, though, since it a practice that at least in fundamentalist churches presupposes having proclaimed one's faith in Jesus. In most of the fundamentalist churches where women wear skirts, not trousers, I would follow suit – so to speak. In fundamentalist churches where members bring their own bibles, I, too, would bring one.

The service programs across the five churches included many of the same elements and even followed much the same order: pastor's welcome and greetings, invocation, prayer, scriptural readings, hymns, pastor's sermon, offertory, invitation to declare one's faith, and benediction. This traditional structural commonality did not, however, entail similar messages. Subtle behaviors conveyed profound ideological differences between the liberal and conservative churches. Going back to the Bible, for example, it was not only that fundamentalist congregation members would bring their own. Their bibles were stuffed with strips of paper, scribbled notes, and sticky notes – reflecting frequent and careful study. Many women, and some men, kept their bibles in cloth carriers that were elaborately embroidered or quilted – reflecting considerable care. Also, unlike the mainline church, the fundamentalist ones would never type page numbers in the programs for where to find biblical passages, a situation that caused me considerable initial chagrin and fear of embarrassment. The absence of page numbers may partly be because fundamentalist congregation members do not all bring the same version of the Bible, but, more importantly, it undoubtedly signals the deep knowledge of the Bible expected in churches where scriptures are taken to denote divine will.

How behavioral responsibilities are distributed also differentiates the two kinds of religious communities in telling ways. Service activities and rituals at the mainline Baptist church are performed by women and men, as well as children and adults. An attempt to encourage the participation of all individuals is evident from the first to the last moment of service. For example, both women and men serve as church greeters, lead invocations, and recite scripture verses from the pulpit. Also, both women and men speak to the congregation about fund-raising drives, serve as ushers, and provide guidance to persons who make known their intent to join the church during the end-of-service invitation. Children, too, are involved side by side with adults. For example, youth groups perform musical arrangements. Also, services often include children's sermons, where children – and the occasional small group of jesting adolescents – come to the front of the church to chat with the pastor about diverse topics. Both children and adolescents also serve as ushers – another practice that on occasion renders events less than formal with children merrily chewing gum or forgetting the protocol. The involvement of members across age and gender in the worship service signals that hierarchy between children and adults and women and men is deemphasized. There is, instead, encouragement of individual expression, equality, and inclusiveness.

In the fundamentalist churches, congregation members participate in service rituals and activities with exuberance and enthusiasm, but all members do not partake equally in responsibilities. Both women and men sing in the choir, give witness, and come to the front of the church to kneel and pray. Women, however, do not serve as church greeters or ushers, lead in prayer, or speak from the pulpit on matters of faith. This division of gender roles within the churches is one manifestation of a conservative worldview that prescribes gender role divisions in many areas of life – church, family, and society. Also, children and adolescents have virtually no responsibility for service activities and rituals.

They do not typically perform musical arrangements. They do not serve as ushers. There are no children's sermons. In fact, children are sometimes dismissed to various classes during service. It is primarily at special times, such as Christmas, that children are actively involved through musical and theatrical performances. In one church, a children's Christmas play featured the conversion of Kermit the Frog from hedonism to fundamentalism – in a rendition that seemed pretty far from Jim Henson's otherwise vivid imagination. The fundamentalist division of church labor conveys a hierarchical worldview in terms of the relations between children and adults, women and men, parishioners and pastor, and – of course – humans and God.

Finally, an analysis of pastors' sermons, too, helps us to see the different values and worldviews that guide these religiously liberal and conservative communities. Naturally, the subjects of pastors' sermons varied and pertained to a wide variety of issues. When I analyzed themes across about a hundred sermons, three consistent messages emerged in the fundamentalist Baptist ministers' sermons. These pertained to sin, salvation, and evangelizing. The sinfulness of human nature and the sinfulness of the present world were consistent concerns. In the words of two pastors, "lust" and proneness to "temptation" are ineradicably part of human nature. Moreover, this day and age is a time when lust is promoted rather than curtailed. For example, one pastor in a sermon spoke of how present day media and laws encourage sinful behaviors. Focusing upon "sexual lusts," he argued that our current society promotes promiscuity, which in turn has led to the evils of abortion and sexually transmitted diseases. In his and the other pastors' view, we must refrain from giving in to temptations – sexual or otherwise. We must "do battle" against temptation in our individual lives and in society.

The goal of salvation was another consistent theme of the pastors' sermons. They often spoke of the goal of becoming saved. They explained that only through faith and a personal commitment to Christ can humans enter heaven. When we "receive" Christ, we experience a new birth. The pastors emphasize that being saved means that we strive to become righteous and "Christ-like" in this world, for example, by battling temptation. It also means that after this world we are ensured of entry into heaven.

The third consistent theme of the pastors' sermons was the necessity of evangelizing. The fundamentalist pastors conceive of evangelizing as a first step toward a person's salvation. It is a dead serious task – literally – aimed at saving family members, friends, acquaintances, and strangers from the fires of hell and granting them entry into a glorious heaven. In sermons, the pastors repeatedly invoked the necessity of evangelizing in the course of one's daily life. They also provided favorable depictions of missionary life. In one sermon, for example, the pastor described missionary work as an arduous but noble endeavor. He explained that missionaries must sever their ties to their homes and families – they must be willing to "go anywhere, bear any burden, and sever any tie." Yet, the lives of missionaries are ennobled by the fact that their tie to God is fortified. In the words of the pastor, God becomes "my all, my life." The pastors' sermons on sin, salvation, and evangelizing indicate the centrality of divine authority and the divine realm in the religiously conservative worldview. In this psychologically powerful view, the self has a divine purpose.

The mainline pastor's top three themes were different from those of the fundamentalist ministers, as was the underlying notion of self revealed by the themes. The first prominent theme in the mainline church was the importance of respecting diverse people and their rights. The pastor's sermons sometimes included general statements to the effect that his church welcomes all persons and does not require uniformity. At times he contrasted this to the "pushy closed-mindedness" of more conservative congregations. At the more specific level, the pastor spoke, for example, of the necessity of supporting the rights of gays and lesbians.

A second prominent sermon theme pertained to caring for both self and others. This theme was given an imaginative elaboration in one sermon when the pastor spoke of the danger of falling into the "messiah trap." As he explained it, this is the trap where one begins to fancy oneself a messiah. He described two ways in which one may get caught. One way is to think that one can create one's own religion and be entirely self-sufficient. The second messiah trap involves an exclusive devotion to the lives of others. It is the trap of sacrificing the self for others. The pastor, in essence, was calling for a delicate balance between individual and community considerations.

On the surface, the third theme preached by the mainline Baptist minister – evangelizing – overlapped with those of the fundamentalist ministers. Evangelizing is at the heart of Christian faith, and it is an imperative task of mainline Protestant congregations that are shrinking and aging (PewResearch, 2014). The mainline Baptist pastor often encouraged his parishioners to evangelize, but he was at pains to distance himself and his congregation from the kind of evangelizing carried out by evangelicals and fundamentalists. A telling sermon was entitled: "Reframing the troublesome task." The task, of course, is evangelizing. According to the pastor, it is troublesome because his church must clearly distinguish itself from "Bible-thumping fundamentalists" who push a "quasi-religio-politico" agenda that "eventually will defame our faith." In the pastor's view, the evangelizing approach of fundamentalists and others akin to them is "confrontational," "manipulative," and "simplistic." It seeks to convert persons into a faith that is "oppressive." In order to set themselves apart from this form of evangelizing and outlook, the pastor suggested that his church bury the word *evangelizing* and instead begin to employ the term "disciple making." He also suggested that two key concerns to be spoken of during "disciple making" should be those of justice and love.

We see, then, from the ethnographic research, that religious liberals and conservatives frame the self differently. To religious conservatives, the self has divine purpose in this world and the hereafter. The self may become godly, but humans are not on par with God. This hierarchical relationship between God and humans is one that also extends to and is mirrored in other relations between humans, including between men and women. To religious liberals, in comparison, the self is what might be termed a "social individual," whose primary purposes involve balancing care for self and for others and treating all individuals in an equitable manner.

We see, too, that the cultural clash between liberals and conservatives is potent. The mainline Baptist pastor's sermons unmistakably delineated the division and portrayed the other side in antagonistic terms. Fundamentalist pastors, meanwhile, made their view plain that hell is for real and that the modern world seems eager to get there as fast as possible. It is evident that the two sides are competing with the other each to claim its own worldview as the better one and to promote it as widely as possible.

Interviewing adults: two hierarchies of ethics

But how do ordinary individuals on the two competing sides see things? That was my next question. The sociological research had addressed group dynamics (Bellah, 1987; Hunter, 1991; Wuthnow, 1989). My own ethnographic work provides insight into behaviors and beliefs as expressed in church. Aiming to delve deeper into individuals' own perspectives and explanations, I decided to interview adult members of the congregations about moral issues, especially those that seemed at the heart of the cultural clash such as family, gender relations, and views on the purpose of life (Jensen, 1997, 1998a, 1998b).

Over the course of several months, I visited the homes of forty adults who were in midlife, half from the mainline congregation and half from the fundamentalist ones.[2] They volunteered to take part in interviews that addressed a variety of moral issues, including divorce, abortion, and suicide in the case of terminal illness. I would ask them to tell me whether they thought these behaviors were right or wrong and to explain their reasoning. For example, "Do you think it is morally wrong to divorce, or do you not think so?" "Why is that? What are your reasons for thinking so?" "Would you try to stop a person from divorcing?" As I have found across many interview studies on morality by now, almost everyone was open and had quite a lot to say. People are often engrossed by moral questions. Here, the official part of the interviews, the part I recorded for analysis, lasted about an hour and half on average. Often, though,

---

[2] The age range was 35 to 55 years old. The mean age was 42.9 years ($SD = 6.8$) for fundamentalist Baptists and 48.6 years ($SD = 6.8$) for mainline Baptists.

people wanted to chat both before and after the interview, something I was happy to do.

The only truly knotty moment I experienced during all of the interviews occurred fairly early in the course of one visit with a fundamentalist woman. I could tell from the moment that I pulled into her driveway that she held strong convictions. Her parked car was plastered with bumper stickers, including "Life is short. Pray hard. Read the Book!" Once inside the front door, there were religious items all over – crosses on the wall, a bible on the coffee table, plenty of sofa pillows with scripture in needlepoint. After some lemonade and friendly small talk, I started my recording device, but I had barely gotten halfway through the questions for the first issue when she suddenly gripped my arm and implored me to kneel down on the floor with her and ask Jesus to come into my heart. She was warm, passionate, beseeching. Desperately casting about in my mind for a graceful reply to a plea that I had never encountered, I finally gave her hand a gentle squeeze and said that now was not the right time. The experience was entirely outside my research protocol or anything I had learned from graduate school courses and textbooks on research methods. But it was perhaps the single most revealing moment in my research because I understood that while I had come to her house in search of knowledge about human psychology, she had opened her door to try to save my soul.

My other thirty-nine interviews were also thought-provoking but seldom as interpersonally intense. After I had transcribed all interviews, I coded the interviewees' moral reasoning in terms of the three Ethics of Autonomy, Community, and Divinity proposed by Shweder and his colleagues (Jensen, 1995; Shweder, 1990; Shweder, Much, Mahapatra, *et al.*, 1997; see also Appendix A of this volume). These ethics entail different conceptions of the moral self. The Ethic of Autonomy defines the self as an autonomous individual who is free to make choices, being restricted primarily by concerns with inflicting harm on other individuals and encroaching on their rights. Moral reasoning within this ethic centers on an individual's rights, interests, and well-being and on equality between individuals. The Ethic of Community defines the moral self through membership in social groups such as family and nation and through responsibilities that ensue from this membership. Moral reasoning within this ethic includes a focus on a person's duties to others and promoting the interests and welfare of groups to which the person belongs. The Ethic of Divinity defines the self as a spiritual entity. Here, moral reasoning centers on divine and natural law, injunctions and lessons found in sacred texts, and the striving on the part of a person to avoid spiritual degradation and come closer to moral purity.[3] I decided to analyze my data in terms of the three ethics

---

[3] A stratified random sample consisting of 20 percent of the interviews was coded by an independent rater. Reliability using Cohen's kappa was 0.90.

because, unlike other major approaches in moral psychology at this time, they incorporated a wide variety of moral concepts and explicitly included a divinity dimension.

What I found was that although the two groups of religious liberals and conservatives showed overlap in their moral concepts and reasoning, they were also strikingly different. The groups were similar in making frequent mention of the Ethic of Community. Liberals, however, reasoned significantly more in terms of the Ethic of Autonomy for almost all of the moral issues than did religious conservatives. Meanwhile, the conservatives reasoned more in terms of the Ethic of Divinity for every issue than did liberals. Listening to the interviewees, the differences in where the dial was set on their moral compass was clear. In response to the issue of suicide in the case of terminal illness, for example, a religiously conservative man said: "I leave that in God's hands . . . He gave us life, He can take the life when he wants to, and He can give us grace to go through difficulties in life while we're here." In contrast, a liberal interviewee approached the issue from the vantage point of the individual and the loss of autonomy. Rhetorically, she asked: "Who wants to lay in bed for even one extra day of their life just to be alive, if they can't communicate, they can't eat by themselves?"

Ordinary individuals who belong to religiously liberal and conservative Baptist congregations care deeply about moral issues. But what comes clear is that they have different hierarchies of ethics. For conservatives, Ethics of Divinity and Community are well above the Ethic of Autonomy. For religious liberals, Ethics of Autonomy and Community are above the Ethic of Divinity. While both sides share communal concerns and values, even this commonality is not uncomplicated because, as we already saw from the ethnographic research, some of the specifics of the communities that each side values and wishes to pass on to the next generation differ markedly. Their views of what constitutes a good family and a good society diverge on crucial questions such as how much individual expression to allow for, how to divide the roles and responsibilities of women and men, and the extent of authority invested in parents, pastors, and other familial and social leaders (see also Jensen, 2006).

More research: replicating the two hierarchies

Interviews, especially when conducted in people's homes, are very high on my list of ways to conduct psychological research. People say the most interesting things. They are thoughtful and often eloquent. Unfortunately, interviews are also incredibly time consuming, both to conduct and analyze. So, while what we learn has depth and complexity, we are left to wonder how broadly the findings apply. Asking myself this question, I next decided to survey a larger sample. I constructed a questionnaire pertaining to the same moral issues used in my interviews. For each issue, respondents indicated whether they judged it as right or wrong. Then, they selected from a list of six moral reasons the ones they thought were most important in supporting their judgment. I had formulated these reasons on the basis of the most common word choices and key concepts that I had heard in the course of conducting the interviews. For each list, two of the six reasons represented each of the three Ethics of Autonomy, Community, and Divinity (see Appendix D for the questionnaire, Three Ethics Reasoning Assessment, TERA).[4]

I recruited 120 respondents, 60 mainline and 60 fundamentalist Baptists. Also, each Baptist group included even numbers of young, midlife, and older adults.[5] The findings replicated those from the interviews. Again, religious liberals hierarchized the Ethics of Autonomy and Community as more important than the Ethic of Divinity, whereas conservatives placed Divinity and Community above Autonomy. This was true across all three age groups.

Interestingly, these two different hierarchies of ethics have also been found in research with religious liberal and conservative Hindus in India (Jensen, 2008) and religiously liberal and conservative Lutherans in Finland (Vainio, Chapter 3, this volume). These findings are suggestive of the moral psychologies that might underlie the post–World War II worldwide differentiation that social observers have noted between modernism and fundamentalism. However, I would hasten to add that we should not simply conclude that, for example, liberal American Baptists, liberal Finnish Lutherans, and liberal Hindu Indians are one and the same. That would gloss over important diversity between religions and nations, even as they appear to share a similar hierarchy of ethics.

Subsequent research by social psychologists, using a coding system derived from the three ethics, has also extended the research to political liberals and conservatives as well as continued research with ministers of liberal and conservative congregations. They have either found the same two hierarchies of ethics as in my interview and questionnaire research with religious groups (McAdams, Albaugh, Farber, *et al.*, 2008) or something fairly similar (Graham, Haidt, & Nosek, 2009; Haidt, 2013).

Thinking about psychology: what about development?

We know, then, that religious liberals and conservatives, from young through older adulthood, have two different hierarchies of ethics. What soon puzzled me about this finding was how to reconcile it with almost a century's worth

---

[4] Respondents were also provided with the option of writing their own reasons in addition to selecting from the lists. This was in case some respondents did not think the list included what they considered important reasons. Only 2 percent of all reasons in the study, however, were self-generated.

[5] The young adults were 19 to 27 years old (mean $= 23.2$, $SD = 0.58$), the midlife adults were 35 to 56 years old (mean $= 46.5$, $SD = 1.49$), and the older adults were 65 to 84 years old (mean $= 72.7$, $SD = 1.30$).

of developmental research on morality (Freud, 1930/1961; Kohlberg, 1984; Piaget, 1932/1965; Turiel, 1983). All of this work postulates one universal pathway of moral development. The argument, with some variations among theories, is that young children are self-focused, then broaden their horizons to consider others as they grow older, and then come to think in terms of concepts of rights and equity in the course of adolescence or adulthood.

When I first came over to the United States from Denmark, perhaps I, too, thought that adult moral development looked one kind of way. But my research with mainline and fundamentalist Baptist adults shook me out of this cocooned conviction. Clearly, the two groups of adults are not the same. Over the course of their development they have not ended up in the same place, and it stands to reason that there must be more than one developmental pathway of moral psychology. I was not the first researcher to realize that adults from different cultures and religions varied vastly in their moral reasoning. In the early 1990s, as I collected my dissertation data, scholars working in many parts of the world were increasingly writing about a plethora of moral concepts (e.g., Edwards, 1997; Huebner & Garrod, 1991; Miller, 1994; Shweder, Mahapatra, & Miller, 1990; Zimba, 1994). The Three Ethics formulation (Shweder, 1990) and coding manual (see Appendix A), in fact, sprang from a survey of all of these kinds of concepts.

The question remained, however, of how to describe the development of morality as a multiplicitous phenomenon. I was convinced of the validity of cultural research findings showing multiplicity. At the same time, I also thought that almost a century's worth of moral development research had generated valuable knowledge. The question was how to bridge the findings from the cultural and universalistic research traditions (Jensen, 2011a, 2012). To me, the answer lay with a new kind of theoretical approach – one that was not unitary and static, but flexible and dynamic.

With the goal of formulating such a theory, I reviewed a large set of findings pertaining to moral reasoning, emotions, values, and judgments. As described in the introductory chapter to this book (Jensen, Chapter 1, this volume), the findings come from diverse disciplines. Based on a synthesis and some reinterpretation of the findings, I proposed the cultural-developmental approach (Jensen, 2008, 2011b). The central new idea is that there is a *template* for the development of each of the Ethics of Autonomy, Community, and Divinity. In other words, there is a certain ontogenetic trajectory across the life course for each. These trajectories place boundaries on the impact of culture, but they are not determinative because the trajectories are also shaped by culture.

Let's first look at the ontogenetic templates. Figure 8.1 illustrates the trajectories across the life course for each ethic. In previous writing, I have described extensively the research basis for each trajectory (Jensen, 2008, 2011b). Here, then, I give the elevator talk version. The proposal is that Ethic of Autonomy reasoning emerges early in childhood and stays relatively, if not entirely, stable

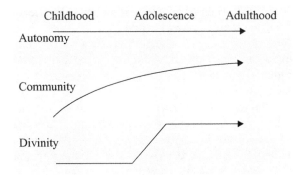

Figure 8.1   The cultural-developmental template of moral reasoning
(Reprinted from *Developmental Review* 28[3], Jensen, L. A., 'Through two
lenses: A cultural-developmental approach to moral psychology,' © 2008,
with permission from Elsevier.)
Note. Each line shows developmental patterns across the life span, from
childhood to adulthood. The positions of the lines do *not* indicate their
frequency in relation to one another (e.g., Autonomy being more frequent
than Community and Divinity).

across adolescence and into adulthood. Some types of Autonomy reasoning go
down after childhood but are then supplanted by other Autonomy considerations. Thus large amounts of research have shown that children in different cultures focus on harm to individuals and individual needs in regard to both self and
others (Bloom, 2013; Carlo, 2006; Gilligan, 1982; Miller, Bersoff, & Harwood,
1990; Snarey, 1985; Turiel, 2002; Walker, 1989; Warneken & Tomasello, 2006).
In adolescence and adulthood, some consideration of the welfare of the self and
other individuals remains, but now consideration of individual rights and equity
also emerges – even if these concepts do not prevail across cultures (Eisenberg,
Carlo, Murphy, *et al.*, 1995; Gilligan, 1982; Killen, 2002; Miller & Luthar,
1989; Piaget, 1932/1965; Snarey, 1985; Vasquez, Keltner, Ebenbach, *et al.*,
2001; Walker, 1989; Walker, Pitts, Hennig, *et al.*, 1995; Zimba, 1994). While
the proposal is that Ethic of Autonomy reasoning remains fairly stable across the
life span, it is also plausible that in cultures where there is a very strong push for
collectivity or submission to divinity, there may be somewhat of a decline with
age. In such cultures, considerations of the needs, desires, and interests of individuals – especially the self – would be seen as either irrelevant or even morally
objectionable, and hence by adulthood such considerations might diminish.
      Turning to the Ethic of Community, my review of the research indi-
cates a rise throughout childhood and into adolescence and adulthood. Findings have consistently indicated that younger children in diverse cultures
invoke Community reasons such as family interests and customs (Kohlberg,
1984; Miller, Bersoff, & Harwood, 1990; Olson & Spelke, 2008; Shweder,

Mahapatra, & Miller, 1990; Thompson, 2012). Moral reasoning related to the family is likely to find continued expression past childhood and probably even more so in the course of adolescence and adulthood as a person's experiences with duty to family and family interests go up (Miller, Bersoff, & Harwood, 1990). By late childhood and adolescence, Community reasons that pertain to social groups other than the family are added, including concern for friends, peers, and authority figures in places such as school and work (Carlo, 2006; Rubin, Bukowski, & Parker, 2006; Schlegel, 2011; Whiting & Edwards, 1988). Research has also shown that by late adolescence or adulthood even more Community reasons are added, such as a focus on societal organization (Eisenberg, Carlo, Murphy, *et al.*, 1995; Nisan, 1987; Walker, 1989; Zimba, 1994).

My proposal for the Ethic of Divinity is somewhat more tentative because research on divinity considerations in people's moral psychology is scarce (Trommsdorff, 2012). Psychology has long eschewed the religious and spiritual sides of people's lives, going back at least to Freud's (1927/2010) declaration that religion is an "illusion." Bearing in mind the caveat regarding scarcity of research findings, my proposal is that this ethic will often be low among children but will rise in adolescence and become similar to adult use. To me, it is telling that diverse religions have ceremonies in early or midadolescence that confer moral responsibility on adolescents and link that responsibility to knowledge of religious teachings (Mahoney, Pargament, Murray-Swank, *et al.*, 2003; Schlegel & Barry, 2015). Just to give a few well-known examples, there is the Hindu sacred thread ceremony, the Jewish bar mitzvah, or the Protestant confirmation. Furthermore, research has also indicated that adults often explain their moral behaviors in terms of divinity concepts, including adults from relatively secular communities (Colby & Damon, 1992; McAdams, Albaugh, Farber, *et al.*, 2008; Shweder, Mahapatra, & Miller, 1990; Walker, Pitts, Hennig, *et al.*, 1995). I think the potential infusion of Divinity reasoning in adolescence may especially characterize religious groups that emphasize scriptural authority or regard supernatural entities as largely distinct from humans. In these communities, beliefs in omniscience and omnipotence, for example, are of such an abstract nature that they may be readily translated into moral reasoning only by adolescents whose cognitive skills allow for more abstraction than those of younger children (Adelson, 1971; Keating, 1990; Kohlberg, 1976; Piaget, 1972). In short, children in these communities may well believe in God, but converting this belief into moral reasoning takes additional development. However, in religious traditions and cultures where the divine and human realms are regarded as intermeshed, it is possible that Divinity concepts are more accessible to and hence used more by children in their moral reasoning (Saraswathi, 2005). Then in the course of adolescence and adulthood, additional Divinity concepts may get added on.

As I mentioned, the templates for the ethics are flexible rather than one-size-fits-all. How early each ethic emerges and their slopes across development

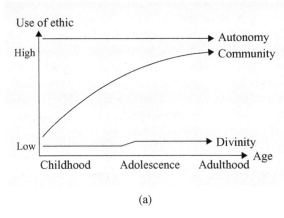

(a)

Figure 8.2A Hypothesized expression of template among religious liberals (Reprinted from *Developmental Review* 28[3], Jensen, L. A., 'Through two lenses: A cultural-developmental approach to moral psychology,' © 2008, with permission from Elsevier.)

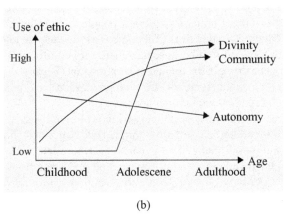

(b)

Figure 8.2B Hypothesized expression of template among religious conservatives (Reprinted from *Developmental Review* 28[3], Jensen, L. A., 'Through two lenses: A cultural-developmental approach to moral psychology,' © 2008, with permission from Elsevier.)

depend on the hierarchy of ethics within a culture. So, let us return now to what we know about the hierarchies of religiously liberal and conservative adults and see how culture shapes the trajectories. I have illustrated this in Figures 8.2A and 8.2B. Within religiously liberal groups, the expectation is that children, adolescents, and adults frequently will use the Ethic of Autonomy. The Ethic of Community will be rarer among children but will then become quite common among adolescents and adults. The Ethic of Divinity will be used infrequently at all ages, and if it emerges, this will occur only in the course of adolescence. For religiously conservative groups, my expectation is that children, adolescents, and adults will use Autonomy infrequently. There may be some decrease over the life span because of the strong emphasis on renouncing self-interest among religious conservatives. With respect to Community, the expectation is that its prevalence will rise steadily from childhood to reach a high level in adulthood. The Ethic of Divinity will be low among children but will then rise markedly in adolescence and remain high throughout adulthood.

Back to interviewing: how liberals and conservatives are alike and grow apart

To test the hypotheses represented by Figures 8.2A and 8.2B, I decided to return to my favorite pastime of interviewing. For this study, graduate students and I embarked on visiting the households of sixty mainline and sixty evangelical Presbyterians in a metropolitan area on the East Coast of the United States. Within each of these two religiously liberal and conservative groups, we interviewed even numbers of children, adolescents, and adults.[6] Even though it requires a lot of driving, I prefer to interview people in their homes because it gives a sense of their everyday lives. This time around when we interviewed children, it was also a good idea because they were very comfortable at home. They could go to get a drink in the middle of an interview (Pepsi was popular), show you around their room (some did this with great pride), and jump up and down on the couch (one boy with tremendous zest).

For this study, we asked everyone about two kinds of moral issues. As in my earlier work with liberal and conservative congregants, we asked about issues such as divorce and giving money to a panhandler, where interviewees made moral judgments for people in general. For example, "Do you think that it is morally right or morally wrong for people to give money to a panhandler?" I term these "public" issues, since they involve judgments and reasoning in regard to the general public. We also asked everyone about an experience from their own life that they considered to have involved a moral decision. I term these "private" issues. We quickly found that our interviewees recounted a huge range of private moral issues, from fairly mundane matters of deciding whether to give back excess change at the grocery store to shocking accounts of being convicted for child molestation. As a research group, we met weekly to review and process what we had heard.

---

[6] The children were 7 to 12 years old (mean $= 10.03$, $SD = 1.38$), the adolescents were ages 13 to 18 years old (mean $= 15.03$, $SD = 1.60$), and the adults were 36 to 57 years old (mean $= 45.88$, $SD = 4.65$).

The reason why I wanted to include private moral issues in addition to public ones is that I was concerned that research on liberals and conservatives was missing a significant part of the picture in regard to their moral lives and the nature of the so-called culture wars division. For example, some scholars have claimed that liberals, unlike conservatives, do not speak in terms of Ethic of Divinity considerations at all. The assertion is that they lack this "language" (Graham, Haidt, & Nosek, 2009).

Yet, from my ethnographic research, I knew that religious liberals value religion and spirituality. Many attend church with some regularity. Many are involved in volunteer work that seems in part motivated by their faith. Also, in some other research where I had asked liberals to describe God, they provided extensive and detailed descriptions that touched on questions about the purpose of life and the extent of free will – in short, matters of morality (Jensen, 2009).

So, what were we missing? Thinking back to my earlier review of the research literature on moral psychology, I remembered that some of my colleagues had found that adults, even relatively secular ones, would invoke religion and spirituality when talking about private moral issues (Colby & Damon, 1992; McAdams Albaugh, Farber, et al., 2008; Walker, Pitts, Hennig, et al., 1995). In fact, I, too, had found this in my first study in graduate school with alumni of the University of Chicago, few of whom were particularly conservative (Jensen, 1995). In contrast, the researchers who claim that liberals lack the moral language of divinity use surveys that address only highly hypothetical moral situations where all judgments are made for the general public. This highlights a fundamental research method truism: what researchers learn from their participants depends on what they ask about in the first place. So, in hopes of learning something complex, real, and nuanced, I decided to ask people about their everyday lives.

What did we find? Three key points stood out. First, religious liberals and conservatives share important developmental features. Children – whether they lived in a liberal or conservative household – reasoned more in terms of the Ethic of Autonomy and less in terms of the Ethic of Community as compared with adolescents and adults. The children especially focused on the physical and mental well-being and interests of self and other individuals. In response to the question of whether to give money to a panhandler, a conservative girl, for example, thought it best not to give money to a panhandler, "because they could go out to the store and buy, like, cigarettes or something that's not good for them. So it would be better to just give them some kind of food." A liberal girl sounded similarly concerned for the physical well-being of panhandlers, "If you give them food and water . . . and stuff they'll be able to live for a longer amount of time."

Second, there is much more to moral development than age or common maturation alone. Culture indeed shapes moral trajectories. Cultural differences were already evident by about age 10, which was the mean age of the children. Conservative children thought in terms of the Ethic of Divinity, whereas liberal children did not. A 9-year-old boy from the conservative community supported giving money to a panhandler, "because God tells us to give things." In contrast, a 10-year-old girl from the liberal community emphasized fairness, an Ethic of Autonomy concept that was superpopular among liberal children. She explained that a panhandler is just as deserving as anyone else: "just like if you took all [of] Queen Elizabeth's stuff away, she'd be just as poor as the panhandler. It's just they don't have enough stuff to get as far as Queen Elizabeth."

Third, the role of culture in moral development becomes even more evident when comparing public and private spheres of reasoning. As compared to conservative children, not only did conservative adolescents and adults reason more in terms of Divinity but they showed a bifurcation where they invoked Divinity more for public than private issues. In other words, they not only thought of their own moral lives in terms of considerations pertaining to God and scriptures but especially emphasized these considerations in terms of how they believed everyone ought to think and behave. When I first saw this result in my statistical output, I had an instant flashback to my days of attending fundamentalist Baptist churches. Of course — evangelism! To conservative adolescents and adults, the Ethic of Divinity belongs not only in the private sphere but also decidedly in the public one. Bearing witness to God, as the pastor had implored his congregants, should be "my all, my life."

Among liberals, in contrast, age intersected in a different way with spheres of morality for Divinity. Whereas liberal children and adolescents scarcely reasoned in terms of Divinity, liberal adults did. In contrast with the claims that they simply lack this language (Haidt, 2013), liberal adults primarily spoke of Divinity when contemplating their private moral issues. Here is an example of many where a liberal woman recounted her decision to find her adoptive mother against the advice of friends: "I thought it was something that in the eyes of God it was right for me to do." Another liberal woman described how she had returned $10 to Borders bookstore that the cashier mistakenly had refunded her. She said: "God knows and so it hurts Him when you cheat. He didn't cheat on me, and I shouldn't cheat on other people. By doing the right thing, the world becomes a better place. It's not enough just to do it in bigger things, you've gotta do it in little things." Some liberal adults clearly think about moral matters in terms of religion and spirituality. It is just that liberal adults have privatized the Ethic of Divinity.

Conclusions: on "culture wars" and moral psychology

So, what does this tell us about the psychology of the culture wars? From two decades of research with religious liberals and conservatives, I have come to the conclusion that the culture wars are much more public than private. That's good. It may well be why it is not truly a "war" in the United States. We can all think of the daily clashes in Congress and in the media between liberals and conservatives. But for ordinary Americans, there is an everyday moral life, too, that is more complex, more nuanced, less conflictual. While bumper stickers proclaim that "Friends don't let friends vote _____" – fill in either democrat or republican – the fact is that most people have friends across the culture wars divide. While we may get heated about public policy, things are less divided and more peaceful on the private front.

The research also tells us something basic about the psychology of morality. Moral psychology has witnessed a virtual "fall of reason [to the] current trend in psychology and neuroscience . . . in favor of gut feelings," according to Yale psychologist Paul Bloom (2013). In a nutshell, the argument in vogue is that humans make moral decisions solely based on emotions, and our thoughts are but rationalizations of what we already felt like doing. But I really think that humans have evolved to be something more than, say, chipmunks (although they probably think and plan, too). Undoubtedly, we all rationalize from time to time, but it is not all that we do. Our tremendous and distinctive capacity for reasoning is not just an epiphenomenon. In my view, the research findings indicate that the development of moral reasoning in humans involves intra- and interpersonal dialogical processes. Morality in part is a process in which we have internal dialogues with some distinct private moral reasons for weighing our behaviors – such as Ethic of Divinity reasons for liberal adults. Morality is also a social process in which we dialogue, debate, and argue with others. We do this person-to-person. We also do this at the level of groups and through public representatives – as in the culture wars.

As an immigrant who has now lived longer in the United States than in my native Denmark, I still sometimes feel apart. Over time, though, I have come to think that being a kind of anthropologist-in-residence may have virtues. I am at a close distance. It makes for a research approach with which people are at once familiar and remarkable. Certainly, I hope that my research, while not telling people how they should live their lives, nonetheless might make us more thoughtful about how we all – alike and apart – develop and live our individual and collective lives.

REFERENCES

Adelson, J. (1971). The political imagination of the young adolescent. *Daedalus*, 100, 1013–1050.

Ammerman, N. T. (1987). *Bible believers.* New Brunswick, NJ: Rutgers University Press.

Arnett, J. J. and Jensen, L. J. (2015). *There's more between heaven and earth, but who knows what it is: Danish emerging adults' views of religious and moral questions* (Unpublished manuscript). Clark University, Worcester, MA.

Bellah, R. N. (1987). Conclusion: Competing visions of the role of religion in American society. In R. N. Bellah & F. E. Greenspahn (Eds.), *Uncivil religion: Interreligious hostility in America* (pp. 119–232). New York, NY: Crossroads.

Bloom, P. (2013). *Just babies: The origins of good and evil.* New York, NY: Crown.

Carlo, G. (2006). Care-based and altruistically-based morality. In M. Killen & J. Smetana (Eds.), *Handbook of moral development* (pp. 551–580). Mahwah, NJ: Erlbaum.

Colby, A., & Damon, W. (1992). *Some do care: Contemporary lives of moral commitment.* New York, NY: Free Press.

Crabtree, S. (2010). Religiosity highest in world's poorest nations. Gallup. Retrieved from http://www.gallup.com/poll/142727/religiosity-highest-world-poorest-nations.aspx

Edwards, C. P. (1997). Morality and change: Family unity and paternal authority among Kipsigis and Abaluyia elders and students. In T. S. Weisner & C. Bradley (Eds.), *African families and the crisis of social change* (pp. 45–85). Westport, CT: Bergin & Garvey.

Eisenberg, N., Carlo, G., Murphy, B., & Van Court, P. (1995). Prosocial development in late adolescence. *Child Development*, 66, 1179–1197.

Freud, S. (1961). *Civilization and its discontents.* New York, NY: W. W. Norton. (Original work published 1930)

(2010). *The future of an illusion.* Seattle, WA: Pacific Publishing Studio. (Original work published 1927)

Gilligan, C. F. (1982). *In a different voice: Psychological theory and women's development.* Cambridge, MA: Harvard University Press.

Graham, J., Haidt, J., & Nosek, B. A. (2009). Liberals and conservatives rely on different sets of moral foundations. *Journal of Personality and Social Psychology*, 96, 1029–1046.

Haidt, J. (2013). *The righteous mind.* New York, NY: Vintage Books.

Huebner, A., & Garrod, A. (1991). Moral reasoning in a karmic world. *Human Development*, 34, 341–352.

Hunter, J. D. (1991). *Culture wars: The struggle to define America.* New York, NY: Basic Books.

Jensen, L. A. (1995). Habits of the heart revisited: Ethics of Autonomy, Community and Divinity in adults' moral language. *Qualitative Sociology*, 18, 71–86.

(1997). Different worldviews, different morals: America's culture war divide. *Human Development*, 40, 325–344.

(1998a). Different habits, different hearts: The moral languages of the culture war. *American Sociologist*, 29, 83–101.

(1998b). Moral divisions within countries between orthodoxy and progressivism: India and the United States. *Journal for the Scientific Study of Religion*, 37, 90–107.

(2006). Liberal and conservative conceptions of family: A cultural-developmental study. *International Journal for the Psychology of Religion*, 16, 253–269.

(2008). Through two lenses: A cultural-developmental approach to moral reasoning. *Developmental Review*, 28, 289–315.

(2009). Conceptions of God and the devil across the lifespan: A cultural-developmental study of religious liberals and conservatives. *Journal for the Scientific Study of Religion*, 48, 121–145.

(2011a). *Bridging cultural and developmental psychology: New syntheses in theory, research, and policy*. New York, NY: Oxford University Press.

(2011b). The cultural-developmental theory of moral psychology: A new synthesis. In L. A. Jensen (Ed.), *Bridging cultural and developmental psychology: New syntheses in theory, research, and policy* (pp. 3–25). New York, NY: Oxford University Press.

(2012). Bridging universal and cultural perspectives: A vision for developmental psychology in a global world. *Child Development Perspectives*, 6, 98–104.

Keating, D. (1990). Adolescent thinking. In S. S. Feldman & G. Elliott (Eds.), *At the threshold: The developing adolescent* (pp. 54–89). Cambridge, MA: Harvard University Press.

Killen, M. (2002). Early deliberations: A developmental psychologist investigates how children think about fairness and exclusion. *Teaching Tolerance*, 22. Retrieved from www.tolerance.org/magazine/number-22-fall-2002/feature/early-deliberations

Kohlberg, L. (1976). Moral stages and moralization: The cognitive-developmental approach. In T. Lickona (Ed.), *Moral development and behavior*. New York, NY: Holt, Rinehart and Winston.

(1984). *The psychology of moral development*. San Francisco, CA: Harper & Row.

Mahoney, A., Pargament, K. I., Murray-Swank, A., & Murray-Swank, N. (2003). Religion and the sanctification of family relationships. *Review of Religious Research*, 44, 220–236.

Marty, M. E., & Appleby, R. S. (1995). *Fundamentalisms comprehended*. Chicago, IL: University of Chicago Press.

McAdams, D. P., Albaugh, M., Farber, E., Daniels, J., Logan, R. L., & Olson, B. (2008). Family metaphors and moral intuitions: How conservatives and liberals narrate their lives. *Journal of Personality and Social Psychology*, 95, 978–990.

Miller, J. G. (1994). Cultural diversity in the morality of caring: Individually oriented versus duty-based interpersonal moral codes. *Cross-Cultural Research*, 28, 3–39.

Miller, J. G., Bersoff, D. M., & Harwood, R. L. (1990). Perceptions of social responsibility in India and in the United States: Moral imperatives or personal decisions? *Journal of Personality and Social Personality*, 58, 33–47.

Miller, J. G., & Luthar, S. (1989). Issues of interpersonal responsibility and accountability: A comparison of Indians' and Americans' moral judgments. *Social Cognition*, 7, 237–261.

Nisan, M. (1987). Moral norms and social conventions: A cross-cultural study. *Developmental Psychology*, 23, 719–725.

Olson, K. R., & Spelke, E. S. (2008). Foundations of cooperation in young children. *Cognition*, 108, 222–231.

PewResearch. (2014). U.S. religious landscape survey. Retrieved from http://religions.pewforum.org/affiliations.

Piaget, J. (1965). *The moral judgment of the child*. New York, NY: Free Press. (Original work published 1932)

(1972). Intellectual evolution from adolescence to adulthood. *Human Development,* 15, 1–12.

Rubin, K., Bukowski, W., & Parker, J. (2006). Peer interactions, relationships and groups. In W. Damon & R. M. Lerner (Eds.), *Handbook of child development.* New York, NY: Wiley.

Saraswathi, T. S. (2005). Hindu worldview in the development of selfways: The "Atman" as the real self. *New Directions for Child and Adolescent Development,* 109, 43–50. doi:10.1002/cd.136

Schlegel, A. (2011). Adolescent ties to adult communities: The intersection of culture and development. In L. A. Jensen (Ed.), *Bridging cultural and developmental approaches to psychology: New syntheses in theory, research, and policy* (pp. 138–157). New York, NY: Oxford University Press.

Schlegel, A., & Barry, H. (2015). Leaving childhood: The nature and meaning of adolescent transition rituals. In L. A. Jensen (Ed.), *The Oxford handbook of human development and culture: An interdisciplinary approach.* New York, NY: Oxford University Press.

Shweder, R. A. (1990). In defense of moral realism: Reply to Gabennesch. *Child Development,* 61, 2060–2067.

Shweder, R. A., Mahapatra, M., & Miller, J. G. (1990). Culture and moral development. In J. W. Stigler, R. A. Shweder, & G. Herdt (Eds.), *Cultural psychology* (pp. 130–204). Cambridge, United Kingdom: Cambridge University Press.

Shweder, R. A., Much, N. C., Mahapatra, M., & Park, L. (1997). The "Big Three" of morality (Autonomy, Community, Divinity), and the "big three" explanations of suffering. In A. Brandt & P. Rozin (Eds.), *Morality and health* (pp. 119–170). New York, NY: Routledge.

Snarey, J. R. (1985). Cross-cultural universality of socio-moral development: A critical review of Kohlbergian research. *Psychological Bulletin,* 97, 202–232.

Suárez-Orozco, C. (2015). Migration between and within countries: Implications for families and acculturation. In L. A. Jensen (Ed.), *The Oxford handbook of human development and culture: An interdisciplinary approach.* New York, NY: Oxford University Press.

Thompson, R. A. (2012). Whither the preconventional child? Toward a life-span moral development theory. *Child Development Perspectives,* 6, 423–429.

Trommsdorff, G. (2012). Cultural perspectives on values and religion in adolescent development: A conceptual overview and synthesis. In G. Trommsdorff & X. Chen (Eds.), *Values, religion, and culture in adolescent development* (pp. 3–45). Cambridge, United Kingdom: Cambridge University Press.

Turiel, E. (1983). *The development of social knowledge: Morality and convention.* Cambridge, United Kingdom: Cambridge University Press.

(2002). *The culture of morality.* Cambridge, United Kingdom: Cambridge University Press.

Vasquez, K., Keltner, D., Ebenbach, D. H., & Banaszynski, T. L. (2001). Cultural variation and similarity in moral rhetorics: Voices from the Philippines and the United States. *Journal of Cross-Cultural Research,* 32, 93–120.

Walker, L. J. (1989). A longitudinal study of moral reasoning. *Child Development,* 51, 131–139.

Walker, L. J., Pitts, R. C., Hennig, K. H., & Matsuba, M. K. (1995). Reasoning about morality and real-life moral problems. In M. Killen & D. Hart (Eds.), *Morality in everyday life: Developmental perspectives* (pp. 371–407). New York, NY: Cambridge University Press.

Warneken, F., & Tomasello, M. (2006). Altruistic helping in human infants and young chimpanzees. *Science*, 311, 1301–1303.

Whiting, B. B., & Edwards, C. P. (1988). *Children of different worlds: The formation of social behavior.* Cambridge, MA: Harvard University Press.

Wuthnow, R. (1989). *The struggle for America's soul: Evangelicals, liberals, and secularism.* Grand Rapids, MI: William B. Eerdmans.

Zimba, R. F. (1994). The understanding of morality, convention, and personal preference in an African setting: Findings from Zambia. *Journal of Cross-Cultural Psychology*, 25, 369–393.

Zuckerman, P. (2008). *Society without God: What the least religious nations can tell us about contentment.* New York: New York University Press.

Commentaries

9 Taking culture and context into account in understanding moral development

Joan G. Miller

This volume presents a timely set of chapters addressing the question of how to understand the development of morality through a cultural lens. This requires going beyond facsimile models of enculturation to take into account that children's understandings may differ from those emphasized in their cultural community in ways that reflect both children's developmental needs and concerns as well as their experiences and cognitive capacities. This type of focus also entails adopting a culturally broadened understanding of the scope of the moral domain and recognizing that developmental trajectories involve both common and culturally variable paths.

In terms of its central agenda, the volume adopts a developmental perspective in testing the claims of Shweder's Big Three Ethics (Shweder, Much, & Mahapatra, *et al.*, 1997). Pointing to the need to broaden the scope of the moral domain, Shweder and his colleagues argue that conceptions of morality include not only ideas of autonomy that are privileged in the universalistic perspectives that dominate contemporary models of morality within psychology (e.g., Turiel, 2006) but as well notions of community and of divinity. Arguing for a cultural-developmental approach to morality, Jensen (2008) extended work on the Big Three Ethics to more fully take into account issues of development (see also Jensen, Chapter 1, this volume). She forwarded an ambitious theoretical model that calls for greater attention to the developmental emergence of these diverse forms of morality and that forwards broad predictions regarding how the various moralities may be expected to change in emphasis and in nature with development. The predictions encompass claims about common developmental trends that are anticipated to occur in reliance on the moral perspectives and developmental differences in the specific types of ethical considerations taken into account. Thus, it is predicted that an emphasis on the Ethic of Autonomy will arise early in development and remain relatively stable with age in all cultural communities, though the specific types of autonomy concerns raised, such as self-interest versus other's interest, will reflect age-related changes. In turn, it is predicted that the morality of Community will show an age increase in the degree to which it is emphasized and in the types of considerations individuals take into account, whereas the morality of Divinity will be given little attention early in development but show an age increase starting in adolescence. Notably, whereas the model forwards these types of distinctive predictions, it also acknowledges that the predictions may need to be qualified depending on cultural context. For example, it is noted that moral outlooks emphasizing Divinity may be evident early in development in cultures emphasizing spiritual concerns. It is a central goal of the present volume not only to provide evidence on which to ground the cultural-developmental approach but to inspire future theory and research. In my commentary, I underscore the important contributions of the work presented in this volume and what I see as promising directions for future theory and research on these issues.

As a background for understanding the present chapters, it is important to note how research on culture and morality has developed in social and developmental psychology in following up on Shweder's Big Three Ethics model (Shweder, Much, Mahapatra, *et al.*, 1997). Shweder's argument for the Big Three Ethics assumed that the three ethics represent outlooks that coexist, overlap, as well as vary in their usage in relation to different types of issues. In this model, Shweder also assumed that moralities entail culturally specific perspectives and thus need to be understood in emic terms. For example, in arguing for the morality of Divinity, Shweder presented in-depth discussion of Hindu Indian outlooks, with specific attention to practices in the Old Temple town of Bhubaneswar in which he and his colleagues conducted their research (e.g., Shweder & Much, 1987). Importantly, although Shweder and his colleagues make use, in cases, of cross-cultural comparisons (e.g., Shweder, Mahapatra, & Miller, 1990), they tap outlooks in relation to local cultural practices and attend to respondents' qualitative reasoning. Whereas Shweder presents his theoretical perspective as a challenge to the exclusive focus on autonomy of the distinct domain perspective, he retains the formal distinctions between morality, convention, and personal choice made within the distinct domain perspective (e.g., Turiel, 1983). In their research, Shweder and his colleagues thus included criterion probe judgments to assess empirically whether individuals treat concerns involving Autonomy, Community, and/or Divinity as matters of morality as compared with matters of social convention or personal choice (Shweder, Mahapatra, & Miller, 1990).

However, as research on the Big Three Ethics of morality has gained in popularity within both social and developmental psychology, it has developed in directions that deviate from Shweder's formulation. There has been a tendency in this recent research to treat the different moralities as discrete rather than overlapping outlooks. Also, researchers increasingly rely on scale measures as the preferred method for tapping the different moralities, with the researchers operationalizing outlooks on morality in terms of general etic statements given in scale items or coding schemes. Also, in this recent work, researchers commonly assess morality in terms of broad dimensions, such as perceived wrongness, without making formal distinctions between issues of morality, convention, and personal choice.

Contributions

In terms of contributions of the chapters in the present volume, the strengths and limitations of scale measures are made clear in the chapter by Guerra and Giner-Sorolla (Chapter 6, this volume) that presents results from cross-cultural comparisons undertaken in Brazil, Israel, Japan, the United Kingdom, and New Zealand on responses to the Community, Autonomy, and Divinity Scale (CADS) (Guerra & Giner-Sorolla, 2010). The examination of outlooks on morality in such a wide range of cultural communities represents a strength of the approach of Guerra and Giner-Sorolla that is facilitated by their use of a common assessment instrument. However, their reliance on the CADS limits the sensitivity of the assessment of morality possible. As in other similar scale measures in this tradition (e.g., Graham, Nosek, Haidt, *et al.*, 2011), morality is operationally defined only in terms of actions considered as either "morally right" or "morally wrong," with no criteria offered to assess how respondents define the linguistic terms of *moral* or *right/wrong*. Also, the scale taps summary judgments about moral behavior in general, providing little insight into the types of moral evaluations made in specific cases. The research by Guerra and Giner-Sorolla (Chapter 6, this volume) importantly corroborates certain past related research findings that have used similar scale measures. However, it yields results that the authors themselves acknowledge may reflect, in part, limitations in the issues assessed, such as the items on the CADS tapping Divinity tending to center on religious rules and institutions and not encompassing conceptions of natural law that may be more relevant for Japanese. Whereas the chapter uncovers intriguing empirical trends among the Japanese, who show the lowest endorsements of Autonomy, Community, and Divinity of all the cultural groups compared, the absence of assessment of qualitative reasoning and possible skewing in certain scale items do not make it possible to gain insight into the processes underlying such findings.

The importance of attention to local cultural sensitivities is further highlighted in the chapters examining Hindu Indian outlooks, including the chapters presenting the research conducted in Baroda by Pandya and Bhangaokar (Chapter 2, this volume) among third and sixth graders and Kapadia and Bhangaokar (Chapter 4, this volume) among adolescents and middle-aged adults. The research by Pandya and Bhangaokar (Chapter 2, this volume) highlights respects in which moral outlooks are embedded in everyday sociocultural practices in such a way that they not only emerge early in development but are so taken for granted that they remain implicit. For example, in striking findings, Pandya and Bhangaokar demonstrate that whereas third-grade Hindu Indian children emphasize punishment concerns that are congruent with claims made by Piaget (1932) about the existence of an early focus by young children on objective consequences, the Indian children's focus on punishment entails a wide range of both explicit and implicit divinity concepts, such as convictions about the omnipotence of God and beliefs that one's moral conduct has consequences for the afterlife. Likewise, in their chapter, Kapadia and Bhangaokar (Chapter 4, this volume) highlight respects in which certain key concepts have a different meaning for Indian respondents than captured in the *Coding Manual: Ethics of Autonomy, Community, and Divinity* (Jensen, 2004), such as the link of concepts of reciprocity to an Ethic of Community among Indians rather than its link to Autonomy, as assumed in the coding manual (see, e.g., Miller, Bland, Kallberg-Shroff, *et al.*, 2014). They also underscore the inattention paid in the coding manual to culturally specific concepts, such as *karma, paap,* and *dharma/kartavya.* More generally, both chapters provide evidence that Hindu Indian outlooks reflect a monistic outlook in which Autonomy, Community, and Divinity concerns are understood as coterminous and mutually constitutive rather than as discrete perspectives. Thus, whereas their research supports the relevance of all three forms of morality, it also points to limitations entailed in a scoring system that treats the forms of morality as discrete.

The importance of giving greater attention to the interdependence of the moral perspectives is further underscored in the chapter by Hickman and DiBianca Fasoli (Chapter 7, this volume), who make a powerful case for the need to recognize the overlap in moral orientations and the distortion and oversimplification entailed in treating them as discrete types. The authors point out that treating the three ethics as discrete embodies an etic perspective that fails to capture ways the outlooks interrelate in everyday reasoning. As Hickman and DiBianca Fasoli argue in reference to the three ethics, "while we find these distinctions to be analytically useful as Weberian ideal types ... these ideas so deeply interpenetrate one another that it calls into question the empirical utility of these distinctions in characterizing a cultural moral code on its own terms." Hickman and DiBianca Fasoli support their claims in research conducted in a wide range of cultural settings, including an American evangelical Christian community in Boston (DiBianca Fasoli, 2013) and among Hmong families in both Thailand and the United States (Hickman, 2011). Their findings employ methodological approaches that have considerable ecological validity in that they are based on discourse analysis of conversations undertaken by respondents about realistic examples of everyday breaches. Hickman and DiBianca Fasoli (Chapter 7, this volume) present empirical evidence that the ethics provide parallel justifications in cases in which they offer distinct rationales for a particular position and provide divergent justifications in cases in which they offer incompatible rationales. However, they also show, interestingly, that the ethics may provide "imbricated" justifications that inseparably weave the diverse ethics into a single rationale and in which the ethics cannot be meaningfully separated analytically without dismantling the coherence of an individual's response.

Finally, a major contribution of the present set of chapters is to provide insight into ways the ethics may conflict with – rather than be congruent with – cultural values and practices and may give rise to increasingly divergent outlooks with increasing age. For example, in their chapter assessing the moral outlooks of Mormon emerging adults from Utah, Padilla-Walker and Nelson (Chapter 5, this volume) document that members of this community struggle with negotiating the worldviews associated with the moralities of Divinity and Autonomy. While the authors demonstrate that the Ethic of Autonomy is important for Mormon emerging adults and is linked to positive adaptive implications, such as being negatively associated with depression, they show that the Ethic of Divinity is positively associated with the family centeredness that is emphasized in Mormon culture and takes on more importance in this community than has been found in research conducted among emerging adults from secular US communities. Likewise, in research conducted among Finnish adolescents from nonreligious, religiously liberal, and religiously conservative backgrounds, Vainio (Chapter 3, this volume) demonstrates that whereas religiously conservative Finnish adolescents place greater weight on the Ethic of Divinity than do nonconservative Finnish adolescents, the moral outlooks of all of the subgroups of Finnish adolescents reflect values emphasized in the larger society, in this case, notions of shared responsibility based in the Nordic welfare state. In turn, in comparing the moral outlooks of individuals from religiously liberal as compared with religiously conservative backgrounds, Jensen (Chapter 8, this volume) provides evidence for the predicted developmental pattern of greater commonality in moral outlooks early in development and increasing divergence with increasing age. Jensen documents that whereas young children from liberal as compared with conservative religious background share a common emphasis on Autonomy, their responses show greater difference from each other at older ages, as Community concerns increase in all groups and Divinity concerns are given greater emphasis by conservative as compared with liberal adults. This chapter also highlights the impact of content on moral outlooks in contrasting reasoning about a spontaneously generated moral issue from one's real life experience, termed "private" issues, as compared with issues supplied by the researchers, termed "public" issues. Thus, for example, the findings show that whereas conservatives tended to invoke Community reasons for public issues, liberals tended to invoke Community concerns for private issues, with the reverse group difference observed in the case of a subset of Autonomy reasons.

Future directions

In terms of valuable directions for future research, it is important to give greater attention to the context and content under consideration in the assessment of moral outlooks. It is problematic to make claims about general cross-cultural differences in the emphasis placed on each type of morality, given the contextual dependence of all forms of moral reasoning. For example, in her introductory chapter, Jensen (Chapter 1, this volume) refers to comparative research in Taiwan and the United States (Li, 2011; Miller, Fung, Lin, *et al.*, 2012) that she portrays as indicating that "there is a more pronounced emphasis on the Ethic of Community in Taiwan than in the United States, and a stronger emphasis on the Ethic of Autonomy in the United States than Taiwan." However, given the focus in these studies on child socialization practices, any such conclusion needs to be understood as limited to the context under consideration and not to be portrayed as a general cultural difference. For example, in research that my colleagues and I undertook examining moral outlooks on helping family and friends among Americans and Indians, we uncovered tendencies for Americans to give greater weight to personal decision making than did Indians (e.g., Miller & Bersoff, 1992, 1995, 1998; Miller, Bersoff, & Harwood, 1990). However, we concluded not that Indians give greater weight to community concerns than do Americans but rather that each cultural group tends to approach community in qualitatively distinctive ways (Miller, 1994). Our research also documented that the type of cultural variation observed depends on the content under consideration, with considerable cross-cultural commonality in moral outlooks on community found in cases involving parental care for their young children (Miller & Bersoff, 1998) and in situations involving urgent need for help (Miller, Bersoff, & Harwood, 1990). It must be recognized that moral reasoning in all instances is sensitive to the content under consideration and thus that it is problematic to make context-free claims of general developmental patterns or context-free claims of cultural or subgroup differences. In this regard, a scale measure, such as the CADS, that asks respondents to indicate considerations that they view as important in morality in general may be tapping lay theories about the nature of morality but is likely to have limited predictive relationship to everyday moral judgment.

It will also be valuable in future research to give greater attention to distinguishing among morality, social convention, and personal choice rather than only to focus on coding qualitative themes endorsed by respondents. Whereas these kinds of formal distinctions are assessed by some of the authors of the present chapters, in several chapters the authors center exclusively on tapping the moral themes of Autonomy, Community, and Divinity and do not attempt to distinguish between moral versus nonmoral outlooks. In arguing for the need to go beyond approaches that treat in moral terms anything labeled as wrong or as moral, I am not proposing that researchers should necessarily adopt the specific types of criterion judgment probes developed within the distinct domain tradition (e.g., Turiel, 1983). However, I am asserting that in focusing exclusively on qualitative moral themes and in not attempting to distinguish between whether individuals view an issue as a conventional as compared with moral concern, investigators are reverting to an earlier approach to morality that predates the work of Kohlberg (e.g., Kohlberg, 1971) and that is arguably less informative than subsequent theoretical perspectives on morality in developmental psychology.

Finally, a valuable direction for future research is to go beyond a focus on Autonomy, Community, and Divinity as the units for cross-cultural and developmental comparison. Whereas it is important to recognize that morality encompasses all of these types of considerations and thus that a focus exclusively on issues of autonomy is problematic, it is limiting to treat the categories of Autonomy, Community, and Divinity per se as the units for understanding cultural and developmental variation. Research has already established that these types of concerns are reflected in moral outlooks universally and vary over development in the types of qualitative considerations taken into account. However, what remains important to explore through a cultural-developmental lens, such as in the chapters by Pandya and Bhangaokar (Chapter 2, this volume), Kapadia and Bhangaokar (Chapter 4, this volume), and Jensen (Chapter 8, this volume), is the nature of moral decision making in different contexts and how this varies with age and with the particular content under consideration. Also, it is important to give greater attention to the enculturation processes entailed in moral socialization, such as considered in the chapter by Hickman and DiBianca Fasoli (Chapter 7, this volume). To achieve these goals, research must be directed to testing new theoretical claims, exploring new phenomena relevant to the development of morality, and going beyond a stance that treats the tripartite Three Ethics scheme as the central rubric for cross-cultural comparison.

Conclusion

The present volume is highly successful in achieving its aspiration of bringing a cultural-developmental lens to testing the claims of the Big Three Ethics model. The chapters not only provide support for the central claims of Jensen's cultural-developmental approach to morality but uncover new findings and point to valuable directions for future theory and research. Adopting a developmental lens in cultural research remains a relatively underexplored topic, and the chapters in this volume point to the importance of such a perspective and to the many valuable insights it can provide.

REFERENCES

DiBianca Fasoli, A. (2013). *Moral psychology and the socialization of helping among evangelical Christian families* (Doctoral dissertation). University of Chicago, Chicago, IL.

Graham, J., Nosek, B. A., Haidt, J., Iyer, R., Koleva, S., & Ditto, P. H. (2011). Mapping the moral domain. *Journal of Personality and Social Psychology*, 101(2), 366–385.

Guerra, V. M., & Giner-Sorolla, R. (2010). The Community, Autonomy, and Divinity Scale (CADS): A new tool for the cross-cultural study of morality. *Journal of Cross-Cultural Psychology*, 41(1), 35–50.

Hickman, J. R. (2011). *Morality and personhood in the Hmong diaspora: A person-centered ethnography of migration and resettlement* (Doctoral dissertation). University of Chicago, Chicago, IL.

Jensen, L. A. (2004). *Coding manual: Ethics of Autonomy, Community and Divinity (Revised)*. Retrieved from www.lenearnettjensen.com

   (2008). Through two lenses. A cultural-developmental approach to moral psychology. *Developmental Review*, 28, 289–315.

Kohlberg, L. (1971). From is to ought: How to commit the naturalistic fallacy and get away with it in the study of moral development. In T. Mischel (Ed.), *Cognitive development and epistemology* (pp. 151–236). New York, NY: Academic.

Li, J. (2011). Cultural frames of children's learning beliefs. In L. A. Jensen (Ed.), *Bridging cultural and developmental psychology: New syntheses in theory, research, and policy* (pp. 26–48). New York, NY: Oxford University Press.

Miller, J. G. (1994). Cultural diversity in the morality of caring: Individually oriented versus duty-based interpersonal moral codes. *Cross Cultural Research*, 28, 3–39.

Miller, J. G., & Bersoff, D. M. (1992). Culture and moral judgment: How are conflicts between justice and interpersonal responsibilities resolved? *Journal of Personality and Social Psychology*, 62, 541–554.

   (1995). Development in the context of everyday family relationships: Culture, interpersonal morality and adaptation. In M. Killen & D. Hart (Eds.), *Morality in everyday life: A developmental perspective* (pp. 259–282). Cambridge, United Kingdom: Cambridge University Press.

Miller, J. G., & Bersoff, D. B. (1998). The role of liking in perceptions of the moral responsibility to help: A cultural perspective. *Journal of Experimental Social Psychology*, 34, 443–469.

Miller, J. G., Bersoff, D. M., & Harwood, R. L. (1990). Perceptions of social responsibilities in India and in the United States: Moral imperatives or personal decisions? *Journal of Personality and Social Psychology*, 58(1), 33–47.

Miller, J. G., Bland, C., Kallberg-Shroff, M., Tseng, C.-Y., Montes-George, J., Ryan, K., . . . Chakravarthy, S. (2014). Culture and the role of exchange versus communal norms in friendship. *Journal of Experimental Social Psychology*, 53, 79–93.

Miller, P. J., Fung, H., Lin, S., Chen, E. C.-H., & Boldt, B. R. (2012). How socialization happens on the ground: Narrative practices as alternate socializing pathways in Taiwanese and European-American families. *Monographs of the Society for Research in Child Development*, 77, 1–140.

Piaget, J. (1932). *The moral judgment of the child*. London, United Kingdom: Routledge & Kegan Paul.

Shweder, R. A., Mahapatra, M., & Miller, J. (1990). Culture and moral development. In J. W. Stigler, R. A. Shweder, & G. Herdt (Eds.), *Cultural psychology: Essays on comparative human development* (pp. 130–204). New York, NY: Cambridge University Press.

Shweder, R. A., & Much, N. C. (1987). Determinants of meaning: Discourse and moral socialization. In W. M. Kurtines & J. L. Gewirtz (Eds.), *Moral development through social interaction* (pp. 197–244). New York, NY: Wiley.

Shweder, R. A., Much, N. C., Mahapatra, M., & Park, L. (1997). The "Big Three" of morality (Autonomy, Community, Divinity) and the "big three" explanations of suffering. In A. M. Brandt (Ed.), *Morality and health* (pp. 119–169). New York, NY: Routledge.

Turiel, E. (1983). *The development of social knowledge: Morality and convention.* Cambridge, United Kingdom: Cambridge University Press.

Turiel, E. (2006). *The development of morality: Handbook of child psychology: Vol. 3, Social, emotional, and personality development* (6th ed.). Hoboken, NJ: Wiley.

10 The next step for the cultural-developmental approach: from moral reasoning to moral intentions and behavior

Gisela Trommsdorff

The main goal of this volume is to present a cultural-developmental approach to moral psychology. The volume addresses the divergent and multiple ways that morality develops in diverse cultures, thus synthesizing developmental and cultural perspectives. It draws attention to the question of how to bridge the lenses of developmental and cultural psychology. The authors expand current theoretical approaches by including conceptualizations of morality beyond Western traditions and highlighting more than one kind of moral reasoning. The goal of this volume is to lay the groundwork for a theoretical approach to moral development that is valid both across and within cultures.

Overview of the volume

Little is known about the development of moral reasoning across the life course in diverse cultures. This volume includes contributions by scholars from a variety of countries who present findings on diverse contexts of moral development. The volume, however, avoids the problem of presenting heterogeneous theoretical approaches. All contributions share the cultural-developmental approach to moral reasoning, and, more specifically, they share Jensen's (2008, 2011, 2015, and Chapter 1, this volume) assumptions of the template model.

Jensen conceptualizes moral development based on a cultural-developmental template describing developmental patterns of moral reasoning across the life course in terms of three Ethics of Autonomy, Community, and Divinity. The idea of the template model is that the general developmental patterns for the ethics emerge somewhat differently in different cultural contexts and vary on how prominent they become in the course of development in different cultures. For example, the model predicts a peak in the development of Ethic of Autonomy reasoning among American emerging adults. The model also predicts early and prominent development of Ethic of Community reasoning in collectivistic

This chapter is related to the project "Development of Intentionality" (Tr 169/14-3) as part of the Research Group Limits of Intentionality, University of Konstanz, supported by the German National Research Council (DFG).

cultures and low levels of development of Ethic of Divinity in individualistic, religiously liberal Western contexts.

This cultural-developmental theoretical model that unifies the volume is also useful because the authors come from diverse disciplines, including anthropology, social psychology, and developmental psychology. Furthermore, the authors make use of different research approaches, including highly diverse samples and diverse qualitative and quantitative measurement techniques for collecting data. While there is theoretical unity across the chapters, the heterogeneity of disciplines and research samples and assessment techniques also allow for promising challenges, modifications, and expansions of the underlying theoretical model. In all, this allows for the advancement of cultural-developmental research on morality.

The volume consists of a foreword by Richard Shweder, eight chapters, and two commentaries. The first, introductory chapter by Jensen (Chapter 1, this volume) presents a theoretical overview, explains the main ideas of the template model, and provides integration of key findings from the chapters in the volume. The cultural side of the present theoretical approach goes back to Richard Shweder, who has challenged Western theorizing on religion and morality (Shweder, Much, Mahapatra, *et al.*, 1997). The next seven chapters present data from diverse cultures and developmental periods. Most chapters include samples that differ on religiosity, thus highlighting the complex role of religion in moral reasoning.

Specifically, two chapters include religious samples from the United States (religiously conservative emerging adults in Padilla-Walker & Nelson, Chapter 5, this volume; religiously liberal and conservative children, adolescents, and adults in Jensen, Chapter 8, this volume). One chapter compares nonreligious and religious Finnish adolescents (Vainio, Chapter 3, this volume). Two chapters examine developmental patterns among Indian samples, focusing on children (Pandya & Bhangaokar, Chapter 2, this volume) and on adolescents and adults (Kapadia & Bhangaokar, Chapter 4, this volume). One chapter investigates the moral codes of emerging adults in five countries (Guerra & Giner-Sorolla, Chapter 6, this volume). Finally, Hickman and DiBianca Fasoli (Chapter 7, this volume) draw on culturally relevant moral vignettes for their discourse analyses among American Evangelical Christian families and Hmong families in both Thailand and the United States. The Appendices to the volume include three questionnaires and a coding manual used by the authors of this volume for their empirical studies on moral reasoning.

As a whole, then, the volume entails a novel theoretical approach to moral reasoning by pointing to the phenomenon of multiple ethics in culture and development. It also provides tools to study moral development in future research. The individual chapters offer specific and original contributions to the general topic of moral development on the basis of the cultural-developmental template.

Most chapters study developmental patterns of moral reasoning in terms of the three Ethics of Autonomy, Community, and Divinity, in line with the editor's theoretical starting point. Furthermore, the chapters focus on development in cultural context, discussing cultural specificities as well as universalities. With respect to the concept of culture, most chapters also address religiosity as a component of culture and a major factor in moral development.

In sum, the diverse methods and samples of the volume may seem a limitation at first sight, but in my view turn out to be a strength. The great advantage of this otherwise heterogeneous volume is that the chapters are organized around the template model approach. This theoretical frame is appealing, and the chapters represent a significant theoretical improvement to moral psychology by enabling the study of more than one kind of moral reasoning through the inclusion of culture and religion (e.g., Shweder, 1990). Thereby, the volume also builds on progress achieved in the study of moral development by cultural scholars (Miller, Bersoff, & Harwood, 1990).

There is some repetition across chapters (the definitions of the three ethics), but the meaning of major concepts (culture, religiosity, moral reasoning, moral code) is also developed somewhat differently in different chapters. Many of the chapters address hypothetical dilemmas, whereas predictions of *moral behavior* is the focus of but one chapter. Also, the cross-sectional data of most chapters limit the discussion of developmental issues. I also think that future theoretical and empirical work would profit from taking into account alternative research on culture, religion, and morality in individual development. However, the major strength of this volume is that it opens the door for a new and promising cultural-developmental approach to moral psychology, thus contributing to the science of moral development in a global world.

In the following, I therefore first focus on moral intentions and behavior, conceiving of moral development as an aspect of agency. Self-regulation, an indicator of intentionality, is viewed here as an important aspect for the development of moral behavior. Second, I address moral agency and behavior as related to self- and worldviews. I discuss Jensen's approach of the three ethics in relation to cultural differences in self- and worldviews, focusing on the value of autonomy and relatedness underlying different approaches to moral behavior in terms of cultural fit.

From moral reasoning to moral intentions and behavior

Moral behavior as agency

In the following, I conceptualize moral development as an aspect of agency that aims to achieve a fit between the self and the world in line with moral standards or rules of the community. This view allows for an extension of the study of moral development to moral behavior. Moral behavior (e.g., helping, cooperation) is based on agency and goes beyond cognitive and motivational processes of moral reasoning. Basic preconditions for the development of moral behavior are intentionality (Tomasello, 1999) and self-regulation (including behavior and emotion regulation; Trommsdorff, 2015).

The question for the development of moral behavior is how a fit between the self and the world can be achieved in such a way that culturally valid and internalized moral standards of the community are met. Once the individual develops the goal to achieve this fit, this fuels the motivation to organize the goal-directed behavior in line with moral standards. Elements of this moral motivation are expectations of successful goal achievement (e.g., due to self-efficacy beliefs), which promote agency in moral behavior. Other elements of this moral motivation are self-regulatory processes. The development of self-regulation implies behavioral regulation (e.g., executive control) and the regulation of internal mental processes (control of emotions, motivation, cognitions; for an overview, see Heikamp, Trommsdorff, & Fäsche, 2013; Karoly, 1993). So far, little is known about the developmental processes of agency and intentionality in moral behavior. Even less is known about the impact of cultural factors on the development of agency and intentionality (including motivation and self-regulation) in moral behavior (Trommsdorff, in press).

In their culture-informed research on moral psychology, Miller, Bersoff, and Harwood (1990) have pointed to the role of agency in moral behavior. There is room for individual interpretation and decision making (depending on the person and the situation) even in cases of moral obligations and regulations. Duty-based moral behavior may focus on conformity or on caring, as a recent study on the influence of cultural values has shown (Becker, Vignoles, Owe, et al., 2014).

A child develops a self-view and a worldview and related values and rules for moral behavior that are dependent on the cultural context. *Worldviews* are subjective and focus on the material (social, physical, and natural) and the non-material and supernatural ("other") world where religious beliefs and spiritual experiences become relevant (Trommsdorff, 2015). Depending on whether the material and nonmaterial worlds are seen as fixed or malleable, different *control beliefs* (Rothbaum & Wang, 2011) and related qualities of *agency* are activated by adapting to the given circumstances ("secondary control") or by changing the situation according to one's own goals ("primary control"). Self- and worldviews are fueled by cultural values, and they influence moral standards and enter into religious and moral intentions (Trommsdorff, 2015).

Cultural values inform the development of self- and worldviews and the respective moral standards and "systems" of meaning (Molden & Dweck, 2006). Moral standards influence goal setting and motivate behavior. Cultural values thus function as motivational orientations that underlie self- and world-views. For example, cultural values prioritizing an independent self are related to moral standards of autonomy, focusing on the individual internal characteristics, whereas cultural values prioritizing an interdependent self are related to moral standards of community, focusing on situational (social) factors. In some cultural contexts, moral standards and rules are clearly defined, they have a specific meaning, and they are related to specific behavior; in other contexts, moral standards and rules have to be interpreted, they may be negotiated, and they can vary among different contexts. For example, children's prosocial behavior varies according to their cultural background (European American, Asian) and their interpretation of the situation: is the child's prosocial intervention helpful or undesirable (losing face) for a stranger who needs help (Trommsdorff, Friedlmeier, & Mayer, 2007)? This implies that nonoccurrence of prosocial intervention may be motivated by empathic concern. This also implies agency when deciding between intervention and inhibition (or promotion and avoidance goals). Further, during individual development the definition and options for moral behavior change depending on sociocultural expectations and implicit developmental theories of the socializing agents. During the life course, moral rules change as a result of developmental tasks or sociocultural changes. Furthermore, in a changing society, old and new values may conflict in decision making and moral behavior. Immigrants often experience such conflicting moral rules during acculturation processes. In general, in the present globalized world, individuals face the developmental task to coconstruct moral guidelines and organize their moral behavior accordingly. Jensen's template model of the three ethics becomes relevant again.

For example, in several East Asian cultures (such as Japan), the young child is perceived as being directly related to God or the Other World. The moral imperative is that parents refrain from negative sanctions of the young child's lack of conformity to rules. Instead, the child learns to distinguish "good" from "bad" and to identify moral behavior through observation or guided participation in everyday practices. Thereby, the child develops a self-construal influenced by cultural values and moral orientations, and, further, moral behavior develops in a way that fits the sociocultural self.

The contexts and the respective options for moral behavior are to a certain degree actively selected by the individual. For example, moral behavior may imply choosing between "Self's Interest" and "Other's Interest" (see the standard coding manual for the three ethics in Appendix A). However, such intentional, goal-oriented, agentic moral development is limited by biological and sociocultural boundaries. Therefore, research on agency in moral development has implications for the study of agency and intentionality in a cultural-developmental framework (Trommsdorff, 2012b).

To summarize, so far, Jensen's model of the three ethics has been largely tested for moral reasoning. When testing the relation between moral reasoning and moral behavior in future research, the role of agentic self-regulation in cultural context will be of major concern. The development of both moral reasoning and moral behavior is guided by cultural values and culture-informed moral standards and may be studied according to Jensen's template framework of the three ethics. Research on the development of moral *behavior* should take into account agency and therefore focus on intentionality, decision making, and self-regulation processes. The cultural context influencing the child's socialization and the development of the child's intentionality conveys cultural values, related moral standards, and moral reasoning, thus influencing the child's development of moral agency, including moral motivation, emotions, and moral behavior.

Development of self-regulation

One aspect of moral agency and intentionality is the development of self-regulation, especially behavioral (such as delay of rewards, focus of attention, impulse control) and emotion regulation (such as modulating the experience and expression of positive and negative emotions; Trommsdorff, 2009). Self-regulation is motivated to reach goals in the face of difficulties and over time. Self-regulation is shaped by cultural models of independence or interdependence and is related to self- and worldviews (e.g., people's entity or incremental theories in stability or malleability of self; Dweck, 2000; Molden & Dweck, 2006), control beliefs (e.g., primary, secondary, harmony control; Morling & Evered, 2006; Weisz, Rothbaum, & Blackburn, 1982), and the preference for approach/promotion– or avoidance/prevention–focused goals (Higgins, 2012). Self-regulation guides culturally adaptive behavior in development (Trommsdorff, 2009, 2012b, 2015; in press). On the one hand, self-regulation results from the internalization of rules in line with the expectations and goals of socializing agents. Thereby, it is relevant for moral judgment. On the other hand, self-regulation is relevant for pursuing culturally valued goals and for the construction of a moral identity based on the internalization of moral values and norms.

Successful internalization is influenced by the quality of the parent-child relationship (Grusec & Goodnow, 1994). Kochanska, Coy, and Murray (2001) view "committed compliance" as an early precursor of moral internalization, strongly related to the internalization of parental rules and values, whereas "situational compliance" is mostly sustained by parental control depending on external factors. Since parenting, including beliefs, goals, and behavior, is influenced by the cultural context (Rothbaum & Trommsdorff, 2007), the goals for moral behavior (indicated by parental rules) should largely be consistent with cultural values guiding the children's moral goals. Here, self-regulation and willpower are necessary, that is, postponing desired rewards to a later time (delay of gratification; Mischel, 1996), inhibiting aggressive behavior, and using effortful control of one's impulses. Agentic self-regulation in the development of morality therefore serves to pursue internalized culturally valued moral goals.

Moral agency as related to self- and worldviews

Broadly conceptualized, the moral goals for moral behavior may focus on "changing the self," that is, changing one's motives, needs, and emotions, or the focus may be on "changing the world," that is, influencing other persons, animals, or objects. For both kinds of goals, agentic self-regulation is needed. However, depending on culture, different aspects of intentionality and agency are activated (Trommsdorff, 2007, 2009).

Three ethics and moral agency

In relation to cultural tasks, cultural models of self, and individual development, the broad question guiding moral development is whether primarily to change the world ("primary control") or change the self ("secondary control") (Rothbaum & Wang, 2011). An individual's preference is part of that person's self-view and worldview: is the self or the world seen as malleable? For example, the Ethic of Autonomy may be related to achieving independence and self-reliance by primary control. The Ethic of Community may be related to achieving interdependence by secondary control; thus, changing oneself serves the goal of maintaining interpersonal harmony in one's social group. However, whether the Ethic of Divinity is related to either primary or secondary control depends on various factors, such as whether the divine order focuses on disciplining nonbelievers or on regulating individual desires and needs or on accepting fate control. Here, basic differences in religious orientations may impact moral motivation and related behavior.

Thus, the development of morality is interrelated with a specific self- and worldview and depends on the normative value priorities and the socialization experiences of children and adolescents (Trommsdorff, 2012a). The self- and worldview give "meaning" (Molden & Dweck, 2006) to moral values and to related agentic self-regulation. However, moral values are not necessarily distinct and exclusive. For example, both the Ethics of Autonomy and Community can be socialized within cultures and can coexist within individuals. Depending on the situation (e.g., private or public sphere) and the developmental stage, the use of either ethic may differ, as several of the contributions to this volume based on Jensen's template model show.

The psychological theorizing underlying the two ethics of Autonomy and Community has its roots in a long line of psychological research. Ryan and Deci (2000), for example, assume the driving quality of three basic needs: autonomy, relatedness, and competence. The need for autonomy has been assumed to be a driving force in most mainstream developmental and social psychological research. The relevance of relatedness (and belonging) was "discovered" in the psychology of religion (Bakan, 1966) and of gender and achievement (Spence, 1985), and later it was acknowledged in personality and developmental research (Guisinger & Blatt, 1994). While autonomy has been considered a basic need in most research carried out in Western countries, the impact of relatedness and interdependence has been discussed in culture-informed social psychological and developmental research (e.g., Markus & Kitayama, 1991).

The value of interdependence resembles Jensen's (2015) description of the Ethic of Community. The value of relatedness organizes moral thinking and behavior around the goals of taking care of the well-being of others (preferably group members such as one's family) and maintaining and fostering social harmony. When social-oriented values of relatedness organize morality, appropriate moral behavior requires emotional and behavioral self-regulation. For example, when frustration arises, anger expression is avoided or inhibited in order not to affect social harmony. Moreover, the experience of anger is less prevalent and occurs only later in development as a result of socialization conditions of anger inhibition (Kornadt, 2011). In Java and Japan, for example, the expression of anger is conceived of as immature and therefore is discouraged (Cole & Tan, 2007; Trommsdorff, 2012b). Self-regulation in the expression of negative emotions is regarded as a "prosocial" moral value. From a European American cultural perspective, in contrast, self-regulation and inhibition of negative emotions and behavior are often seen as running counter to the value of authentic emotions and behaviors. The Ethic of Community, then, may serve individual needs for relatedness and the needs of group members to maintain group harmony. These needs could induce conflicting motivations and goals in cases of adhering to an independent self-construal. In cases of prioritizing cultural values of interdependence, such conflicting motivations are less probable (Trommsdorff, 2012b).

In culture-informed research, the notion of interdependence (often contrasted with independence) may capture the specific moral values characterizing the Ethic of Community. Some cultural-developmental studies acknowledge the coexistence of autonomy and relatedness (e.g., Kagitcibasi, 2005). However, studies focusing on the culture-specific meaning of autonomy and relatedness have shown cultures that prioritize interdependency as a normative cultural value in socialization to have a stronger preference for relatedness (Rothbaum & Trommsdorff, 2007). The development of relatedness is based on emotional bonding and assurance (Rothbaum & Trommsdorff, 2007). That said, relatedness in Asian cultures such as Japan also entails autonomy. For example, in our studies we have found that the Japanese mother allows her child to continue playing even though she wants her child to comply and go home. Her actively "giving in" (model for secondary control) induces empathic concern in her child and the motivation to actively restore harmony in the mother-child relation; accordingly, the child complies without frustration (secondary control; Trommsdorff & Kornadt, 2003). Thus, the Ethic of Community may foster the development of interdependence, empathy, and prosocial behavior while individuals engage Autonomy to repair or to stabilize the interpersonal relationship. This dynamic co-occurrence of ethics that I have seen in Japan is in line with the suggestions by Hickman and DiBianca Fasoli (Chapter 7, this volume). Empirical data on the functional relation between autonomy and relatedness have also been gathered in a study on distress and prosocial behavior in German, Israeli, Indonesian, and Malaysian preschool children (Trommsdorff, Friedlmeier, & Mayer, 2007). This study suggested that the Ethic of Community (prosocial behavior) can be inhibited by an imbalance in the value of autonomy and relatedness in preschool children. Further research should deal with questions of value change, the "successful" transmission of values during socialization (Trommsdorff, 2012a), and conditions for discrepancies in the preference of autonomy or community values and for possible parent-child conflict (in contrast with family relatedness) during development.

My colleagues and I have found that family relatedness (an aspect of the Ethic of Community) was closely associated with religiosity in a study of adolescents from eighteen countries (Mayer & Trommsdorff, 2012). In this volume, Hickman and DiBianca Fasoli show how the moral reasoning of American evangelical parents legitimizes their child's Ethic of Autonomy reasoning while simultaneously recasting it into Ethic of Divinity concepts. In other cultural contexts, too, boundaries between secular and religious life are permeable (Snibbe & Markus, 2002; Trommsdorff, 2012a). For example, in Indonesia, religion is experienced by Muslim adolescents as interwoven with collectivistic values (French, Eisenberg, Purwono, *et al.*, 2012). Similarly, religion in India permeates everyday life and is intertwined with Hindu children's and adolescents' self-construals (Jensen, Chapter 1, this volume; Mishra, 2012; Pandya & Bhangaokar, Chapter 2, this volume). The key Hindu moral concept of *dharma* is understood "as performing of duties pertaining to one's station in life" (Kapadia & Bhangaokar, Chapter 4, this volume). The Hindu culture conceptualizes the self as a spiritual and an embodied entity interrelated with the divine, with nature, and with all living beings. This view does not make for an easy distinction of self's and others' interests in moral behavior, while values of interdependence and acceptance of rules in line with the Ethic of Divinity underlie agency in children's and adolescents' development (Mishra, 2012; Trommsdorff, 2012a).

In turn, this may suggest that the meanings of the concepts of "autonomy" and "relatedness" may change when studied as aspects of the Ethic of Divinity instead of as aspects of the Ethics of Autonomy and Community. Accordingly, from a cultural-developmental approach these concepts and their impact on moral behavior should be studied from an indigenous perspective, for comparing the impact of the three ethics on moral behavior across cultures and developmental periods, their relative importance, and, moreover, the degree of their interrelations may induce a dynamic process-oriented approach to moral development.

When the development of morality is guided by religious normative beliefs (e.g., Ethic of Divinity), a closer look at the kind of religiosity in question is needed for predicting the kind of moral behavior (such as its relation to the Ethic of Community). Religious beliefs based on the sanctification of life can fundamentally transform the awareness of one's self and the world (Rothbaum & Wang, 2012; Trommsdorff, 2012a). For example, the belief in sacred, unquestionable moral rules and values originating in "holy demands" may evoke a sharp contrast between believers and nonbelievers. Accordingly, moral behavior may entail cooperation with one's in-group members and opposition or even fighting against out-groups of nonbelievers. The Ethic of Divinity may be regarded as a legitimate basis for aggression against nonbelievers (Kornadt, 2012). Dynamic processes of commitment to one's in-group may increase the moral legitimacy of aggression and violence against the out-group (Trommsdorff, 2012a; in press). In a secular understanding, community values are understood as universalistic values (as human rights) that are not confined to an in-group of believers. However, secular worldviews can as well entail opposition to out-groups and activate "nonmoral" behavior such as aggression. This line of reasoning opens the door to question under which conditions the three general ethics can predict moral and immoral behavior.

While the general ethics (Divinity, Community, Autonomy) cannot alone predict moral behavior, more has to be known about their interrelations, the predominant cultural values, the individual self- and worldviews, and the specific context for moral agency. Co-occurrence of the Ethics of Divinity, Community, and Autonomy may be related to primary control (changing nonbelievers' beliefs) or to secondary control (changing oneself by self-regulation, suffering, undergoing hardships). Shweder, Much, Mahapatra, and Park (1997) have suggested a culture-informed view on the "big three explanations of suffering." In the Indian culture, suffering plays an important role in the Ethic of Divinity. Numerous rituals practiced individually and collectively permeate everyday life, with certain rituals inducing physical and psychological hardships (e.g., walking long distances without consuming water or food; walking over fire). However, enduring these ritual ordeals contributes to the participant's happiness (Fischer, Xygalatas, Mitkidis, *et al.*, 2014). This process is related to secondary control (or changing the self) by extending one's self-regulation to accept extreme suffering.

A culture-informed approach allows us to better understand the impact of the Ethic of Divinity on moral behavior. The religious concepts promoted by Christianity in the European American contexts do not suffice, as is illustrated by the contributions of Pandya and Bhangaokar (Chapter 2, this volume) and by Kapadia and Bhangaokar (Chapter 4, this volume), suggesting a merger of indigenous psychology and a cultural-developmental perspective. The latter authors, in fact, point out that the cross-cultural validity of the Three Ethics framework partly is due to the ethics' interrelations with self-construal and its components. This view is in line with my assumption that the development of moral reasoning and moral behavior is guided by one's self-construal influencing agency and self-regulation; the development of moral reasoning and moral behavior in cultural contexts is shaped by cultural values.

Conclusion and outlook

Future research is needed to study the culturally preferred modes of moral agency and its transmission into individual development and moral behavior. Assuming that individuals choose developmental contexts and behavioral options with optimal cultural fit, focus on the study of agency as part of moral development in cultural contexts is suggested. A cultural fit should enhance self-evaluation. In their cross-cultural study on the cultural value of self-esteem Becker, Vignoles, Owe, *et al.* (2014) showed that the basis of self-evaluations depends on cultural normative value priorities. The implication points out the need to pay more attention to value orientations and individual motivation in future research with the template model approach. For example, doing one's duty may be based on different motivations (e.g., promoting social approval and self-esteem; prevention of social rejection) that require choice and intentionality, thereby fostering agency. Conforming to prescribed moral behavior such as helping a person in need may be primarily motivated by empathic concern and less by perceived moral duty, depending on the meaning of the situation. Further research should distinguish emotion-based and duty-based agency for predicting moral behavior. Both kinds of agency may be activated in secular cultures prioritizing Ethics of Autonomy and Community and also in transcendent cultures prioritizing ethics of spirituality.

To recapitulate, Jensen's template model approach draws on Shweder and his colleagues' (1997) tripartite distinction among Ethics of Autonomy, Community, and Divinity to propose culturally malleable developmental patterns of moral reasoning. In future theoretical and empirical work, this cultural-developmental template model may be fruitfully extended by focusing on moral motivation and moral behavior and by building on theory of agency and the development of intentionality in cultural contexts. This cultural-developmental and motivational approach will gain from research on the development of self- and other-oriented worldviews contributing to the area of agentic moral development as a motivation to achieve fit between the self and the world in line with moral standards.

REFERENCES

Bakan, D. (1966). *The duality of human existence: An essay on psychology and religion.* Chicago, IL: Rand McNally.

Becker, M., Vignoles, V. L., Owe, E., Easterbrook, M. J., Brown, R., Smith, P. B.,... Koller, S. H. (2014). Cultural bases for self-evaluation: Seeing oneself positively in different cultural contexts. *Personality and Social Psychology Bulletin*, 40(5), 657–675. doi:10.1177/0146167214522836

Cole, P. M., & Tan, P. Z. (2007). Emotion socialization from a cultural perspective. In J. E. Grusec & P. Hastings (Eds.), *Handbook of socialization: Theory and research* (pp. 516–542). New York, NY: Guilford Press.

Dweck, C. S. (2000). *Self-theories: Their role in motivation, personality, and development.* Philadelphia, PA: Psychology Press.

Fischer, R., Xygalatas, D., Mitkidis, P., Reddish, P., Tok, P., Konvalinka, I., & Bulbulia, J. (2014). The fire-walker's high: Affect and physiological responses in an extreme collective ritual. *PLoS ONE*, 9(2), e88355. doi:10.1371/journal.pone.0088355

French, D. C., Eisenberg, N., Purwono, U., & Sallquist, J. A. (2012). Indonesian Muslim adolescents and the ecology of religion. In G. Trommsdorff & X. Chen (Eds.), *Values, religion, and culture in adolescent development* (pp. 146–163). New York, NY: Cambridge University Press.

Grusec, J. E., & Goodnow, J. J. (1994). Impact of parental discipline methods on the child's internalization of values: A reconceptualization of current points of view. *Developmental Psychology*, 30(1), 4–19. doi:10.1037/0012-1649.30.1.4

Guisinger, S., & Blatt, S. J. (1994). Individuality and relatedness: Evolution of a fundamental dialectic. *American Psychologist*, 49(2), 104–111. doi:10.1037/0003-066X.49.2.104

Heikamp, T., Trommsdorff, G., & Fäsche, A. (2013). Development of self-regulation in context. In G. Seebaß, M. Schmitz, & P. M. Gollwitzer (Eds.), *Acting intentionally and its limits: Individuals, groups, institutions* (pp. 193–222). Berlin, Germany: De Gruyter.

Higgins, E. T. (2012). *Beyond pleasure and pain.* Oxford, United Kingdom: Oxford University Press.

Jensen, L. A. (2008). Through two lenses: A cultural-developmental approach to moral psychology. *Developmental Review*, 28(3), 289–315. doi:http://dx.doi.org/10.1016/j.dr.2007.11.001

(2011). The cultural-developmental theory of moral psychology: A new synthesis. In L. A. Jensen (Ed.), *Bridging cultural and developmental approaches to psychology: New syntheses in theory, research, and policy* (pp. 3–25). New York, NY: Oxford University Press.

(Ed.). (2015). *The Oxford handbook of human culture and development: An interdisciplinary approach.* New York, NY: Cambridge University Press.

Kagitcibasi, C. (2005). Autonomy and relatedness in cultural context: Implications for self and family. *Journal of Cross-Cultural Psychology*, 36(4), 403–422. doi:10.1177/0022022105275959

Karoly, P. (1993). Mechanisms of self-regulation: A systems view. *Annual Review of Psychology*, 44(1), 23–52. doi:10.1146/annurev.ps.44.020193.000323

Kochanska, G., Coy, K. C., & Murray, K. T. (2001). The development of self-regulation in the first four years of life. *Child Development*, 72(4), 1091–1111. doi:10.1111/1467-8624.00336

Kornadt, H.-J. (2011). *Aggression: Die Rolle der Erziehung in Europa und Ostasien* [Aggression: The role of socialization in Europe and East Asia]. Wiesbaden, Germany: VS Verlag.

— (2012). Psychological functions of religion in youth: A historical and cultural perspective. In G. Trommsdorff & X. Chen (Eds.), *Values, religion, and culture in adolescent development* (pp. 46–65). New York, NY: Cambridge University Press.

Markus, H. R., & Kitayama, S. (1991). Culture and the self: Implications for cognition, emotion, and motivation. *Psychological Review*, 98(2), 224–253. doi:10.1037/0033-295X.98.2.224

Mayer, B., & Trommsdorff, G. (2012). Cross-cultural perspectives on adolescents' religiosity and family orientation. In G. Trommsdorff & X. Chen (Eds.), *Values, religion, and culture in adolescent development* (pp. 341–369). New York, NY: Cambridge University Press.

Miller, J. G., Bersoff, D. M., & Harwood, R. L. (1990). Perceptions of social responsibilities in India and in the United States: Moral imperatives or personal decisions? *Journal of Personality and Social Psychology*, 58(1), 33–47. doi:10.1037/0022-3514.58.1.33

Mischel, W. (1996). From good intentions to willpower. In P. M. Gollwitzer & J. A. Bargh (Eds.), *The psychology of action: Linking cognition and motivation to behavior* (pp. 197–218). New York, NY: Guilford Press.

Mishra, R. C. (2012). Hindu religious values and their influence on youths in India. In G. Trommsdorff & X. Chen (Eds.), *Values, religion, and culture in adolescent development* (pp. 424–442). New York, NY: Cambridge University Press.

Molden, D. C., & Dweck, C. S. (2006). Finding "meaning" in psychology: A lay theories approach to self-regulation, social perception, and social development. *American Psychologist* 61(3), 192–203. doi:10.1037/0003-066X.61.3.192

Morling, B., & Evered, S. (2006). Secondary control reviewed and defined. *Psychological Bulletin*, 132, 269–296. doi:10.1037/0033-2909.132.2.269

Rothbaum, F., & Trommsdorff, G. (2007). Do roots and wings oppose or complement one another? The socialization of autonomy and relatedness in cultural context. In J. E. Grusec & P. Hastings (Eds.), *The handbook of socialization* (pp. 461–489). New York, NY: Guilford Press.

Rothbaum, F., & Wang, Y. Z. (2011). Cultural and developmental pathways to acceptance or self and acceptance of the world. In L. A. Jensen (Ed.), *Bridging cultural and developmental approaches to psychology: New syntheses in theory, research, and policy* (pp. 187–211). New York, NY: Oxford University Press.

Rothbaum, F., & Wang, Y. Z. (2012). Fostering the child's malleable views of the self and the world: Caregiving practices in East Asian and European-American communities. In B. Mayer & H.-J. Kornadt (Eds.), *Psychologie Kultur Gesellschaft* (Psychology – Culture – Society) (pp. 101–20). Wiesbaden, Germany: VS Verlag für Sozialwissenschaften.

Ryan, R. M., & Deci, E. L. (2000). Self-determination theory and the facilitation of intrinsic motivation, social development, and well-being. *American Psychologist*, 55(1), 68–78. doi:10.1037/0003-066X.55.1.68

Shweder, R. A. (1990). In defense of moral realism: Reply to Gabennesch. *Child Development*, 61(6), 2060–2067. doi:10.2307/1130859

Shweder, R. A., Much, N. C., Mahapatra, M., & Park, L. (1997). The "Big Three" of morality (Autonomy, Community, Divinity) and the "big three" explanations of suffering. In A. M. Brandt & P. Rozin (Eds.), *Morality and health* (pp. 119–169). New York, NY: Routledge.

Snibbe, A. C., & Markus, H. R. (2002). The psychology of religion and the religion of psychology. *Psychological Inquiry*, 13(3), 229–234.

Spence, J. T. (1985). Achievement American style: The rewards and costs of individualism. *American Psychologist*, 40, 1285–1295. doi:10.1037/0003-066X.40.12.1285

Tomasello, M. (1999). Having intentions, understanding intentions, and understanding communicative intentions. In P. D. Zelazo, J. W. Astington, & D. R. Olson (Eds.), *Developing theories of intention: Social understanding and self-control* (pp. 63–75). Mahwah, NJ: Erlbaum.

Trommsdorff, G. (2007). Intentionality of action in cultural context. In J. Wassmann & K. Stockhaus (Eds.), *Person, space and memory in the contemporary Pacific – Experiencing New Worlds: Vol. 1. Person, space and memory – Theoretical foundations* (pp. 58–77). New York, NY: Berghahn.

(2009). Culture and development of self-regulation. *Social and Personality Psychology Compass*, 3(5), 687–701. doi:10.1111/j.1751-9004.2009.00209.x

(2012a). Cultural perspectives on values and religion in adolescent development: A conceptual overview and synthesis. In G. Trommsdorff & X. Chen (Eds.), *Values, religion, and culture in adolescent development* (pp. 3–45). Cambridge, NY: Cambridge University Press.

(2012b). Development of 'agentic' regulation in cultural context: The role of self and world views. *Child Development Perspectives*, 6(1), 19–26. doi:10.1111/j.1750-8606.2011.00224.x

(2015). Cultural roots of values, and moral and religious purposes in adolescent development. In L. A. Jensen (Ed.), *The Oxford handbook of human culture and development: An interdisciplinary approach*. New York, NY: Oxford University Press.

(in press). Entwicklung von Intentionalität: Implikationen für moralische Entwicklung im kulturellen Kontext. In J. Sautermeister (Ed.), *Moralpsychologie: Transdisziplinäre Perspektiven*. Stuttgart, Germany: Kohlhammer.

Trommsdorff, G., Friedlmeier, W., & Mayer, B. (2007). Sympathy, distress, and prosocial behavior of preschool children in four cultures. *International Journal of Behavioral Development*, 31(3), 284–293. doi:10.1177/0165025407076441

Trommsdorff, G., & Kornadt, H.-J. (2003). Parent-child relations in cross-cultural perspective. In L. Kuczynski (Ed.), *Handbook of dynamics in parent-child relations* (pp. 271–304). London, United Kingdom: Sage.

Weisz, J. R., Rothbaum, F. M., & Blackburn, T. C. (1984). Standing out and standing in: The psychology of control in America and Japan. *American Psychologist*, 39, 955–969. doi:10.1037/0003-066X.39.9.955

Appendices

Appendix A
Coding manual: Ethics of Autonomy, Community, and Divinity

Lene Arnett Jensen

Index of subcategories within each ethic

Ethic of Autonomy

1. Punishment Avoidance (to self)
2. Reward Seeking (to self)
3. Self's Physical Well-Being
4. Self's Psychological Well-Being
5. Self's Interest
6. Other Individual's Physical Well-Being
7. Other Individual's Psychological Well-Being
8. Other Individual's Interest
9. Fairness and Reciprocity
10. Conscience (guilt)
11. Virtues (autonomy-oriented)
12. Responsibility (for self)
13. Means-Ends Consideration: Ends of an Individual
14. Rights
15. Other Autonomy

Ethic of Community

1. Punishment Avoidance: Social Sanctions
2. Reward Seeking: Social Benefits
3. Others' Physical Well-Being
4. Others' Psychological Well-Being
5. Others' Interest
6. Important Socially Defined Person's Authority
7. Customary or Traditional Authority
8. Legal Authority (of social institution)
9. Virtues (community-oriented)
10. Duty (to others)

11. Means-Ends Considerations: Ends of Social Group
12. Social Order or Harmony Goals
13. Other Community

Ethic of Divinity

1. Punishment Avoidance (from God[s])
2. Reward Seeking (from God[s])
3. Self's Physical Well-Being (body as God's temple)
4. Interest of Self's Soul
5. Other's Physical Well-Being (body as God's temple)
6. Interest of Other's Soul
7. Important Spiritually Defined Person's Authority
8. Customary or Traditional Authority (of spiritual/religious nature)
9. Legal Authority (of religious institution)
10. Authority of Natural Law
11. Scriptural Authority
12. God(s)' Authority
13. Conscience (when God-given)
14. Virtues (divinity-oriented)
15. Duty (as spiritual/religious being)
16. Other Divinity

Coding guidelines

1. A justification is defined as a statement that can be coded within the manual as a subcategory.
2. Code every justification that participant (P) provides to explain his/her moral evaluation. Do not code justifications that P may mention but which support another (e.g., an opposing) moral evaluation not endorsed by participant.
3. Code parsimoniously. Give only one code if a P elaborates on a justification by giving multiple examples or mentions different but related aspects of an argument. (Though see also 4.)
4. The same subcategory may be assigned more than once to P's justifications of his/her moral evaluation. This should be done only when the P clearly is describing different justifications; for example, that divorce is wrong because it often leaves children to be raised under poor financial conditions (Community – Other's Interest) and that divorce is wrong because it is bad for society (Community – Other's Interest).
5. A justification should be assigned only one subcategory. Do not assign multiple codes to one justification, but choose the one code that is most applicable. (Though see also 2.)

6. Do not assign a final code to justifications that are insufficiently described. For example, a justification may be an example of one subcategory that could be classified within two or more ethics (e.g., divorce is wrong because it shows a lack of respect. This is a case of a Virtues subcode, but without knowing in regard to whom or what divorce shows a lack of respect, a final Ethics code cannot be assigned. For example, a lack of respect for God would be classified within the Ethic of Divinity, whereas a lack of respect for one's spouse would be classified within the Ethic of Community).

7. Ethic of Community subcategories may be further differentiated. Specifically, a differentiation between family, peers, and society may be useful for the subcategories. For example, one may differentiate whether "Others' Interest" pertains to family, peers, or society at large.

8. New subcategories (e.g., characteristic of a culture or of theoretical importance) may be added by researchers.

Reliability coding

Provide the transcribed interview to a second rater with the coded justifications underlined or otherwise marked. The second rater assigns a code (ethic and subcategory) to each of the underlined justifications. Reliability is assessed on the ethic, typically using Cohen's kappa. (Reliability may also be assessed for subcategories.)

ETHIC OF AUTONOMY

Moral discourse within the Ethic of Autonomy defines the person as an autonomous individual who is free to make choices, with few limits. Justifications within this ethic center on an individual's rights, needs, feelings, and well-being. What restricts a person's behavior is mainly a prohibition on inflicting harm to oneself and others and encroaching upon the rights of other people. The ethic also includes a concern with equality.

Subcategories, definitions, and examples[1]

Punishment Avoidance (to self)
Definition: Avoidance of adverse consequences where focus is on harm or cost to self rather than on the social context of sanctions experienced by self.

Example

> "The child would know never to do that again because he'll just get hit again."

---

[1] All examples in the manual are from interviews with participants of different ages and cultural backgrounds.

Reward Seeking (to self)

Definition: Action is done so that actor can receive immediate benefits. The focus is on the benefits to the self rather than on who provides the benefits or the relationship within which the action-benefit exchange takes place.

Example

> "I cheated on the exam because I hoped to get a better grade."

Self's Physical Well-Being

Definition: Hurting the body, causing or failing to relieve hunger or thirst, injury, discomfort, pain, etc., of the self. This category includes references to the absence of physical harm and to the promotion of physical well-being. (It does not address when the body is described as belonging to God, or as a temple of God. See Ethic of Divinity.)

Examples

> "People who are terminally ill may commit suicide. They should be taken out of their pain and misery. They have no hope of enjoying life."
> "Abortion is wrong in that it has a lot of ramifications; for example, a lot of times it can affect a woman's ability to conceive children."

Self's Psychological Well-Being

Definition: Causing or failing to alleviate unpleasant emotional states to one's own psyche, such as sadness, frustration, fear, and anger. The category includes references to the absence of psychological harm and to the promotion of psychological well-being.

Examples

> "Incest is destructive to the perpetrators as it encourages the sick part of them."
> "When you do what is right, you get a certain peace of mind."

Self's Interest

Definition: Advancing or protecting (or failing to do so) interests, goals, wants, or the general welfare of the self.

Examples

> "By committing suicide, one is not giving oneself a chance to obtain a better life."
> "Abortion is wrong. You have to consider that children give so much more than they take. They give so much purpose to your life."

Other Individual's Physical Well-Being
Definition: Hurting the body, causing or failing to relieve hunger or thirst, injury, discomfort, pain, etc., to individuals other than oneself. This category includes references to the absence of physical harm and to the promotion of physical well-being. The Ethic of Autonomy is used when the harm is caused to an individual that the actor has immediate interaction with regarding the issue at hand. (See also Ethic of Community for cases of third person's well-being.)

Example

> "If I divorce my husband, it might really hurt him, including even physical ramifications."

Other Individual's Psychological Well-Being
Definition: Causing or failing to alleviate unpleasant emotional states to individuals other than the self, such as sadness, frustration, fear, and anger. The category includes references to the absence of psychological harm and to the promotion of psychological well-being. The Ethic of Autonomy is used when the harm is caused to an individual that the actor has immediate interaction with regarding the issue at hand. (See also Ethic of Community for cases of third person's well-being.)

Examples

> "In the case of incest between consenting adults, there does not seem to be any emotional harm to others."
> "My decision to divorce my wife was right because it was psychologically destructive to her to stay in the marriage."

Other's Individual's Interest
Definition: Advancing or protecting (or failing to do so) interests, goals, wants, or the general welfare of individuals other than the self. The Ethic of Autonomy is used when the interests pertain to liberties and a person's freedom to make choices. (See also Ethics of Community and Divinity.)

Example

> "It didn't have an impact on anyone's life except my own."

Fairness, Reciprocity, Golden Rule
Definition: Treating like cases alike and different cases differently; proper ratio or proportionality of give and take in an exchange; doing to others what you would have them do to you.

Example

> "She was not treated fairly. She was fired without justification and was given no opportunity to defend herself."

Conscience (guilt)

Definition: Your conscience will feel bad because you know you have done wrong or will not feel bad because you do not believe you have done wrong or think you have done right. Use Ethic of Autonomy when the conscience is seen as a psychological part of the person. When conscience is described as a psychological feeling of guilt. (See also Ethic of Divinity.)

Examples

> "There would be a sense of guilt if I did not tell her the truth, it would bother me unconsciously."
> "Abortion is wrong because afterward people have great problems with guilt. So they are doing themselves a disservice."

Virtues (autonomy-oriented)

Definition: Attitude or trait that, if manifested in the situation, would make behavior right and, if not manifested, would make behavior wrong. If informant talks about vice, then manifestation of attitude or trait would make the behavior wrong, and absence of trait or attitude would make it right. Also habitual manner of action. Virtues include gratitude, respect, devotion, loyalty, sympathy, love, etc. Use Ethic of Autonomy when the virtues pertain to individuality and freedom, such as respecting another's choice. When the virtues are not related to a person's dignity or social role. Virtues related to handling of individual property. (See also Ethics of Community and Divinity.)

Examples

> "I didn't tell her full story out of respect for her boundaries."
> "It was all right for me not to reference the source in my essay because I was creative and came up with things of my own."
> "Committing suicide is a sign of weakness. You are running away from life, but you have to face life."

Responsibility (for self)

Definition: Taking responsibility for one's own actions (or failing to do so). The code does not include taking responsibility for others. (See Ethic of Community.)

Example

> "Abortion is wrong because if they made the choice to have sexual relations and got pregnant, then they should take responsibility for their actions."

Means-Ends Considerations: Ends of an Individual

Definition: When means serve ends that are beneficial or pertain to an individual.

Example

> "Physical discipline is a good way to teach a child right from wrong. It helps them learn about life and gain self-control."

Rights

Definition: Entitlement to be treated or not treated in a certain way or to act or abstain from acting in a certain way. The category includes references to a person's right not to be forced to engage in an activity and the absence of voluntary consent.

Examples

> "Ending one's life is one's own decision. It's one's right to make that decision."
>
> "Abortion is wrong because the child has a right to life."

Other Autonomy

Definition: Any other justifications centered on the self or other individuals.

ETHIC OF COMMUNITY

Moral discourse within the Ethic of Community describes the person in terms of membership in groups, such as the family, the community, or the nation. Persons are described as acting in terms of their social roles, such as mother, scout leader, or American. The view is that our roles bind us together in intricate relations of differing obligations. The ethic also includes a concern with promoting the welfare, goals, needs, and interests of social groups.

Subcategories, definitions, and examples

Punishment Avoidance: Social Sanctions

Definition: Avoiding adverse reactions from other people in one's social group; includes gossip, rumors, fines, beatings, prison, loss of job, salary cut, etc.

Example

> "Incest will have a lifelong effect on the girl in the form of social condemnation."

Reward Seeking: Social Benefits

Definition: Action is done so that actor can receive social benefits.

Example

> "When you do what is right, you get more respect from others in the long run."

Others' Physical Well-Being

Definition: When physical harm is caused to a collective entity. This category includes references to the absence of physical harm and to the promotion of physical well-being. When physical harm is caused to persons, third parties, who are not directly involved in the decision making pertaining to the moral issue.

Example

> "Divorce is wrong because it is harmful to all family members. It preys upon their physical health."

Others' Psychological Well-Being

Definition: When psychological harm is caused to a collective entity. This category includes references to the absence of psychological harm and to the promotion of psychological well-being. The category also applies to a case where a person is not directly involved in the issue at hand but will be affected due to her relationship with an actor who is directly involved in the issue.

Examples

> "When a terminally ill person commits suicide, the family will know that there is nothing they could have done and will not feel insecurity."
> "My decision to divorce my wife was right because the situation was psychologically destructive to my children."

Others' Interest

Definition: When the focus is on the interests of society or some other form of collective entity. When the focus is on someone who is not directly involved in the issue at hand but who will be affected due to her relationship with an agent who is directly involved in the issue.

Examples

> "Suicide is wrong as society needs its people."
>
> "To have an affair with a married man would be mitigated by the fact that it would not affect the wife if she did not know."
>
> "Divorce is wrong because it does a lot of harm to society. You miss a key element if you're a single family and this ends up harming society."

Important Socially Defined Person's Authority

Definition: Important persons, such as parents or social leaders, have taught or exemplified that it is wrong or right.

Example

> "Abortion is wrong from the way that I have been taught by my parents."

Customary or Traditional Authority

Definition: Our practices or traditions or customs go against it and indicate it is wrong, or encourage it and indicate it is right. It is what we do, or what we do not do. When focus is on custom or tradition as socially derived, as opposed to instituted by a transcendental authority. (See also Ethic of Divinity.)

Examples

> "There is a cultural taboo against incest."
>
> "I did not remarry because society does not accept it."

Legal Authority (of social institutions)

Definition: When one must obey the law because it is of social origin.

Example

> "I shouldn't have taken the candy at the store because it's against the law."

Virtues (community-oriented)

Definition: Attitude or trait that, if manifested in the situation, would make behavior right and, if not manifested, would make behavior wrong. If informant talks about vice, then manifestation of attitude or trait would make the behavior wrong, and absence of trait or attitude would make it right. Also habitual manner of action. Virtues include gratitude, respect, devotion, loyalty, sympathy, love, etc. (Use Ethic of Community when the virtues pertain to familial and communal relationships, such as familial loyalty. See also Ethics of Autonomy and Divinity.)

Examples

> "It is questionable whether one can love one's kin as it is proper for intimate partners to love each other."
> "I didn't want to go back on my word that I had given to my sister."
> "Divorce is wrong because when you make a promise you should keep it. Honesty and integrity are traits. They are valuable and valued in the community."

Duty

Definition: An obligation of station to behave in certain ways in certain circumstances due to one's status or position (e.g., father, son). The category includes absolution from duty. Use Ethic of Community when the duty in question derives from a familial, social, or communal role, not when duties transcend society and culture or pertain to a person's duties to a divine or higher order. (See also Ethic of Divinity.)

Example

> "When a parent commits incest, he abdicates his responsibility to look after his child's welfare."

Means-Ends Considerations: Ends of Social Groups

Definition: When means serve familial, social, or communal ends.

Examples

> "Lying about my Jewish identity does not alleviate the problem and make people realize that their conceptions of Jews are false."
> "*Sati* is not rational. It was for another time, now a days ladies are no longer confined to the home and remarriage is also possible."

Social Order or Harmony Goals

Definition: Avoiding chaos or disorder. May imply the extremity, if not the violence, of the war of all against all. Promoting to perpetuation of order within any social group.

Examples

> "Suicide is very impractical, if everyone just killed themselves when others weren't doing what they wanted, we'd have a real mess on our hands."

> "Divorce is wrong. The goal is to unite and bring a house together. You can't stand there divided because you'd create turmoil."

Other Community
Definition: Any other justification centered on social groups or the ways that actions have ramifications beyond those immediately involved.

ETHIC OF DIVINITY

Moral discourse within the Ethic of Divinity envisions the person as a spiritual entity. A person's behaviors are to be in accordance with the guidelines rendered by a given spiritual or natural order. Thus the person avoids degradation and comes closer to moral purity.

Subcategories, definitions, and examples

Punishment Avoidance (from God[s])
Definition: Avoiding punishment from God(s) or unmentioned Higher Order(s). Includes avoiding consequences such as a decline in one's relationship with God.

Examples

> "One reason that I would not have an affair with a married man is that I'm afraid of God's punishment."
> "We couldn't keep the money that wasn't ours, because to purposely choose to do what's wrong it sets us up for one bad thing after another."
> "To divorce is not God's first choice, and therefore if you're not going to live God's first choice, you can't expect God's first blessings either."

Reward Seeking (from God[s])
Definition: Action is or should be done so that actor can receive benefits from God(s).

Examples

> "In heaven, I will see the bird again that I rescued. I will go to heaven."
> "*Sati* is a good act; it will ensure the woman's salvation."

Self's Physical Well-Being (body as God's temple)

Definition: When the self's body is described as God's rather than the person's. (See also Ethic of Autonomy.)

Example

> "It's wrong to take drugs because it would harm my body, and your body is God's temple."

Interest of Self's Soul

Definition: When the interest promoted or hindered pertains to the self's spiritual interests, status, or soul. (See also Ethics of Autonomy and Community.)

Example

> "It would be degrading to my soul."

Other's Physical Well-Being (body as God's temple)

Definition: When another person's body is described as God's rather than the person's. (See also Ethic of Autonomy.)

Example

> "I told her not to drink alcohol because it would harm her body, which is like a temple to God."

Interest of Other's Soul

Definition: When the interest promoted or hindered pertains to another person's spiritual interests, status, or soul. (See also Ethics of Autonomy and Community.)

Examples

> "Remarriage is wrong because children that are born to that union are illegitimate children. This has lifelong ramifications, in that it hinders their witnessing for Christ."
>
> "*Sati* is wrong. The wife should remain alive and finish the work her husband has not completed. In this way, his soul will find peace."

Important Spiritually Defined Person's Authority

Definition: Important persons have taught or exemplified that it is wrong or right. Use Ethic of Divinity when the person is seen as a representative of God or the divine. (See also Ethic of Community.)

Example

> "According to the Pope, abortion is wrong."

Customary or Traditional Authority (of spiritual/religious nature)
Definition: Practices or traditions or customs go against it and indicate it is wrong or encourage it and indicate it is right. It is what we do or what we do not do. Use Ethic of Divinity when the tradition or custom is religious, when a tradition or custom is seen as having a divine origin or being divinely sanctioned. (See also Ethic of Community.)

Example

> "As a Brahmin it is right for me to work as a cook. Most of us choose our occupation according to our tradition."

Legal Authority (of religious institution)
Definition: When the law is regarded as instituted or sanctioned by divine authority. (See also Ethic of Community.)

Example

> "The religious law commands us to observe certain guidelines regarding food preparation and consumption."

Authority of Natural Law
Definition: It is wrong because it is unnatural or right because it adheres to natural law.

Example

> "Suicide is wrong because it is unnatural. That's just not the way it was supposed to happen. That's not the way life was supposed to end."

Scriptural Authority
Definition: The scriptures have stated in the form of injunction or as revealed truth that it is wrong or right.

Examples

> "The Bible says that incest is wrong."
> "Thou shalt not steal."

God's Authority
Definition: God has indicated or exemplified by action or otherwise that it is wrong or right. Doing what is pleasing or not pleasing to God. This category includes references to violating the sacred, committing sacrilege.

Examples

> "We are given life by a Supreme Being and it is not in our hands to end it."
> "Divorce is wrong because the two people coming together is a picture of Christ and his bride. That's supposed to be a sacred picture."
> "Abortion is wrong because God gives life and it's a God-given privilege to raise the child."

Conscience (when God-given)

Definition: Your conscience will feel bad because you know you have done wrong or will not feel bad because you do not believe you have done wrong or think you have done right. Use Ethic of Divinity when the conscience is the soul or a part of the self through which a higher authority is experienced. (See also Ethic of Autonomy.)

Example

> "Our God-given conscience tells us that it is wrong to take one's own life."

Virtues (divinity-oriented)

Definition: Attitude or trait that, if manifested in the situation, would make behavior right and, if not manifested, would make behavior wrong. If informant talks about vice, then manifestation of attitude or trait would make the behavior wrong, and absence of trait or attitude would make it right. Also habitual manner of action. Virtues include gratitude, respect, devotion, loyalty, sympathy, love, etc. Use Ethic of Divinity when the virtues pertain to a person's status as a transcendental being or when the virtues pertain to traditions that have a divine basis. (See also Ethics of Autonomy and Community.)

Examples

> "To commit suicide shows a lack of respect for human life."
> "You should strive to be holy as God is holy."
> "You should honor the marriage vow. I respect the institution of marriage as sanctioned by God."

Duty (as spiritual/religious being)

Definition: An obligation of station to behave in certain ways in certain circumstances due to one's status or position (e.g., Muslim, Brahmin). The category includes absolution from duty. Use Ethic of Divinity when the duties obtain due to a person's status as a human being or as a faithful person or result from being sworn to uphold a divine order. (See also Ethic of Community.)

Examples

> "Since we will die, there is an obligation to do something while we are alive."
> "Taking one's life is wrong because God created man that we might serve Him and love Him and glorify Him."

Other Divinity

Definition: Any other justification centering on God(s), divine being, spirituality, religion, the soul, sin, sanctity, purity, pollution, etc.

OTHER CODES

Justifications that *cannot* be coded as Ethics of Autonomy, Community, or Divinity:

Involuntarism

Definition: The actor is judged not to be a moral agent because of age, acting under duress or compulsion, infirmity, incapacity, etc. If the actor is simply judged not to be a moral agent and no reference is made to who might step in the actor's place, the justification cannot be coded as an Ethic of Autonomy, Community, or Divinity.

Categorically Right or Wrong

Definition: When the participant only states that an action is right or wrong and that no reason is necessary or can be given.

Appendix B
The Community, Autonomy, and Divinity Scale (CADS)

Valeschka M. Guerra and Roger S. Giner-Sorolla

Instructions: With what frequency do the phrases below justify someone's action as MORALLY right? Using the 7-point rating scale, please rate each justification for acts that are RIGHT.

1	2	3	4	5	6	7
Never	Almost never	Rarely	Sometimes	Often	Almost always	Always

An action/behavior is right if . . .
1. . . . it is a religious tradition.
2. . . . by doing it, the person gains respect from the family.*
3. . . . it follows nature's law.*
4. . . . it is a customary practice of the community.
5. . . . it allows a person to defend herself/himself.
6. . . . it expresses someone's autonomy.*
7. . . . it is socially accepted.
8. . . . it is God's will.*
9. . . . by doing it, the person gains respect from society.
10. . . . it is socially approved.*
11. . . . it respects the natural order.*
12. . . . it respects family traditions.*
13. . . . it is in accordance with the scriptures.*
14. . . . it expresses personal choice and liberty.*
15. . . . it respects someone's privacy.*
16. . . . it is in accordance with religious authority.*
17. . . . it follows the rules of one's social group.
18. . . . people will gain God's approval from it.
19. . . . it is in accordance with true faith.
20. . . . it is accepted by the family.*
21. . . . people respect the social order.
22. . . . it protects someone's interests and needs.*

With what frequency do the phrases below justify someone's action as MORALLY wrong? Using the 7-point rating scale, please rate each justification for acts that are WRONG.

An action/behavior is wrong if . . .
23. . . . it opposes religious authority.
24. . . . it pollutes the spirit.*
25. . . . it is against the scriptures.
26. . . . it is degrading to the soul.
27. . . . it is unnatural.*
28. . . . it brings disorder to society.
29. . . . it is socially condemned.*
30. . . . it is against true faith.*
31. . . . the family considers it unacceptable.*
32. . . . it restricts the individual's rights.*
33. . . . it is against the rules of one's social group.*
34. . . . society considers it unacceptable.*
35. . . . it opposes the rules of society.*
36. . . . it is against God's will.*
37. . . . it restricts the freedom of choice of a person.*
38. . . . it opposes the beliefs of the family.*
39. . . . it is against the natural order.*
40. . . . it restricts someone's privacy.*
41. . . . it restricts personal choice and liberty.*
42. . . . it is considered a sin.
43. . . . it restricts the possibility of a person to defend her/himself.*
44. . . . it is against nature's law.*

Note. * Items to include for the CADS – Short Version.

Coding scheme

Community: All items: 2, 4, 7, 9, 10, 12, 17, 20, 21, 28, 29, 31, 33, 34, 35, 38
Community: Social rules: 4, 7, 9, 10, 17, 21, 28, 29, 33, 34, 35
Community: Family: 2, 12, 20, 31, 38
Autonomy: All items: 5, 6, 14, 15, 22, 32, 37, 40, 41, 43
Autonomy: Positive rights: 5, 6, 14, 15, 22
Autonomy: Negative rights: 32, 37, 40, 41, 43
Divinity: All items: 1, 3, 8, 11, 13, 16, 18, 19, 23, 24, 25, 26, 27, 30, 36, 39, 42, 44
Divinity: Religious rules: 1, 8, 13, 16, 18, 19, 23, 24, 25, 26, 30, 36, 42
Divinity: Nature: 3, 11, 27, 39, 44

SOURCES

Standard Version: Guerra, V. M., & Giner-Sorolla, R. (2010). Community, Autonomy, and Divinity Scale: A new tool for the cross-cultural study of morality. *Journal of Cross-Cultural Psychology*, 41, 35–50. doi:10.1177/0022022109348919

Short Version: Guerra, V. M. (2013). Community, Autonomy, and Divinity Scale: Identifying facets of moral codes. In A. Roazzi, B. Campello, & W. Bilsky (Eds.), *Proceedings for the 14th Facet Theory Association Conference* (pp. 347–360). Retrieved from http://dspace.uevora.pt/rdpc/bitstream/10174/10933/1/Facet%20Theory%20-%20Proceedings%2014FTC.pdf

Appendix C
Ethical Values Assessment (EVA)

Lene Arnett Jensen and Laura M. Padilla-Walker

Ethical Values Assessment (EVA – Long Form)

What moral values do you think are important to how you should live **at this time in your life?**

	Not at all important	Slightly important	Moderately important	Very important	Completely important
1. I should take responsibility for myself.*	1	2	3	4	5
2. I should take care of my family.*	1	2	3	4	5
3. I should aim for spiritual salvation.*	1	2	3	4	5
4. I should take good care of my body.	1	2	3	4	5
5. I should be a good member of society.	1	2	3	4	5
6. I should take care of my soul.	1	2	3	4	5
7. I should feel good about myself.	1	2	3	4	5
8. I should be cooperative.*	1	2	3	4	5
9. I should have a spiritual compass.	1	2	3	4	5
10. I should try to achieve my personal goals.*	1	2	3	4	5
11. I should fulfill my responsibilities to others.	1	2	3	4	5

(cont.)

	Not at all important	Slightly important	Moderately important	Very important	Completely important
12. I should be fair to other individuals.*	1	2	3	4	5
13. I should know my place or role in a group.*	1	2	3	4	5
14. I should strive for social harmony.*	1	2	3	4	5
15. I should strive for spiritual purity.*	1	2	3	4	5
16. I should aim to live a holy life.*	1	2	3	4	5
17. I should respect other individuals' rights.*	1	2	3	4	5
18. I should follow God's law.*	1	2	3	4	5

Indicate the *three* moral values from the above list that you consider the *most* important to how you should live at this time in your life. Indicate the number that is written in front of the statement.

Most important: #_____
Most important: #_____
Most important: #_____

In your own words, indicate if there are moral values that you consider *completely important* to how you should live at this time in your life which are *not* mentioned on the list above.

1. _____
2. _____
3. _____

Ethical Values Assessment (EVA – Short Form)

*Designates the 12 items used for the Short Form.

Listing the 3 most important items, and the open-ended questions may be excluded.

Coding

AUTONOMY ITEMS:
I should take good care of my body
I should feel good about myself
I should try to achieve my personal goals
I should be fair to other individuals
I should take responsibility for myself
I should respect other individuals' rights
COMMUNITY ITEMS:
I should take care of my family
I should be a good member of society
I should be cooperative
I should fulfill my responsibilities to others
I should know my place or role in a group
I should strive for social harmony
DIVINITY ITEMS:
I should aim for spiritual salvation
I should take care of my soul
I should follow God's law
I should have a spiritual compass
I should strive for spiritual purity
I should aim to live a holy life

Alternate or additional prompts

The prompt "What moral values do you think are important to how you should live **at this time in your life?**" may be changed.

For example, surveys have also assessed "What moral values do you want **to pass on to the next generation?**"

Appendix D
Three Ethics Reasoning Assessment (TERA)

Lene Arnett Jensen

This is a survey of your moral views. Please read the questions and instructions carefully. The instructions below are given in capital letters and are underlined.

1. Do you think that generally it is morally wrong or not wrong to divorce? If you have difficulty in deciding, please circle the answer that indicates the position you most agree with.
   a. Yes, it is morally wrong **(GO TO QUESTION 2)**
   b. No, it is not morally wrong **(GO TO QUESTION 3)**

2. If you think any of the following are *exceptions to divorce being wrong*, please circle all that apply:
   a. Adultery
   b. Physical abuse of spouse
   c. Mental abuse of a spouse
   d. Other: _____

2. (*Continued*) Following is a list of statements that people sometimes make in order to explain why divorce is morally wrong. Please read all of these statements carefully, then circle the statements that you think are true and the most important. You must circle at least <u>one</u> statement, but you may not circle more than <u>four</u> statements.
   a. Divorce is morally wrong because it is very emotionally damaging to the husband and wife, for example, they may lose their ability to trust others.
   b. Divorce is morally wrong because it hampers your relationship with God, you can no longer expect all of his blessings.
   c. Divorce is morally wrong because it is harmful to children and to families, and this leads to societal problems related to crime, welfare, and so forth.
   d. Divorce is morally wrong because it is very emotionally damaging to the children, for example, they often feel abandoned.
   e. Divorce is morally wrong because it causes economic hardship on one or both of the divorcees.

f. Divorce is morally wrong because the Bible states that "what God has joined together, let no man put asunder."

g. Other: _____

_____

_____

(Go to question 4)

3. If you think there are any *particular cases* where divorce is wrong, please indicate what these are:

a. _____

b. _____

3. (*Continued*) Following is a list of statements that people sometimes make in order to explain why divorce is not morally wrong. Please read all of these statements carefully, then circle the statements that you think are true and the most important. You must circle at least <u>one</u> statement, but you may not circle more than <u>four</u> statements.

a. Divorce is not morally wrong because if parents are forced to stay together, they will be poor role models to their children.

b. Divorce is not morally wrong because to stay in an unhappy marriage is destructive to the husband and wife, their emotional well-being and sense of self-worth.

c. Divorce is not morally wrong because while the Bible says to avoid divorce if possible, it does not state that two people must stay together under all circumstances. So if two people are incompatible, divorce is justified.

d. Divorce is not morally wrong because the husband and wife have the right to make their own decision.

e. Divorce is not morally wrong because it is not wrong in the eyes of God.

f. Divorce is not morally wrong because it is better for the children not to see their parents being unhappy together.

g. Other: _____

_____

_____

(Go to question 4)

4. Do you think that generally it is morally wrong or not wrong for terminally ill persons to end their life through suicide? If you have difficulty in deciding, please circle *the position you most agree with*.

a. Yes, it is morally wrong (**GO TO QUESTION 5**)

b. No, it is not morally wrong (**GO TO QUESTION 6**)

5. Following is a list of statements that people sometimes make in order to explain why suicide in the case of terminal illness is morally wrong. Please read all of these statements carefully, then circle the statements that you think are true and *the most important*. You must circle at least *one* statement, but you may not circle more than *four* statements.
   a. Suicide in the case of terminal illness is morally wrong because even a person who is ill may still experience some happiness.
   b. Suicide in the case of terminal illness is morally wrong because there are many situations where people who have been in hard times have caused others to reflect about their lives. Someone with a terminal illness might help other people change their lives for the better.
   c. Suicide in the case of terminal illness is morally wrong because the Bible says that "Thou shalt not kill," which includes not killing oneself.
   d. Suicide in the case of terminal illness is morally wrong because contrary to expectations you might suddenly get better, and if you commit suicide, you will miss out on the rest of your life.
   e. Suicide in the case of terminal illness is morally wrong because it cheapens life, and once society goes down that path there is no knowing where it will end in terms of whose lives will be dispensable.
   f. Suicide in the case of terminal illness is morally wrong because even when we are ill God still has a purpose for us.
   g. Other: _____
   _____
   _____

(Go to question 7)

6. Following is a list of statements that people sometimes make in order to explain why suicide in the case of terminal illness is not morally wrong. Please read all of these statements carefully, then circle the statements that you think are true and *the most important*. You must circle at least *one* statement, but you may not circle more than *four* statements.
   a. Suicide in the case of terminal illness is not morally wrong because it puts an end to the physical pain and suffering that the person is likely to experience.
   b. Suicide in the case of terminal illness is not morally wrong because it is emotionally damaging to the family to watch a loved one suffer and grow weaker and more incapacitated.
   c. Suicide in the case of terminal illness is not morally wrong because it is not wrong in the eyes of God.
   d. Suicide in the case of terminal illness is not morally wrong because God will not make a judgment on you and punish you for that.

e. Suicide in the case of terminal illness is not morally wrong because it is a financial burden on society to keep someone alive who will soon die.

f. Suicide in the case of terminal illness is not morally wrong because a person has the right to make that decision.

g. Other: _____

_____

_____

(Go to question 7)

7. Excluding the case of terminal illness, do you think that generally it is morally wrong or not wrong for persons to end their life through suicide? If you have difficulty in deciding, please circle the answer that indicates *the position you most agree with*.

a. Yes, it is morally wrong (**GO TO QUESTION 8**)

b. No, it is not morally wrong (**GO TO QUESTION 9**)

8. If you think any of the following are *exceptions to suicide being wrong*, please circle all that apply:

a. Someone has completely lost control of their actions and mind and commits suicide in such as state.

b. Other: _____

8. (*Continued*) Following is a list of statements that people sometimes make in order to explain why suicide is morally wrong. Please read all of these statements carefully, then circle the statements that you think are true and *the most important*. You must circle at least *one* statement, but you may not circle more than *four* statements.

a. Suicide is morally wrong because we have a duty to glorify God and to serve Him, and you are not doing that by ending your own life.

b. Suicide is morally wrong because you ought to develop your resources, skills, and personality to the fullest.

c. Suicide is morally wrong because you have responsibilities to the people around you, such as your spouse, children, friends, colleagues, and so forth.

d. Suicide is morally wrong because of the emotional harm it causes those people left behind, such as family and friends.

e. Suicide is morally wrong because the Bible speaks of trusting God and seeking God in times of trouble; suicide shows a lack of trust in God.

f. Suicide is morally wrong because the person is going to miss out on a whole lot of things that are worthwhile.

g. Other: _____

_____

_____

(Go to question 10)

9. If you think there are any *particular cases* where suicide is wrong, please indicate what these are:

   a. _____

   b. _____

9. (*Continued*) Following is a list of statements that people sometimes make in order to explain why suicide is not morally wrong. Please read all of these statements carefully, then circle the statements that you think are true and the most important. You must circle at least <u>one</u> statement, but you may not circle more than <u>four</u> statements.

   a. Suicide is not morally wrong because the individual has the right to make that decision.

   b. Suicide is not morally wrong because it does not threaten the stability of society, the way violent acts against others do.

   c. Suicide is not morally wrong, in fact it shows a tremendous amount of courage to be able to end your own life.

   d. Suicide is not morally wrong because it is not a sin for which a person will suffer God's punishment.

   e. Suicide is not morally wrong because while family and friends will suffer they will be able to overcome that.

   f. Suicide is not morally wrong because it is not wrong in the eyes of God.

   g. Other: _____

      _____

      _____

(Go to question 10)

10. Do you think that generally it is morally wrong or not wrong to have an abortion? If you have difficulty in deciding, please circle the answer that indicates the position you most agree with.

    a. Yes, it is morally wrong **(GO TO QUESTION 11)**

    b. No, it is not morally wrong **(GO TO QUESTION 12)**

11. If you think any of the following are *exceptions to abortion being wrong*, please circle all that apply:

    a. The mother's life is endangered by continuing the pregnancy

    b. The pregnancy is a result of incest

    c. The pregnancy is a result of rape

    d. The fetus is seriously deformed

    e. It is a teen pregnancy

    f. Other: _____

11. (*Continued*) Following is a list of statements that people sometimes make in order to explain why abortion is morally wrong. Please read all of these

statements carefully, then circle the statements that you think are true and *the most important*. You must circle at least *one* statement, but you may not circle more than *four* statements.

a. Abortion is morally wrong because society loses someone who could have been a productive and contributing person.

b. Abortion is morally wrong because the baby has a right to life.

c. Abortion is morally wrong because of the psychological consequences to the woman. She will have a sense of loss and suffer emotionally.

d. Abortion is morally wrong because the Bible tells us that "Thou shalt not kill."

e. Abortion is morally wrong because only God can give life and only God is allowed to take life. It is not our place to take life.

f. Abortion is morally wrong because once the child is conceived, you have a duty as a parent to care for and protect the child.

g. Other: _____
   _____
   _____

(Go to question 13)

12. If you think there are any *particular cases* where abortion is wrong, please indicate what these are:

a. Abortion is used as a method of birth control

b. The fetus is viable (about 6 months of more since conception)

c. The abortion is wanted because the fetus is of a particular sex

d. Other: _____

12. (*Continued*) Following is a list of statements that people sometimes make in order to explain why abortion is not morally wrong. Please read all of these statements carefully, then circle the statements that you think are true and *the most important*. You must circle at least *one* statement, but you may not circle more than *four* statements.

a. Abortion is not morally wrong because the woman has a right to decide what happens to her body.

b. Abortion is not morally wrong because unwanted children increase society's problems.

c. Abortion is not morally wrong because it is not wrong in the eyes of God.

d. Abortion is not morally wrong because to have a child may put a burden upon a woman, in terms of her education, career, finances, and so forth.

e. Abortion is not morally wrong because if a child is unwanted, the child is less likely to receive proper nurture and care.

f. Abortion is not morally wrong because God will not punish you for that.

g. Other: _____

_____

_____

Thank you for completing this survey.

Coding

Each moral judgment (generally right or generally wrong) is followed by:
- Options where respondents can indicate exceptions to their overall or general moral judgment (except for suicide in the case of terminal illness).
- Six moral reasons, with two from each of the three Ethics of Autonomy, Community, and Divinity (randomized).

Autonomy

2a, 2e, 3b, 3d, 5a, 5d, 6a, 6f, 8b, 8f, 9a, 9c, 11b, 11c, 12a, 12b.

Community

2c, 2d, 3a, 3f, 5b, 5e, 6b, 6e, 8c, 8d, 9b, 9e, 11a, 11f, 12b, 12e.

Divinity

2b, 2f, 3c, 3e, 5c, 5f, 6c, 6d, 8a, 8e, 9d, 9f, 11d, 11e, 12c, 12f.

Index

9 781316 635674